**Concepción Ávila
de Cetina**

Sabores Yucatecos
A Culinary Tour of the Yucatán

*Dedicated to my mother, Concepción Ávila de Cetina, for her wisdom and inspiration;
and to my wife, Blanca Cetina, for her endless love and support.*
—Chef Gilberto Cetina

*Dedicated with love to my parents, Leno and Elisa Díaz,
for their unwavering support.*
—Katharine A. Díaz

Copyright © 2011 by Gilberto Cetina and Katharine A. Díaz
All Rights Reserved. Printed in China. **ISBN 978-1889379-41-8**

While every precaution has been taken in the preparation of this book, the authors and publisher assume no responsibility for errors or omissions, or for damages resulting from the use of the information contained herein. For more about books presented by WPR Publishing, please go to www.WPRbooks.com.

WPR Books: Comida
3445 Catalina Dr., Carlsbad, CA 92010-2856
www.WPRbooks.com 760-434-1223 kirk@whisler.com

SABORES YUCATECOS
A Culinary Tour of the Yucatán

**Chef Gilberto Cetina
Katharine A. Díaz
Gilberto Cetina, Jr.**

WPR BOOKS
COMIDA

CREDITS

Authors: Chef Gilberto Cetina, Katharine A. Díaz and Gilberto Cetina, Jr.
Art direction and layout: Katharine A. Díaz
Plating coordination: Gilberto Cetina, Jr.
Cover design: David Mir
Cover and principal photography: Matthew Fried
Additional photography: Katharine A. Díaz
Photography editing: Marissa Marrufo
Food styling: Angela Pettera

ACKNOWLEDGMENTS

We would like to thank the following people for their tremendous help and support in making this cookbook a reality.

CETINA FAMILY
Concepción Ávila de Cetina, Blanca Cetina and María José Cetina de Sarabia.

DÍAZ FAMILY
Leno and Elisa Díaz, Eduardo Díaz, Micaela Díaz-Sánchez, Siboney Díaz-Sánchez and Yuquita Díaz.

OUR EXPERTS
Kirk Whisler, our publisher, who made a dream come true; Matthew Fried, who took such beautiful photographs of the food; Angela Pettera, a wonderful food stylist; Samuel Mark, for his expert eye and wise observations; and David Mir for a stunning cover.

OUR RECIPE TESTERS AND TASTERS
Pia Franco, Sheila Riddell, Ed Alves, Kathleen Vallee Stein, Ecriselia Gutiérrez, Betty Schaub, Michael Cecka, Beth Rodin, Kevin Rodin, Ryan Erlich, Christian Chaudhari, Mary Christine Daly, Rick Hurvitz, Amy Turk, Fabiano Oyafuso, Lisa Boling, Neil Rippon, Megan Rising, Ivy Chang and Bashir Eustache.

ADDITIONAL SUPPORT
The staff at Chichén Itzá Restaurant, Peggy Hentschke, Richard Vázquez, Sergio López, Iliana Escovedo, Marnie Olmstead, Carol Gilman, Nita Moots Kincaid, Becky García, Ivy Orta, Gloria Herrera, Diana Martínez, and many other supporters.

CONTENTS

Acknowledgments IV

Introduction/From the Authors 6

Chapter 1 **Recados & Salsas** 10

Chapter 2 **Starters/Antojitos** 18

Chapter 3 **Eggs/Huevos** 34

Chapter 4 **Soups & Stews/Sopas y guisos** 44

Chapter 5 **Poultry/Aves** 62

Chapter 6 **Pork/Puerco** 80

Chapter 7 **Beef & Venison/
 Carne de res y venado** 96

Chapter 8 **Seafood/Pescados y mariscos** 112

Chapter 9 **Tamales** 126

Chapter 10 **Sides/Para acompañar** 140

Chapter 11 **Drinks/Refrescos** 152

Chapter 12 **Desserts/Postres** 158

Techniques 174

Tools 175

Glossary 176

Index 184

Map of the Yucatán Peninsula 189

Rule-of-thumb Guide 190

About the Authors 192

Left, from top to bottom: Potaje de lentejas *(page 54);* queso relleno *(page 93),* Kukulkan, the Featured Serpent, in Chichén Itzá, Yucatán; vaporcitos *(page 129);* and tropical beverages *(Chapter 11).*

"La tierra del faisán y del venado"

From top: Pavo en relleno negro; *the Mayan ruins of Chichén Itzá, Yucatán;* sopa de lima; *and bell tower in Campeche, Campeche.*

From top: Door front in Isla Mujeres, Quintana Roo; puerco entomatado; *Tizimín, Yucatán; and* ceviche.

From top: Poc chuc; huipiles *for sale in Valladolid, Yucatán;* pastelitos de atropellado *with* helado de coco; *and Tulúm, Quintana Roo.*

Food photography by Matthew Fried/Location photography by Katharine A. Díaz

6 Sabores Yucatecos: A Culinary Tour of the Yucatán

"The Land of Pheasant and Deer"

INTRODUCTION

Turquoise seas . . . white-sand beaches . . . deep, azure *cenotes* . . . ancient, sky-reaching pyramids . . . aromatic *recados* . . . colorfully embroidered *huipiles* . . . crisp guayaberas . . . the music of strolling trios . . . all invoke images of Mexico's Yucatán Peninsula that encompasses the states of Yucatán, Campeche and Quintana Roo.

Making up part of Mexico's Caribbean along the Gulf of Mexico, the region was relatively isolated from central Mexico due to its geography. As a result, it boasts rich histories, unique cultural traditions . . . and food distinct from other parts of Mexico.

Populated by early Mesoamerican peoples during pre-Columbian times, the area would eventually be dominated by the great Mayan civilization. The Maya developed a calendar more accurate than today's Gregorian calendar. They are considered the first to understand the mathematical concept of "0." Astrology was an intensely studied science.

In the arts, the Maya excelled in building, sculpture, art and pottery. They also had highly stylized and artistic hieroglyphics that detailed their advances in the sciences as well as their complicated histories.

What they shared with the rest of Mesoamerica was an agricultural sophistication that allowed them to cultivate foodstuffs native to the Americas that would transform diets around the world. The list includes maize or corn, beans, tomatoes, chile peppers, cacao (chocolate), pumpkins, and avocados. Vanilla, *chaya*, papaya, *pitaya* and *mamey* also came from the region. The Maya also domesticated a species of turkey.

Although the brilliance of Mayan civilization had dulled by the time of the Conquest, the people of the peninsula were still fiercely independent. Nevertheless, this meeting of the Old World and New World was—for the purposes of this book—revolutionary in terms of everything having to do with food and eating.

Just imagine what happened when the *conquistadores* arrived with cattle and dairy products, pigs, chickens, onion, garlic, flour, citrus fruit, bananas, sugar, cinnamon and other spices, cilantro and other herbs, etc. Not to mention their European culinary technologies, techniques and traditions. Food in the Americas and the entire would never be the same.

As expected, in the Yucatán Peninsula, prideful of its uniqueness, an exciting cuisine would evolve unlike any other in Mexico.

In addition to Mayan and Spanish influences, the Lebanese and Dutch have left their mark on Yucatecan cuisine. Of particular interest is that of the Lebanese.

FROM THE CHEF: GILBERTO CETINA

I grew up in the timber town of Colonia Yucatán, Tizimín, in the state of Yucatán. As a boy, I would watch my mother as she cooked breakfast, lunch and dinner for hard-working loggers. My brothers and I often had to help her with chores. I was fascinated by what she was doing and was always at her side watching and learning.

Later, I moved to Mérida to study engineering in college. I lived with my brothers in a home we had there. We shared duties in the house; mine was to do the cooking. I loved it.

After graduating I worked briefly as an engineer, but cooking was always in the back of my mind. Finally, when I moved to the United States, I was able to focus on working in the food industry.

I worked in various restaurants where I honed my culinary skills. Along the way I never lost my love of preparing traditional Yucatecan foods, just like my mother did. Eventually I began catering as a side business . . . but only preparing Yucatecan dishes.

When I finally had an opportunity to open my own restaurant I jumped at the chance. I was advised that a Mexican restaurant only serving the regional foods of the Yucatán would never make it in Los Angeles. But I took a chance anyway.

That was back in 2001. Today, Chichén Itzá Restaurant has received accolades from food critics and customers who keep coming back for more. You could even say it has a cult following. It has become THE place for the best *panuchos, cochinita pibil, sopa de lima,* etc., etc., etc.

Kathy and I have worked hard on this cookbook that we think, in our humble opinion, best represents the cuisine of the Yucatán. It reflects the region's Mayan influences as well as those traditions that were introduced from other parts of Mexico and the world following the Conquest.

I would also like to recognize my son, Gilberto Cetina, Jr., for his contributions to the book.

We hope you learn not only how to prepare delicious dishes, but also gain an appreciation of my homeland.

Below: Katharine A. Díaz (l.) and Chef Gilberto Cetina.

A large population of Christian Lebanese began to migrate to the Yucatán in the later part of the 19th century. This was the result of a civil war in which the Druze, a Middle Eastern religious sect, was pitted against Christian Maronites. The greatest migration took place between 1880 and 1930, with many Lebanese continuing to arrive to join their relatives who had settled in the Yucatán, particularly in Mérida in the state of Yucatán. That's why *kibis* and other Middle Eastern foods are enjoyed throughout the Yucatán.

The Dutch connection is due primarily to the area's sea trading history and piracy. The best surviving example of this connection is the popularity of baby Edam cheese, which is the cheese of choice in the Yucatán. However, years ago you would have seen other Dutch products in homes in the Yucatán, such as cookies, candies, butter—even Happy Cow cheeses.

Yucatecan cuisine takes its place beside the other great regional foods of Mexico . . . culinary traditions recognized by UNESCO on its list of Intangible Cultural Heritage of Humanity.

We hope you enjoy this culinary tour of the Yucatán.

About the Recipes

We have taken great care to present the recipes in this book as clearly and as straightforward as possible. Any unusual techniques are explained plainly so that they are easy to follow and execute. We also note substitutes for any ingredients that might be hard to find in your local markets.

Will you find any of these recipes difficult to make? Some are more complicated than others; others benefit from that certain touch. However, the carefully written instructions should get you through any dish just fine.

Read each recipe before you begin. There's a good chance that you will be referred to other recipes in the book to complete the one you are planning to make. For example, you made need a *recado*, salsa or garnish. Some of these you might want to make ahead of time and have ready to go. You might also find that several recipes are similar and that a simple change of one or more ingredients or a cooking technique delivers a unique dish.

The measurements given for ingredients are as accurate as possible. Most measurements are given by volume, but in a few instances they are given by weight. Regardless, how do you account for the fact that some bunches of cilantro are bigger than others, that some limes are juicier than others, and that some plum tomatoes are big and some are small?

In addition, some people like their foods saltier, others less so; and some can handle heat from chiles, others can't.

So use your judgment, let your eyes and nose guide you . . . and taste, taste, taste as you prepare a dish. Take a look at Techniques (page 174), Tools (page 175) and the Glossary (page 176). And check out page 190 for some tips.

Sources

Thanks to today's interest in cuisines of the world, ingredients and tools that were once hard to find are now more available. In addition, the Internet will help you locate just about any hard-to-find item. Because of this easy access to find and order ingredients on the Internet, we have not provided a listing of sources.

Stop By for a Visit!

When in the Los Angeles area, please stop by **Chichén Itzá Restaurant** to sample the best of the cuisine of the Yucatán. During the week, our regular menu includes many of the dishes presented in this cookbook. But we also honor our culinary traditions. For example, on Mondays we offer *frijol con puerco* (see recipe), and on the weekends we offer *puchero de tres carnes* and *mondongos* (see recipes). We even roast a whole pig in order to offer *lechón al horno* (roasted pig) with all the trimmings on the weekends.

We also have special holiday menus. To celebrate Hanal Pixan or Día de los Muertos (Day of the Dead), for example, we offer *mucbi pollo* (see recipe). For Thanksgiving and Christmas you can also order a complete meal to go that includes our famous *pavo asado* (see recipe).

Check out our Web site for a schedule of cooking classes that can range from tamal making to seafood dishes that always end with a multiple-course, sit-down dinner.

And while you are there, you may as well pick up some of our Chichén Itzá–brand items: Gourmet Habanero Sauce, Chile Kut Sauce, horchata syrup, *longaniza tipo Valladolid*, *recado rojo*, *recado para bistec* and *recado negro*.

Chichén Itzá Restaurant

3655 S. Grand Avenue
Los Angeles, CA 90007
213-741-1075
www.chichenitzarestaurant.com

From the Writer: Katharine A. Díaz

I'll admit, in my youth I was a fussy eater. Oh, I ate all right and plenty, I was just picky. It took a year as a foreign-exchange student in Brazil to change all that. I began to finally appreciate all cuisines and enjoy challenging my tastebuds. Later travels to Latin America, plus my Mexican heritage, led to a particular interest in Latino cuisine, particularly from a cultural standpoint.

Incidentally, I loved to cook. As a kid, I would clip recipes from magazines and compile them in well-ordered chapters in three-ring binders. I still have them. Then I began to collect cookbooks, a collection that continues to grow and grow. For me, cookbooks are great reads.

As I began to write as a freelancer and as editor of national, Hispanic magazines, I found I enjoyed writing about Latino cuisine. This interest led me to Chef Cetina when I covered Chichén Itzá Restaurant in an article about the top Hispanic restaurants in the United States. Our acquaintance grew into a friendship.

It is his voice you hear here, a voice I was honored to interpret and express in the cookbook. I hope I have captured it because this book reflects his traditions, his life, his livelihood. For me it represents my deep fondness for the foods of the Yucatán and a deep appreciation for the talents of Chef Cetina.

Thanks, Gilberto, for revealing your culinary secrets to me!

Chapter 1
Recados & Salsas

Cooks from the Yucatán have an arsenal of ways to add flavor to their food that gives it its signature tastes and aromas. Topping the list are *recados* (sometimes "*recaudos*"), complex spice blends. Then there is a list of tomato-based salsas and others that are particular to specific dishes. Master these and you are well on you way to becoming an expert in preparing Yucatecan cuisine.

Recados

Recados (spice mixes) represent important and unique flavoring components to the cuisine of the Yucatán. Wet or dry, they are used to give dishes an extra layer and depth of flavor. In the recipes calling for a *recado*, we are generally referring to a paste that is used as a rub or to marinate meats and seafood.

A visit to the Mercado Municipal Lucas de Gálvez in Mérida, Yucatán, makes it clear that *recados* are indispensable to the Yucatecan table. You will see mounds and mounds of earth-tone *recados* for sale at booth after booth. The heady fragrance of the spices wafts overhead. Patrons have their favorite vendor.

In days gone by, *amas de casa* (housewives) would make their own *recados* from scratch, using secret family recipes. Today, family blends are still popular, but it's more likely that patrons take their secret blends to *molinos* or mills to have them ground. In fact, the *recado* vendors in Mérida's markets make theirs the same way. The *molinos,* with their huge, granite, grinding stones, efficiently churn out vendor or family blends.

Be careful buying prepared rubs or pastes. Sometimes manufacturers add ground corn, ground tortillas or flour to add volume; and food coloring to compensate for these fillers. I remember making *mondongo kabic* (see recipe) using a store-bought *recado*. When I added it to the stock, it made an *atole* (gruel) almost immediately. It obviously had flour added to it.

My tip for buying a good *recado*? Smell it and taste it. A good *recado rojo*, for example, should smell of the flower of achiote. What does this smell like? Just sink your nose into a handful of achiote seeds and you'll know.

Salsas, Sauces and More

Yucatecos also appreciate their *salsas frescas*, salsas made with market-fresh ingredients. Many feature the ultra-hot *chile habanero,* which is also iconic to Yucatecan cuisine. These small babies rate 150,000–325,000 on the Scoville scale making them hot, hot, hot. The most familiar color for *habaneros* is a bright orange, but you can also find green and red ones.

As you experiment with dishes in this cookbook, you will find that various sauces represent a key ingredient in a specific dish. These include a number of tomato sauces and pumpkin seed sauces.

Above, from top: Mounds of recados *in the market, Chef Cetina (l.) with the* molinero de recados, *and the infamous* chiles habaneros.

Opposite page, clockwise from top right: Recado negro *(page 12),* recado rojo *(page 12),* pepitas de calabaza tostadas *(page 17) and* recado para bistec *(page 12).*

Chapter 1: Recados & Salsas 11

RECADOS

RECADO ROJO
(OR PASTA DE ACHIOTE, RECADO COLORADO)

Makes about 1 cup (pictured on page 10)

This is the grandddaddy of all the *recados*, playing a major role in the iconic dish of the Yucatán, *cochinita pibil* (see recipe). It also flavors tamales, chicken dishes, stews, *tikin xic* (see recipe), etc. It is probably the most used of all the spice blends, rubs and marinades. Like all the *recados*, it is simple to make.

1/2 cup ground achiote (ground annatto seed)

1 tablespoon ground white pepper

4 tablespoons salt

1 tablespoon garlic powder

1 pinch ground cloves

1 pinch ground allspice

1 pinch ground oregano

1/4 cup white vinegar

1/4 cup water

1. Mix all of the ingredients in a nonreactive bowl (stainless steel or glass) until everything is well blended.

2. Ready to use immediately.

RECADOS: SPICEY SURPRISES *Recados* are to the Yucatán what *moles* are to Oaxaca. They are regional treasures and figure as important ingredients in Yucatecan cooking. *Recados* are distinctive spice and herb blends that are used in rubs and marinades in a wide range of dishes. Some are used more widely than others (see "*recado rojo*"). They are not difficult to make and homemade ones are better than store-bought ones. While some *recados* appear to be matched to a specific dish, experiment by using them with other favorite dishes. They will add a nice punch to those dishes. Store *recados* in a jar or other tightly sealed container. Refrigerated, they keep pretty much indefinitely. See side bar on achiote on page 84.

RECADO NEGRO

Makes about 2 cups (pictured on page 10)

This *recado* captures best the taste that the early Maya had for earthy tastes—or more specifically, burnt or charred ones. It gives food a unique flavor as well as a dark color. It is the recado called for in *buth negro* and *pavo en relleno negro* (see recipes).

3 pounds *chile árbol*, seeded (see Glossary)

2 tablespoons salt

2 gallons water

1 teaspoon (or 4 ounces) black peppercorns

8 whole allspice berries (see Glossary)

10 whole cloves

1 head garlic, peeled

20 leaves fresh oregano

1 tablespoon achiote seeds

1. Burn the chiles on a hot *comal* (or griddle or skillet). The chiles should be black through and through.

2. Dissolve the salt in the water and soak the burnt chiles in the salty water for 1 hour.

3. Drain the chiles and rinse them in clear water (see notes).

4. In a coffee grinder, grind the chiles, peppercorns, allspice, cloves, garlic, oregano and achiote seeds until you get a smooth paste like a dough. If the mixture is too dry, add a bit of water.

Notes: Rinsing the chiles in water reduces some of their heat. If you want the heat, don't rinse, just drain from the salt water. If you want to reduce more heat, rinse the chiles several times in clear water.

RECADO PARA BISTEC
(OR RECADO BLANCO)

Makes about 1 cup (pictured on page 10)

This *recado* makes an excellent rub or marinade for a variety of meats. It is the *recado* of choice for *pollo alcaparrado* (see recipe), and *empanizados* (breaded meats, such as *puerco empanizado*, see recipe). As its name suggests, it is the marinade of choice for *bistec* (steaks).

1/2 cup ground white pepper

1 tablespoon garlic powder

1/4 cup white vinegar

1/4 cup water

1. Mix all of the ingredients in a nonreactive bowl (stainless steel or glass) until everything is well blended.

Recado para escabeche

Makes about 1 cup

This spice blend and marinade is used exclusively for escabeches—pickled seafood, meats and vegetables. Examples are *pollo en escabeche* and *calamares en escabeche* (see recipes).

1/2 cup ground white pepper

1 tablespoon garlic powder

1 pinch ground cloves

1 pinch ground oregano

1 pinch ground cumin

1/4 cup white vinegar

1/4 cup water

1. Mix all of the ingredients in a nonreactive bowl (stainless steel or glass) until everything is well blended.

Recado para puchero

Makes about 1 cup

The name tells you all you need to know about this *recado*. It is used only for *puchero de tres carnes*, a hearty stew (see recipe).

1/2 cup ground white pepper

1 tablespoon garlic powder

1 pinch ground cloves

1 pinch ground oregano

1 pinch ground cumin

1 pinch ground cinnamon

1 pinch saffron

1/4 cup white vinegar

1/4 cup water

1. Mix all of the ingredients in a nonreactive bowl (stainless steel or glass) until everything is well blended.

Salsas

Pico de gallo

Fresh Salsa

Makes about 2 cups (pictured on page 112)

This fresh salsa is known throughout Mexico. It's a classic and just requires some chopping.

4 plum tomatoes, diced

1/2 medium red onion, diced

3 sprigs cilantro, diced

1/2 teaspoon salt

Juice of 1/2 lime

1. Dice the tomatoes, red onion and cilantro into similarly sized bits and mix with salt and lime. Chill.

Notes: This fresh salsa is great as a dip served with tortilla chips or as an accompaniment to all sorts of dishes.

X'nipek

Dog's Nose Salsa

Makes about 2 cups

Despite its exotic name, *x'nipek* is really just *pico de gallo* with *chile habanero* added to it. In Mayan, *x'nipek* means "nose of a dog." That's because if you overindulge in this hot salsa *fresca* your nose will be runny and wet just like a dog's.

1 recipe of *pico de gallo* (see recipe)

1 *chile habanero,* diced (or *chile serrano* or jalapeño)

1. Follow the instructions for making *pico de gallo* (above).

2. Add diced chile. Chill.

Notes: Like *pico de gallo,* you can offer *x'nipek* with every dish and every meal. But if you use *chile habanero,* you should warn your guests that it is HOT.

SALSA DE CHILE HABANERO

Habanero Chile Sauce

Makes about 4 cups

This salsa is one of the most popular featuring *chile habanero.* You can by it bottled, but as you might expect, homemade is best. Again, use caution when handling chiles, especially this one. It is a great salsa to serve on the side. It's wise to allow your guests to choose to use it or not. It's hot!

4 cups water

1 pounds *chiles habaneros* (not green)

1/2 pound diced white onion

4 garlic cloves, peeled

1/3 cup white vinegar

2 tablespoons salt

OPTIONAL (see notes)

4 tablespoons cornstarch

2 tablespoons water

1. Bring the water to a boil and add the chiles, onion and garlic. Boil until the chiles fall apart, about 15–20 minutes.

2. In a blender add the boiled chiles, onion, garlic (with water), vinegar and salt. Blend until you get a fairly smooth mixture.

3. Optional: To thicken the salsa slightly, mix the cornstarch in the tablespoons of water until smooth. Pour the salsa into a pot and over a medium-high heat, add the cornstarch paste a little at a time to the salsa, stirring constantly, until it thickens slightly.

Notes: Step 3 is optional. Thickening the salsa keeps the solids and liquids from separating. If you don't thicken the salsa, just give it a stir or shake before using.

CHILE KUT

Roasted Habanero Chile Salsa

Makes about 1/3 cup

This is an extra-hot chile sauce. So proceed with caution when making, and warn your guests when offering it. No doubt there will be someone you know who boasts just

Left, from top: Salsa de chile habanero, chile kut *and* x'nipek.

how much he or she can eat . . . even as the sweat pours down his or her face. It is at its peak heat on the first day; the heat level diminishes with time. Believe it or not, during the first Chile Kut Eating Contest held in 2011 at Chichén Itzá Restaurant, the winner downed 4 1/2 cups of *chile kut*!

10 whole *chiles habaneros,* roasted

2 cloves garlic, roasted

4 tablespoons white vinegar

4 tablespoons olive oil

1 tablespoon salt

1. Roast chiles and garlic over direct heat or on a hot *comal* (griddle of skillet) until completely charred, but not burned all the way through.

2. Place in a *molcajete* (pestle and mortar, see Glossary) with the rest of the ingredients. Grind until everything is well mixed together. You can also use a blender or food processor. The salsa should be chunky.

Notes: For tips on roasting chiles, garlic and tomatoes, see Techniques. Make sure to work in a well-ventilated area when roasting the chiles as the fumes are choking. And wear plastic gloves when handling.

SALPICÓN
RADISH AND CILANTRO GARNISH

Makes about 1/2 cup (pictured on page 101)

Salpicón is not really a stand-alone *salsa fresca*. But it is an integral part of *salpicón de res* and *salpicón de venado* (see recipes) and a topping or garnish for other dishes. So be prepared to refer to this recipe. It can be tossed together quickly. For aesthetic purposes, finely chop the ingredients.

10 radishes, minced

1 bunch cilantro, finely chopped

Juice of 5–6 *naranjas agrias* (or lime juice) (about 1/2 cup)

1 teaspoon salt

1. In a bowl, toss the radishes, cilantro, juice of *naranja agria* (or lime juice) and salt.

Notes: *Naranjas agrias* have a lot of seeds, so it's best to squeeze them over a strainer into the dish you are preparing. If a seed should slip into your dish, you'll know because it's very bitter, something to avoid.

SALSAS DE TOMATE
TOMATO-BASED SAUCES

SALSA DE TOMATE
YUCATECAN TOMATO SAUCE

Makes about 5 cups (pictured on page 24)

This is a basic tomato sauce used in many dishes, so it's a good idea to learn to make it well. You will note that it is one of the few dishes that uses a standard salad tomato rather than the more commonly used plum tomato.

5 cups water

4 salad tomatoes (about 2 pounds)

3–4 cloves garlic, crushed

1 medium white onion, quartered

2 teaspoons salt

3 tablespoons vegetable oil

1. Boil water in a stockpot. Add the tomatoes (whole), garlic, onion and salt. Bring to a boil, about 30 minutes or until the tomatoes easily break apart.

2. Liquefy in a blender until you get a smooth puree. Do in batches if you have a small blender. The sauce is watery.

3. Heat the oil in a large skillet. Add purée carefully and, stirring occasionally, let it cook over medium heat until it thickens somewhat, about 25-30 minutes. It should still pour easily, only slightly coating a spoon. Adjust salt.

Notes: In the majority of recipes in this book, you will find that the favored tomato is the plum or Roma tomato. But for *salsa de tomate,* your run-of-the-mill salad or beefsteak tomato is used because it is less acidic than the plum tomato.

SOFRITO DE TOMATE
SEASONED TOMATO SAUCE

Makes about 4–5 cups (pictured on page 33)

Sometimes simple things give dishes an extra something. *Sofrito de tomate* is one of those easy-to-make additions that are used to add flavor to various dishes. A classic

CHAPTER 1: RECADOS & SALSAS 15

example is *pan de cazón* (see recipe). Who can imagine it without being smothered in *sofrito de tomate*? You'll also need it for *codzitos* (see recipe), *papadzules* (see recipe) and tamales (Chapter 9).

2 tablespoons olive oil

1/2 medium white onion, chopped

1 clove garlic, finely chopped

6 medium plum tomatoes (about 1 1/2 pounds), chopped

2 cups *salsa de tomate* (see recipe)

1 teaspoon salt

1. Heat the oil in a skillet and add the onions and sauté for about a minute.

2. Add the garlic, tomatoes and salt, and sauté over heat for another 5 minutes or until the tomatoes break up.

3. Add the *salsa de tomate* and cook down until some of the liquid has evaporated.

Notes: This is a slightly chunky sauce as opposed to the more liquid purée that is *salsa de tomate* (see recipe).

Chiltomate

Roasted Tomato Sauce

Makes about 2 cups (pictured on page 88)

You will discover that this salsa is used with specific dishes. But it's a great salsa to have for everyday eating. Again, the *chile habanero* is optional, but it does add a lot of character to the salsa. So maybe you could put in a quarter or half of the chile without much ado.

10 medium plum tomatoes, roasted

1 *chile habanero*, roasted (optional)

3-4 sprigs cilantro, chopped

1/2 teaspoon salt

1. Roast the tomatoes and chile on a *comal* (griddle or skillet) over low to medium heat until they are charred on the outside and soft to the touch. If the heat is too high, the tomatoes will not cook through. Let cool.

2. Add the tomatoes and chile to a food processor. Pulse into small chunks. You can also use a *molcajete*—pestle and mortar. You do not want a purée.

3. In a bowl, toss the chopped cilantro and salt with the chunky tomatoes and chile.

Misc. Salsas

Salsa de Achiote para Tikin Xic
Achiote Sauce for Tikin Xic

Makes about 2 quarts (pictured on page 112)

This is the sauce that is going to contribute to the great flavor and color of your *tikin xic* (see recipe). So you're going to definitely want to have some *recado rojo* on hand.

2 quarts chicken or fish broth

1 ounce (1 1/2 tablespoons) *recado rojo* (see recipe)

2-3 tablespoons *naranja agria* juice (or lime juice)

3-4 tablespoons cornstarch

Salt, to taste

1. Bring the chicken or fish stock to a boil in a stockpot. Dilute the *recado rojo* paste in 1 cup of stock, and strain back into the stockpot.

2. Add the *naranja agria* juice (or lime juice).

3. Dilute the cornstarch in 1 cup of stock until well incorporated. Slowly pour this into the stockpot, stirring constantly until it is incorporated with no lumps.

4. Let cook at a high simmer, stirring occasionally, for 6 to 8 minutes or until the sauce thickens enough to coat a spoon. Adjust salt.

Salsa de Achiote para Tamales
Achiote Sauce for Tamales

Makes about 1 gallon

This is the sauce you will need for fillings for many of Yucatán's tamales. Please see the recipe for *caldo de pollo* (chicken stock) to make the stock needed for this recipe. For the tamal fillings, you will also need the chicken that is stewed at the same time. So reserve the meat.

4 quarts *caldo de pollo* (chicken stock, see recipe) (divided)

1 ounce (1 1/2 tablespoons) *recado rojo* (see recipe)

6 plum tomatoes, quartered (about 1 1/2-2 cups)

4 sprigs epazote

8 ounces *masa de maíz para tortillas* (see Glossary)

Salt, to taste

1. Pour 3 quarts the *caldo de pollo* into a large stockpot. Take 1 cup of that stock and liquefy it with the *recado rojo*. Bring stock to a boil and strain the liquefied *recado rojo* into the pot.

2. Add the tomatoes and epazote to the boiling stock. Reduce heat and let simmer uncovered until the tomatoes easily break apart.

3. In the remaining 1 quart stock, liquefy the *masa de maíz para tortillas.*

4. Stirring constantly, slowly pour the liquefied *masa* into the stockpot. Simmer and stir the sauce until it is thicker than a gravy. You may not have to use all of the liquefied *masa*. Adjust salt.

PEPITAS DE CALABAZA TOSTADAS SIN CÁSCARA
GROUND TOASTED HULLED PUMPKIN SEEDS

Makes about 1 pound ground seeds (pictured on page 10)

These ground seeds are used in pretty much any dish that says "*en pipián*," such as *costillas en pipián* (see recipe). They also serve as a base for *mazapán* (marzipan) sweets. This is the New World take on an Old World sweet in which almonds are used. The ground seeds will keep up to 3 months refrigerated in a tight container.

1 pound, hulled pumpkin seeds

1. Heat a *comal* (griddle or skillet) over medium heat. Spread pumpkin seeds evenly, in one layer, over the bottom of the *comal*. (You may have to do in batches.)

2. Toast the seeds, flipping occasionally with a spatula. The seeds should be golden and crispy and crunchy to the taste. Do not burn.

3. Remove from heat and cool.

4. Place the cooled, toasted seeds in a food processor or coffee grinder and pulse to a fine grind.

Notes: You can also toast and grind unhulled pumpkin seeds the same way to get *pepitas de calabaza tostadas con cáscara*. In most cases either ground seed is OK to use. The difference among Yucatecan cooks is one of economics. Unhulled seeds are cheaper than hulled ones.

SAH KOL
WHITE SAUCE

Makes about 3 cups

This is a simple sauce to make that goes with dishes calling for *sah kol*, like *sah kol de pavo* (see recipe). Call it the Yucatecan béchamel.

6–7 tablespoons margarine

4 cups chicken stock

3–4 tablespoons *masa de maíz* (see Glossary)

Salt, to taste

Ground black pepper, to taste

1. Melt the margarine in a deep saucepan over low to medium heat and add the chicken stock.

2. Dissolve the *masa de maíz* in a bit of stock and pour into the pan, stirring constantly, to thicken the stock. It should be thick enough to coat a spoon without dripping.

3. Add salt and pepper to taste.

SALSA TÁRTARA
TARTAR SAUCE DE CHICHÉN ITZÁ RESTAURANT

Makes about 1 cup (pictured on page 124)

Use to accompany seafood dishes. Obviously, the *chile habanero* gives it a lot of extra punch.

1 cup mayonnaise

2 tablespoons white onion, finely minced

1 teaspoon capers, finely minced

1 teaspoon lime juice

1/2 *chile habanero*, finely minced (optional)

1. Mix all ingredients in a bowl. Chill.

ALLPICE: AN ALL-IN-ONE SPICE
Allspice is one of the few spices native to the New World. The dried seeds reminded the Spanish *conquistadores* of pepper or "pimienta," which confused matters between *pimiento*, black pepper and chile peppers. The name "allspice" refers to the spice's aroma that is a mix of cloves, juniper, nutmeg and pepper. For more on allspice, see Glossary.

CHAPTER 2 ..

STARTERS...
ANTOJITOS

Yucatecos don't envy the Spanish and their tapas or Middle Easterners their mezes, because when it comes to snacks and little dishes, they have plenty to offer. And *yucatecos* do like to *botanear*—go out snacking.

The dishes presented here are excellent starters or appetizers. A couple of dishes may seem more like sides—potato salad (*ensalada de papa*) or rice with fried plantains (*arroz con plátanos fritos*)—but these are indeed offered in bars as snacks. And, yes, they can serve as sides as well.

Among the collection of recipes in this chapter, you will find many that are signature dishes of the Yucatán. These include *panuchos, salbutes, xec* and *sikil pac. Kibis, crema de garbanzo* and *arrolladitos de repollo* clearly illustrate the strong foreign influences that have taken hold on the peninsula.

Opposite page, clockwise from top right: Chile x'catic relleno de cazón *(page 25),* crema de garbanzo *(page 31),* arroz con plátanos *(page 29)* and ensalada de papa *(page 29).*

Right, from top: "Tortillas para panuchos" *ready to take home; the cathedral in Mérida, Yucatán; and jícama for sale by the kilo.*

CHAPTER 2: STARTERS/ANTOJITOS 19

Panuchos
Garnished Corn Tortillas Stuffed with Bean Paste

Serves 6–8; makes 15 *panuchos*

Ingredients

1 pound *masa de maíz para tortillas* (or made from *masa harina*) (see Glossary)

3/4 teaspoon salt

1 cup *frijoles colados* (see recipe)

Vegetable oil

Toppings

Green leaf lettuce, thinly sliced

Shredded *pavo* or *pollo asado* (see recipes)

Cebolla para panuchos (see recipe)

1 plum tomato, thinly sliced

1/2 avocado, thinly sliced

Panuchos are a signature snack of the Yucatán and, well made, are a source of pride to any *yucateco*. They are related to many of Mexico's classic *antojitos* based on small tortillas that are stuffed and/or topped with tasty tidbits. A bit labor intensive, *panuchos* are all about technique, and practice will make perfect. Now, if you were in the Yucatán, you could just stop by a market and buy the prepared tortillas for frying and topping (see photograph on page 19). As that might not be possible, challenge yourself to learn how to handle the *masa de maíz* well and your *panuchos* will be instant hits.

1. Mix or knead the salt into the *masa*. Divide the *masa* into 15 balls. As you work, keep the *masa* balls in a bowl covered with plastic wrap to keep the dough from drying out. Add a bit of water if needed for a pliant *masa*.

2. Line a tortilla press with a piece of plastic wrap. Put one ball of *masa* into the center of the press, cover with another piece of plastic wrap (wax paper will work too). Press down on the tortilla press until the tortilla is about 6 inches in diameter.

3. Carefully peel the plastic wrap off the tortilla and place the tortilla on a hot *comal* (griddle or skillet). When it no longer sticks to the *comal*, flip to the other side. While still on the *comal*, press tortilla with a clean, folded kitchen cloth so that it puffs up. Press around the edges to make sure it puffs up all around. Leave a few seconds more on *comal* before removing the tortilla from the *comal*.

4. Along the side, carefully slit the top layer of the tortilla that puffed up—an opening of 3 inches will do—and lift up all the way inside creating a pocket. The tortilla is still very hot, so be careful. Do not create too wide an opening, separate completely or tear. To cool, place on paper towels or clean towel. Repeat steps 2 to 4 for each tortilla. (Veteran *panucho* makers will give the inside of the *panucho* a strong puff to make sure the top separates to create the perfect pocket.)

5. Take a cooled tortilla, carefully lift the top and, with a teaspoon, smear a spoonful of *frijoles colados* inside the pocket. Press with your fingers to make sure the bean paste is spread evenly all around. Repeat process with each *panucho*.

6. To complete, place the *panucho* on a hot, oiled *comal* (griddle or skillet) and toast until golden on both sides, about 2–3 minutes on each side.

7. Remove to paper towels. Repeat process for each *panucho*. This should be done just before you are ready to serve, as *panuchos* are best eaten freshly prepared.

8. To assemble the *panuchos*: Top each *panucho* with sliced green leaf lettuce, shredded *pavo* or *pollo asado* (see recipes), *cebolla para panuchos*, a slice of tomato and a slice of avocado. Serve *salsa de chile habanero* (see recipe) on the side.

Photo by Gilberto Cetina, Jr.

Tips: Do not smear the bean paste inside the tortillas until they have cooled to avoid tearing the top thin layer of the tortillas. Also, make sure the bean paste is spread evenly all around the inside of the *panucho*. If not, it might tear in the process of toasting. You do this by lightly pressing the top of the *panucho* to spread the bean paste out; just don't let any bean paste seep out. And remember that the toppings should be carefully balanced so as not to overwhelm the flavor of the *panucho* you have so carefully prepared. In the spirit of full disclosure, in the Yucatán, thinly sliced cucumber and slices of jalapeños are often included on the list of toppings.

SACRED TOPPINGS Outside the Yucatán, you will often see *panuchos* topped with *cochinita pibil*. However, no self-respecting *yucateco* would do so; that would be sacrilegious. *Pavo asado* (roasted turkey) is the classic topping with *pollo asado* an acceptable second choice. Roasted turkey is also the classic topping for *salbutes*, but at eateries throughout the Yucatán all sorts of other topping options are offered for *salbutes*. These can range from *huevos cocidos* (chopped, hard-cooked eggs) to *carne molida* (see recipe) and all kinds of *guisos* (stewed meats).

Cebolla para panuchos (page 142) *top a* salbut.

SALBUTES
Garnished Puffed Corn Tortillas

Serves 6–8; makes 15 *salbutes*

Ingredients

1 pound *masa de maíz para tortillas* (or made from *masa harina*) (see Glossary)

3/4 teaspoon salt

2 tablespoons all-purpose flour

Vegetable oil

Toppings

Green leaf lettuce, thinly sliced

Shredded *pavo* or *pollo asado* (see recipes)

Cebolla para panuchos (see recipe)

1 plum tomato, thinly sliced

1/2 avocado, thinly sliced

Notes: You can also deep-fry your *salbutes*. When you drop one into the hot oil (375°F), it will sink to the bottom. Then it will puff up and rise to the top. Flip it over to finish.

Salbutes are other tortilla-based *antojitos* typical of the Yucatán, and they rank up there in popularity along with *panuchos*. Making them involves fewer steps than *panuchos*, but there is also some delicate handling of the *masa* required because you do need to get your tortillas to puff up as you fry them. It's all about the flour.

1. Mix or knead the salt and flour into the *masa*. Divide the *masa* into 15 balls. As you work, keep the *masa* balls in a bowl covered with plastic wrap to keep them from drying out. Add a bit of water if needed for a pliant *masa*.

2. Line a tortilla press with a piece of plastic wrap. Put one ball of *masa* into the center of the press, cover with another piece of plastic wrap (wax paper will work too). Press down on the tortilla press until the tortilla is about 6 inches in diameter. Carefully peel the plastic wrap off the tortilla.

3. Heat oil in a frying pan, about 1/4-inch deep. Drop in a tortilla. With a spoon, sprinkle hot oil on top of the tortilla or *salbut* so that it puffs up. At that point, flip over and continue frying. The *salbut* should be golden on the outside but tender and chewy on the inside. Do not fry until crispy. Remove and drain on paper towels.

4. Repeat steps 1–3 for each *salbut*.

5. To assemble *salbutes*: Top each *salbut* with sliced green leaf lettuce, *pavo* or *pollo asado* (see recipes), *cebolla para panuchos* (see recipe), a slice of tomato and a slice of avocado. Serve *salsa de chile habanero* (see recipe) on the side. Like the *panucho*, toppings should not overwhelm the *salbut*.

Empanadas de Cazón

Fish Turnovers

Serves about 6–8; makes 15 empanadas

Empanadas, or turnovers, make for great party food. Better yet, they adapt to a variety of fillings. While I might prefer *cazón* (dogfish, see Glossary), tuna is just fine as a filling. Regardless, I still call them *empanadas de cazón*.

Preparing the tuna filling

1. Heat the oil in a frying pan. Add the tuna and epazote and sauté 4–5 minutes.

2. Add 1 1/2 cup *salsa de tomate*, and sauté over medium-high heat until most of the moisture is removed. Add salt, if needed, and cool.

Preparing the masa (dough)

1. Mix or knead the salt and flour into the *masa*.

2. Divide the *masa* into 15 balls. As you work, keep the *masa* balls in a bowl covered with a damp cloth to keep the dough from drying out.

2. Line a tortilla press with a piece of plastic wrap. Put one ball of *masa* into the center of the press, cover with another piece of plastic wrap. Press down on the tortilla press until the tortilla is about 5 inches in diameter.

3. Remove the top piece of plastic wrap and place about 1 tablespoon of tuna filling in the center of the tortilla. Fold the tortilla in half and seal the edge of the empanada with the tines of a fork. Place on a plate lined with plastic wrap.

4. Repeat steps 2 and 3 with each ball of *masa*. Cover the empanadas with plastic wrap and place in refrigerator for 20–25 minutes before frying.

5. Heat the vegetable oil in a frying pan, about 1-inch deep. Fry the empanadas on both sides until golden, 2–4 minutes both sides. Drain on paper towels.

To serve: Arrange the empanadas on a serving platter and top with reserved 1/2 cup *salsa de tomate* and *cebolla para cochinita pibil* or place in a basket with toppings on the side. You will want to have extra *salsa de tomate* on hand.

Notes: Other fillings, such as *carne molida* (see recipe) or grated cheese, can be used. Try grated baby Edam or Monterrey Jack cheese. I am particularly fond of *queso panela*.

Tuna filling

Vegetable oil, for preparing the filling and to fry empanadas

1 can (12 ounces) tuna in water, drained, broken up finely with a fork (fine-quality, white albacore or other cooked white fish)

20 *epazote* leaves, chopped

2 cups *salsa de tomate* (reserve 1/2 cup for plating) (see recipe)

Salt, to taste

Masa (dough)

1 pound *masa de maíz para tortillas* (or use *masa harina*) (see Glossary)

3/4 teaspoon salt

2 tablespoons all-purpose flour

vegetable oil

Garnishes

Salsa de tomate (see recipe)

Cebolla para cochinita pibil (see recipe)

Codzitos

Rolled and Fried Tortillitas

Serves about 4–6

Ingredients

1 egg

2–3 tablespoons all-purpose flour

1 dozen, 4-inch tortillas

Vegetable oil

Toppings

1/2 cup *salsa de tomate* (see recipe)

2 tablespoons grated baby Edam cheese (or *queso fresco* or *cotija*)

Who knows why the taste of a crispy fried corn tortilla is so satisfying, it just is. *Codzitos* distill this essence and should "*truenan cuando los comas*". That is, the crunch should "thunder" in your mouth when you bite into one. In the Yucatán, home cooks will put the rolled up *codzitos* outside in the sun to dry for a day or two so that they are extra crispy when fried. Prepare a platter of *codzitos* for your next party and let the "*truenos*" or thundering begin.

1. Make a smooth paste by mixing the egg and flour together in a small bowl.

2. Warm a tortilla on a *comal* (griddle or skillet) to soften. (If the tortilla is not warm, it will break as you roll it in the step that follows.)

3. Dip your fingers in the egg-flour paste and smear along one-half of the outer edge of the tortilla. Roll up the tortilla tightly starting on the side without the egg–flour paste. Set aside, edge-side down. The paste acts as a glue to seal the edge of the *codzito*. Repeat process with remaining tortillas.

4. Heat oil in a frying pan, about 1-inch deep. Fry the *codzitos* until golden and crispy, about 4–6 minutes. Remove and drain on paper towels.

To serve: Arrange *codzitos* on a platter. Top with *salsa de tomate* (see recipe) and sprinkle with grated baby Edam or other cheese.

Notes: No, you did not miss anything; there is no filling like you would find with *taquitos* or *flautas*. But you obviously see the similarities between the three. The difference is also about size. *Codzitos* are diminutive, *taquitos* are next in size, *flautas* are the biggest.

Tips: If you can't find 4-inch tortillas in your local supermarket and don't have a neighborhood *tortillería*, follow directions for making tortillas from *masa harina* (see Glossary). Or just make bigger *codzitos*.

Codzitos are made better with a healthy topping of *salsa de tomate* (page 15).

Chile X'catic Relleno de Cazón

Fish-stuffed Blond Chile

Serves about 6–8 (photo on page 8)

These fabulous stuffed chiles are not easy to find, but I remember seeing recipes for it in cookbooks from the 1950s. Perhaps they are more typical of Campeche. Top-quality ingredients should be used for the filling. This recipe uses tuna, but they are typically made with dogfish or *cazón* (see Glossary), which is why I still prefer to leave *cazón* in the name.

1. Roast chiles on a *comal* (griddle) or open flame until the skin blackens and blisters. Then put in a plastic bag to steam for 10–15 minutes. Leaving stem on, remove skin, slit chiles open lengthwise, and remove seeds and vein.

2. Optional: To rid the chiles of some of their heat, mix the vinegar, salt and water in a bowl. Gently rinse the prepared chiles and pat dry with paper towels. Rinse more than once to remove more of the heat and pat dry again.

3. Heat oil in a frying pan. Add the tuna and epazote (except what is reserved for garnish). Sauté 4–5 minutes or until most of the moisture has evaporated..

4. Add 1 1/2 cups *salsa de tomate* and sauté over medium-high heat to reduce until most of the moisture is removed. Add salt, if needed, and cool.

5. Stuff each chile generously with the tuna mixture. They should be plump yet not with a wide opening. Put aside on paper towels, slit side down.

6. Beat the eggs until they are foamy, and add salt and black pepper. Set aside.

7. Put the flour on a plate and lightly dredge the stuffed chiles in the flour. Then, holding by the stem, dip in the egg batter.

8. Heat the oil in a frying pan, about 1-inch deep. Carefully fry the stuffed and battered chiles in the oil on both sides until the egg batter is cooked and golden, about 3–4 minutes. Drain on paper towels.

To serve: Arrange chiles on a serving platter and top each one with a dollop of *sofrito de tomate*. Pour reserved 1/2 cup *salsa de tomate* around the chiles, and finish with a garnish of the epazote you reserved.

Tips: It's OK to stuff the chiles in advance. But do not flour or dip in the egg batter and fry until you are ready to serve. They just don't hold up well. Two to three of these delectable stuffed chiles can be served as a main course with *arroz blanco* (see recipe) and corn tortillas.

Ingredients

12 *chiles x'catic* (*chiles güeritos* or blond chiles), about 3- to 4-inches long (see Glossary)

2 tablespoons vegetable oil

1 can (12 ounces) tuna in water, drained, broken up finely with a fork (fine-quality, white albacore or other cooked white fish)

20 epazote leaves, chopped (reserve about 5 for garnish)

2 cups *salsa de tomate* (reserve 1/2 cup for plating) (see recipe)

Salt, to taste

Rinse for Chiles

(to remove some heat from the chiles, optional)

2 tablespoons white vinegar

1 tablespoons salt

1/2 gallon water

Batter for Chiles

4 eggs

1/4 teaspoon salt

1/4 ground black pepper

1/3 cup all-purpose flour

Garnish

1/2 cup *sofrito de tomate* (see recipe)

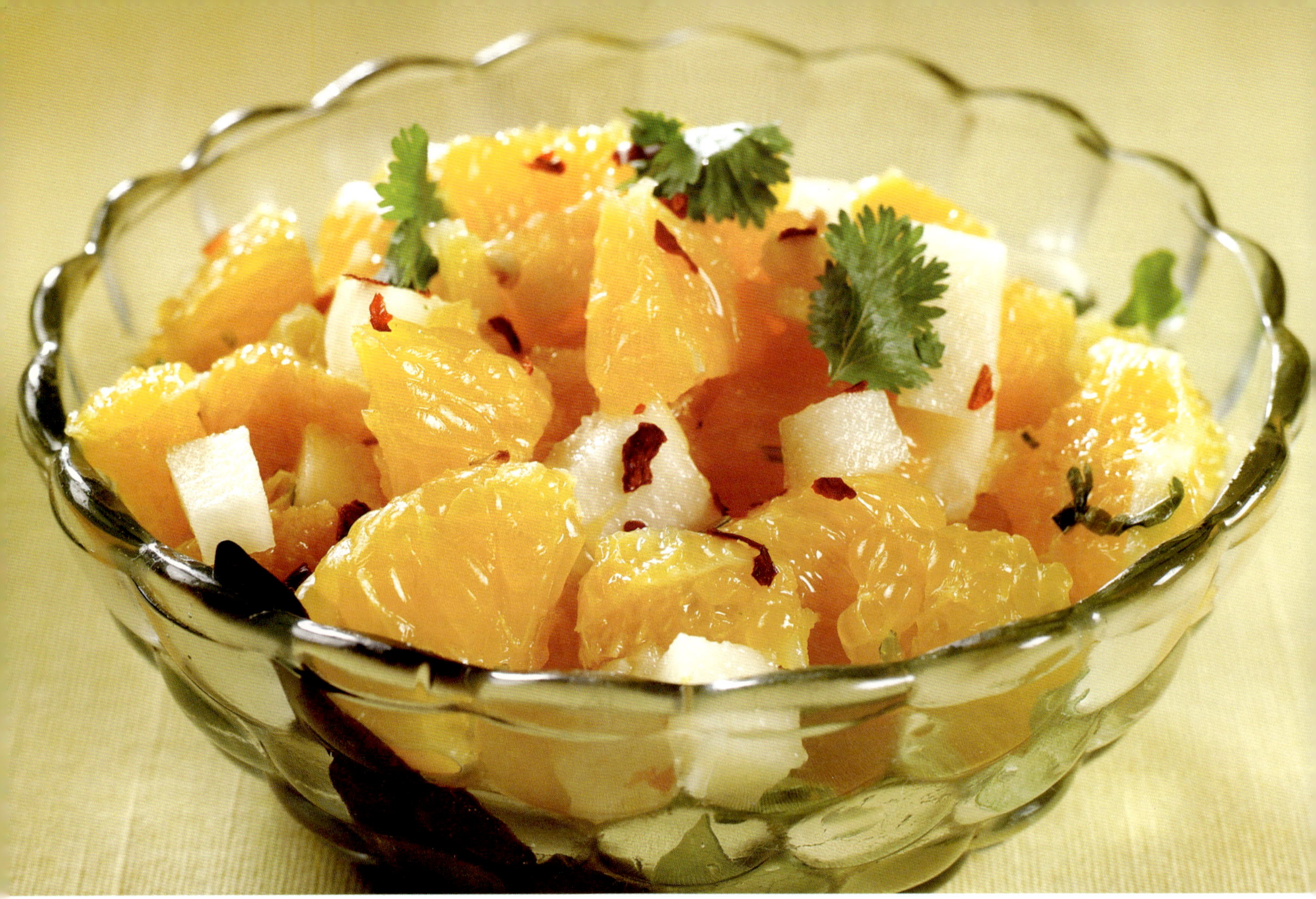

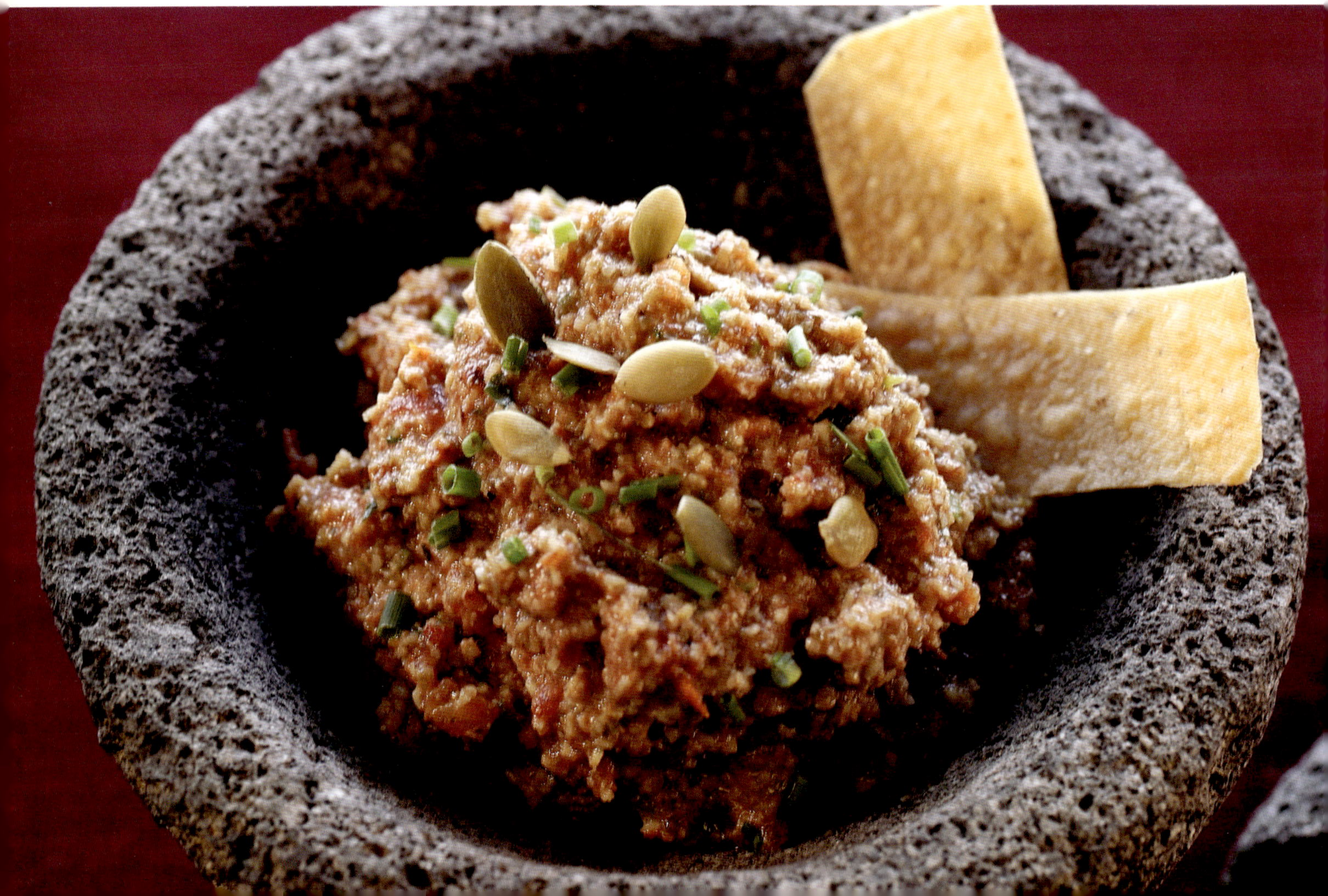

XEC

Jícama Citrus Salad

Serves about 6–8 (top in photo at left)

This salad makes for a refreshing starter or a light side dish. In the Yucatán, it is served in cantinas (neighborhood bars) as an appetizer. Customers pick at it with toothpicks and down it with cold beer.

1. Toss all of the ingredients together in a bowl. Adjust salt.

To serve: Serve family style in a large salad bowl. Or prepare individual servings by placing a single serving over a bed of salad greens on a dish or in a small bowl.

Notes: In the Yucatán, diced grapefruit is sometimes added to the salad. It adds a note of bitter acidity to this refreshing salad. As to dicing, 1/4-inch to 1/2-inch cubes work well.

Ingredients

3 Texas or Valencia oranges, peeled and diced

3 mandarins, peeled and diced (or 1 cup canned mandarins, drained)

1/2–3/4 cup peeled and diced jícama

4 sprigs of cilantro, finely chopped

Juice of 1/2 lime

1/2 teaspoon salt

1/2 teaspoon (or to taste) dried cayenne pepper, crushed or flaked (or toasted and crushed *guajillo chile*)

Salad greens (optional)

SIKIL PAC

Roasted Tomatoes and Ground Pumpkin Seed Dip

Makes about 1 1/2 cups (bottom in photo at left)

Making this dip doesn't require fancy techniques, just fresh ingredients. Guests at my daughter's wedding remember enjoying this dip at the reception in Telchac Puerto following the ceremony in Mérida, Yucatán. They also remember the sultry ocean breezes and moonlit skies.

1. Follow the instructions for the ground *pepitas de calabaza tostadas sin cáscara* (see recipe).

2. In a bowl, mix the ground seeds, *chiltomate*, *chile habanero* (optional), cilantro and chives. Adjust salt.

To serve: Serve with tortilla chips.

Ingredients

3/4 cup ground *pepitas de calabaza tostadas sin cáscara* (ground, toasted, pumpkin seeds, see recipe)

3/4 cup *chiltomate* (see recipe)

1 *chile habanero,* roasted and chopped (optional)

1/4 bunch cilantro, finely chopped

2 tablespoons chives, finely chopped (or scallions or green onions)

1/2 teaspoon salt, or to taste

Ensalada de Pasta

Pasta Salad

Serves about 8–10

For the pasta

1 gallon water

1/2 pound small elbow macaroni

2 tablespoons vegetable oil

1 teaspoon salt

For the salad

1/2 cup pineapple, chopped diced (or canned crushed pineapple) (1/4-inch cubes)

1 can (7.6 ounces) *media crema* (or 3/4 cup heavy cream) (see Glossary)

1/2 cup diced ham (1/4-inch cubes)

1/4 cup diced cheddar cheese (1/4-inch cubes)

1/2 cup canned corn kernels, drained

1/3–1/2 teaspoon salt

1/3–1/2 teaspoon ground black pepper

1 tablespoon chopped pimentos (canned or jarred)

2–3 tablespoons peas (drained if canned or thawed if frozen)

This is another dish that's easy to make. The most time-consuming task is dicing the ham and cheddar cheese into those 1/4-inch cubes. Present it as a starter with saltine crackers, like we do in the Yucatán, or as a side dish.

1. Bring the water to a boil and add the pasta, oil and salt. Cook until al dente (pasta should have a little of resistance when you bite into it). Drain.

2. Mix all of the other salad ingredients—except the peas—in a large bowl and adjust salt.

3. Fold in peas. Chill.

To serve: Serve family style in a large serving dish. For individual servings, serve on a dish lined with lettuce leaf.

28 SABORES YUCATECOS

Ensalada de papa

Potato Salad

Serves about 10–12 (photo on page 18)

This is not your average potato salad. In fact, it's more like a mashed potato salad and can play the role of an appetizer or side dish. In the Yucatán, it's a popular party food.

1. Bring the water to a boil. Add carrots, let boil for 5 minutes.

2. Add the potatoes and let boil for another 15–20 minutes or until you can mash with a fork. Drain water and let vegetables cool.

3. Mash the carrots and potatoes with a folk or potato masher until you get a lumpy mixture.

4. Fold in the salt, black pepper and jalapeño chiles.

5. Fold in the mayonnaise and peas, adjust salt.

To serve: Serve family style in a large bowl. Or prepare individual servings by placing a scoop or two of the salad on a plate lined with a lettuce leaf.

Tip: Don't over mash the carrots and potatoes. You aren't trying to make orange-colored mashed potatoes.

Ingredients

1 gallon water

3 medium carrots, peeled and sliced (1/4-inch slices)

4 medium Russet potatoes, peeled and chopped (1-inch cubes)

1 teaspoon salt

1 teaspoon ground black pepper

2 tablespoons pickled jalapeño chiles, minced (or to taste)

1 cup mayonnaise

1/2 cup peas (drained if canned or thawed if frozen)

Arroz con plátanos fritos

Rice with Fried Plantains

Serves about 6 (photo on page 18)

This is a very pretty plate with its bright colors. The fried plantains add a sweet note. Like other recipes in this chapter, it can be served as an appetizer or side dish.

1. To prepare one serving, place a mound of cooked rice (about 1/2 cup) in the center of a plate.

2. Arrange 6 slices of *plátanos fritos* and 4 slices of red bell peppers on the mound of rice.

3. Top with 1/2 tablespoon of peas. Repeat until six servings are assembled and serve.

Ingredients

3 cups cooked *arroz blanco* (see recipe)

36 slices *plátanos fritos* (see recipe)

24 slices roasted red bell peppers (or jarred or canned pimentos)

3 tablespoons peas (drained if canned or thawed if frozen)

Kibis *top a mound of* curtido de repollo *(page 151)*.

Kibis

Meat and Bulgar Wheat Patties with Mint

Ingredients

1 pound bulgur wheat (#2 or medium)

1 gallon water

1 pound ground beef

30 fresh mint leaves, finely chopped

1 1/2–2 teaspoons salt

1 1/2–2 teaspoons ground black pepper

Vegetable oil

Garnishes

Curtido de repollo (see recipe)

Cebolla para cochinita pibil (see recipe)

Salsa de chile habanero (see recipe)

Serves about 8–10; makes about 25–30 kibis

Sometimes visitors to the Yucatán are surprised to discover how popular *kibis* are. In fact, a long-established Lebanese community has roots in the region going back to the late 19th century. *Kibis* make a great snack food.

1. Soak the bulgur in 4 times the amount of water (about 1 gallon) in a large bowl. Let soak for 1 hour.

2. Drain the bulgur in a colander, applying pressure to squeeze out excess water.

3. Mix the ground beef, chopped mint, salt and pepper into the bulgur with your hands.

4. Moisten your fingertips and palms with vegetable oil. Scoop out 2-ounce balls of the mixture with your hands (or use a #18 scoop). Slap the ball a couple of times between the palms of your hands to compact the meat-bulgar mixture. Shape into a plump disc about 2 inches in diameter (My preferred shape). Repeat the process until all meat-bulgur mixture is used.

5. Heat the oil in a frying pan, about 1-inch deep. Drop several *kibis* into the oil (do not crowd) and fry on both sides until golden and crispy on the outside and soft and tender in the inside, about 2–3 minutes on each side.

You can also deep fry at 375°F.

6. Remove and drain on paper towels. Repeat until all *kibis* are done.

To serve: Layer a serving platter with *curtido de repollo*. Arrange the *kibis* on top. Top the *kibis* with *cebolla para cochinita pibil*. Serve *salsa de chile habanero* on the side.

Tips: The secret to making good *kibis* lies in the soaking of the bulgur. Do not soak too long or the grains will pop like popcorn when you fry your *kibis*; don't under soak or they will be dry and hard. The balance between the meat and bulgar makes a big difference too.

Notes: *Kibis* come in various shapes and can be eaten raw, baked or fried. Beef is preferred over lamb in the Yucatán. The *kibis* you will most often eat from a stall or street vendor in Mérida, Yucatán, is cigar shaped and hallow inside. After it is fried, it is cut open and stuffed with *cebolla para cochinita pibil* or *curtido de repollo*. I am in awe of these because of the skill required to make them.

CREMA DE GARBANZO

GARBANZO DIP

Makes about 2 cups (photo on page 18)

Here's another recipe with Middle Eastern influences. Just don't be surprised when you see how quickly this easy-to-make dip disappears. Best of all, this recipe is flexible. You can switch out the garbanzo bean puree and use another vegetable purée to make an equally tasty dip. And, no, this is not to be confused with hummus.

1. Drain the garbanzo beans and blend until smooth in a food processor or blender.

2. Blend in the eggs.

3. Dribble in the oil, slowly. If too thick, add water just a little at a time until correct consistency like a creamy hummus is reached.

4. Add the salt and pepper, adjusting to taste.

To serve: Serve in a bowl along with wedges of pita bread for dipping. Or serve with vegetable crudités—carrots, jícama, celery, bell pepper, zucchini, etc. No, tortilla chips are not served with this dip.

Notes: Other vegetable purées can be used instead of garbanzo beans. Follow the same instructions here, but prepare the alternate vegetables as noted here. Eggplant—stud a small eggplant with peeled garlic cloves and roast on a griddle or open flame until cooked completely, peel off the skin and purée with the garlic cloves, eggs and oil. Roasted *chile güerito* or *x'catic*—roast 10 chiles as you did the eggplant (without garlic), peel off skin and remove stem, seeds and veins, and purée with eggs and oil. Garlic—roast one large head of garlic, peel and purée with eggs and oil. Cilantro—wash one bunch of cilantro, pat dry with paper towels and cut off roots but leave stems, and purée with eggs and oil.

INGREDIENTS

1 can (15 ounces) garbanzo beans, drained (or 1 cup other vegetable purée, see notes)

2 eggs

1 cup vegetable oil (or olive oil or corn oil)

1/4 teaspoon salt

1/4 teaspoon ground black pepper

ARROLLADITOS DE REPOLLO
STUFFED CABBAGE LEAVES

Serves about 8 to 10; makes about 25–30 *arrolladitos*

INGREDIENTS

Water to steam cabbage and soak rice

1 large head green cabbage

1 pound ground lean pork

1 cup short-grain rice (or Rose rice), raw

2 tablespoons ground black pepper

2 teaspoons salt

4–5 cups *sofrito de tomate* (see recipe)

With their obvious Middle Eastern roots, these *arrolladitos* may be time consuming to make, but they are well worth the effort. This recipe makes some 30 rolled-up bundles. Don't think for a minute that's too much. They will be gobbled up quickly. If you are looking for a vegetarian option, leave out the meat and substitute vegetables, such as carrots and potatoes. And, yes, they are very peppery.

1. Soak the uncooked rice in enough water to completely cover it for 30 minutes. Drain and discard water. Set rice aside.

2. With a paring knife, cut out a big chunk of the thick center stem of the cabbage. About an inch deep will be enough.

3. Place the head of cabbage in the steamer and bring the water to a boil. Steam for 2 to 3 minutes. (A *tamalera* or big steamer will make this process easier.)

4. Carefully lift out the head of cabbage and remove 2 to 3 layers of cabbage leaves. Try not to tear leaves.

5. Place the cabbage back into the steamer, and repeat process until you get more than 15 large leaves. Reserve extra leaves in case you need to make more rolls or need to use as patches and to line the steamer.

6. To trim the cabbage leaves, cut out the center vein and thick end. You will end up with two pieces.

7. Mix the ground pork, soaked rice, black pepper and salt in large bowl.

8. Place about 1 1/2 tablespoons of the meat mixture in the center of a piece of cabbage leaf and fold like a burrito. Fold in two sides of cabbage wrapper and roll up bundle. Don't roll too tight because the rice will expand as it cooks. Use pieces of reserved leaves to patch any tears in the larger leaves.

9. Place a layer of unused leaves of cabbage on the bottom of the insert of a deep steamer pot or *tamalera* to which water has already been added. Accommodate one layer of *arrolladitos* snugly in the steamer. Cover generously with *sofrito de tomate* and repeat.

10. Top the last layer of *arrolladitos* with more *sofrito de tomate* and cover with a layer of unused leaves. Then place the lid on top or cover with heavy foil.

11. Steam for 1 hour. Remove and taste one *arrolladito*. The meat should be cooked and the rice tender. If so, remove all from heat. If not, return *arrolladitos* to heat for another 15–20 minutes and test again.

To serve: Serve family style on a platter with more *sofrito de tomate*. For an individual serving, serve 2–3 on a dish . . . with more *sofrito de tomate*.

Notes: Don't be stingy with the *sofrito de tomate* during the steaming process, so make sure to have plenty on hand (5 cups at least). Also, make sure to use short-grain rice as it is more tender than long-grain rice.

Tip: Use extra caution when removing the hot head of cabbage. A large serving fork inserted into the center stem is helpful in removing it from the the steamer or *tamalera* in order to remove the leaves.

Plenty of sofrito de tomate *(page 15) is a must with* arrolladitos de repollo.

CHAPTER 3

EGGS...
HUEVOS

The Spanish introduced the New World to chickens. That's not to say that the Maya did not appreciate what a great source of protein eggs from other animals represented. Eggs of wild fowl and reptiles were gathered and eaten. But except for one kind of turkey (see turkey in Glossary), they did not have other domesticated fowl. Certainly the regular collection of eggs from domesticated chickens must have been appreciated.

As expected, many of the egg-based dishes here are great for breakfast, but they would also be good for a light lunch or dinner. And one of the most popular vegetarian dishes from the Yucatán features hard-cooked eggs rolled in tortillas and dipped in pumpkin seed sauce—*papadzules* (see recipe).

Opposite page: Papadzules *(page 36).*

Right, from top: A super moncho especial *at Moncho's in Mérida, Yucatán; and* barras de francés *(or* pan francés *or French rolls) right out of the oven.*

PAPADZULES

TORTILLAS STUFFED WITH HARD-COOKED EGGS WITH PUMPKIN SEED SAUCE

Serves about 6–8 (photo on page 34)

PUMPKIN SEED SAUCE

2 quarts water

10 ounces ground *pepitas de calabaza tostadas sin cáscara* (see recipe)

1/2 bunch fresh epazote

1 tablespoon salt

FILLING AND GARNISHES

12 hard-cooked eggs, mashed with pinch salt

24 tortillas

GARNISHES

1–2 cups *salsa de tomate* (see recipe)

1–2 cups *sofrito de tomate* (see recipe)

Pumpkin seed oil, optional

In the days of the grand haciendas, *papadzules* were a favored dish among the *hacendados* or rancher owners. We know this by its name. "*Papa*" means "food," "*dzules*" means "gentlemen of the haciendas." Hence, *papadzules* was food for the *hacendados*. Surprisingly light and filling at the same time, it's one of Kathy's favorite dishes. She loves its jeweled looks and comforting taste. This is also a dish with clear Mayan roots because of its predominant use of pre-Columbian ingredients. It's a perfect dish for vegetarians too.

1. Bring the water to a boil and add the toasted, ground pumpkin seeds, epazote and salt. Let simmer over medium heat for 15 minutes. You'll know the sauce is done when you pinch a few seeds between two fingers and they smear smoothly and are not grainy.

2. Liquefy the sauce in a blender or with a handheld emulsion blender.

3. Return to the pot and simmer until the sauce reduces to the consistency of a thin *mole* (if you dip a tortilla into it, it coats the tortilla). Cover and keep warm.

TO ASSEMBLE AND SERVE

1. Warm a tortilla and dip into the pumpkin seed sauce. Place about 2 tablespoons of the mashed hard-cooked eggs into the tortilla and roll up like an enchilada or *taquito*. Repeat until all tortillas are dipped, stuffed and rolled.

2. Place three to four dipped and stuffed tortilla rolls on a plate. Spoon spoonfuls of *salsa de tomate* around the *papadzules* and top them with spoonfuls of *sofrito de tomate*. Sprinkle with toasted, hulled pumpkin seeds and drizzle with pumpkin seed oil.

Notes: Pumpkin seed oil is kind of a luxurious enhancement for this dish. It is, in fact, my special touch. It does give the dish a classy look and adds an extra bit of nuttiness to the taste. If you feel like splurging, you can find pumpkin seed oil in gourmet markets or order it from on-line sources. (See Glossary.)

TORTILLAS, CORN THAT IS Tortillas—always corn—in the Yucatán tend to be thinner and smaller than those found in the United States. There it is common to take one tortilla, fold it in half, scoop up, say, some *puerco entomatado* (see recipe) with some beans, and eat the whole thing in one bite! It's also common to serve tostada style on *pimes* that are thick corn cakes that have been pinched and heated on a *comal* (griddle). The pinches create mini craters or depressions that keep the meat juices from dripping off the *pime*. (The photograph of *puerco entomatado* on page 180 is pictured served on a *pime*.) Tortillas come in handy in other ways too. I highly recommend using them to check the tenderness of meats. I take a tortilla and try to pinch off some meat. If the meat comes off easily into the tortilla, I know the meat is done. This is my tortilla-testing method (see Glossary). (Also see *masa de maíz* and *masa harina*.)

Huevos con Longaniza

Eggs with Chorizo

Serves about 6

This is Yucatán's equivalent of *huevos con chorizo,* a very popular breakfast option. *Longaniza* (see Glossary) might be the meat of choice, but you can also substitute Mexican-style chorizo that should be easy to find in most supermarkets.

1. Break the eggs into a large bowl, add salt and beat gently to blend. If you like a lot of heat, add the *chile habanero.*

2. Heat a nonstick frying pan over a medium heat, and add the oil. Add the *longaniza,* breaking it up so that it renders its fat.

3. Pour the eggs into the hot frying pan. Stir gently until the eggs are cooked but still soft and moist, about to 3–4 minutes. Do not overcook the eggs.

To serve: Serve with *frijoles negros guisados* (see recipe) and corn tortillas, *barras de francés* or *bolillos.*

Notes: If using *longaniza,* remove the casing before breaking it up in the frying pan. I smoke my own beef and pork *longaniza,* which gets its rich color from *recado rojo.*

Ingredients

12 eggs

1 teaspoon salt

1 *chile habanero,* diced (optional)

1 tablespoon vegetable oil

6 ounces *longaniza,* broken into chunks (or Mexican-style chorizo) (see Glossary)

Huevos motuleños

Eggs Motul Style

Serves 6 (top in photo at right)

Ingredients

2–4 tablespoons vegetable oil

24 slices ripe plantains, cut on a slant in 1/4-inch slices (about 2 plantains)

12 eggs

12 tostadas (see Glossary)

1–1 1/2 cups *frijol colado* (see recipe)

1 cup diced smoked ham (1/4- 1/2-inch cubes)

1 cup diced cheddar cheese (1/4- 1/2-inch cubes)

1/2 cup peas (drained is canned or thawed if frozen)

Pimento slices (canned or jarred)

1 1/2 cups *salsa de tomate* (see recipe)

Sofrito de tomate (see recipe)

I have fond memories of this dish. When I was a youngster, I would visit my grandfather in Yobaín near Motul (about 27 miles from Mérida in the state of Yucatán) during my two-week holiday, I remember eating this dish a lot. While it's most often eaten for lunch, it makes a great and filling breakfast. Yes, it did originate in Motul, the specialty of a restaurant owned by a Lebanese. It's best to make each serving one by one.

1. Heat the oil in a skillet and fry the plantain slices until golden on both sides. Drain on paper towels.

2. Heat more vegetable oil in the skillet and, for each serving, fry two eggs over easy at a time.

3. To assemble each plate, place 4 slices of fried plantains spaced on a plate to serve as a base or "supporting posts" for the tostadas (refer to photograph to right). Place tostadas, slightly overlapping, on top of the plantains, smear generously with *frijol colado,* followed by the two over-easy eggs. Top with the ham, cheese, peas and pimentos. Then top with a generous spoonful of *sofrito de tomate* and surrounded it with *salsa de tomate*.

Huevos con chaya

Eggs with Chaya

Serves about 6 (bottom in photo at right)

Ingredients

12 eggs

1 teaspoon salt

1 cup chopped *chaya* leaves (or spinach), fresh, or thawed and drained if frozen (see Glossary)

1 *chile habanero,* diced (optional)

4 tablespoons vegetable oil

4 small plum tomatoes, chopped

1/2 cup chopped white onion

2 tablespoons diced green bell pepper

2 tablespoons diced red bell pepper

This is a very traditional breakfast dish that uses *chaya* leaves. It is often served in tacos, especially in Valladolid, the city and municipality in the eastern part of the state of Yucatán, where street vendors do a brisk business in *tacos de huevos con chaya*. It also makes for a light lunch. Use fresh or frozen spinach if you are unable to find fresh or frozen *chaya*.

1. Break the eggs into a large bowl, add salt and *chaya,* and beat gently to blend. If you like a lot of heat, add the *chile habanero*.

2. Heat the oil a nonstick, frying pan. Add the tomatoes, onion, and green and red bell peppers. Sauté until the vegetables are cooked.

3. Pour the eggs into the hot frying pan with the sautéed vegetables. Stir gently until the eggs are cooked but are still soft and moist. Do not overcook the eggs.

To serve: Serve with *frijoles negros guisados* (see recipe) and corn tortillas, *barras de francés* or *bolillos*.

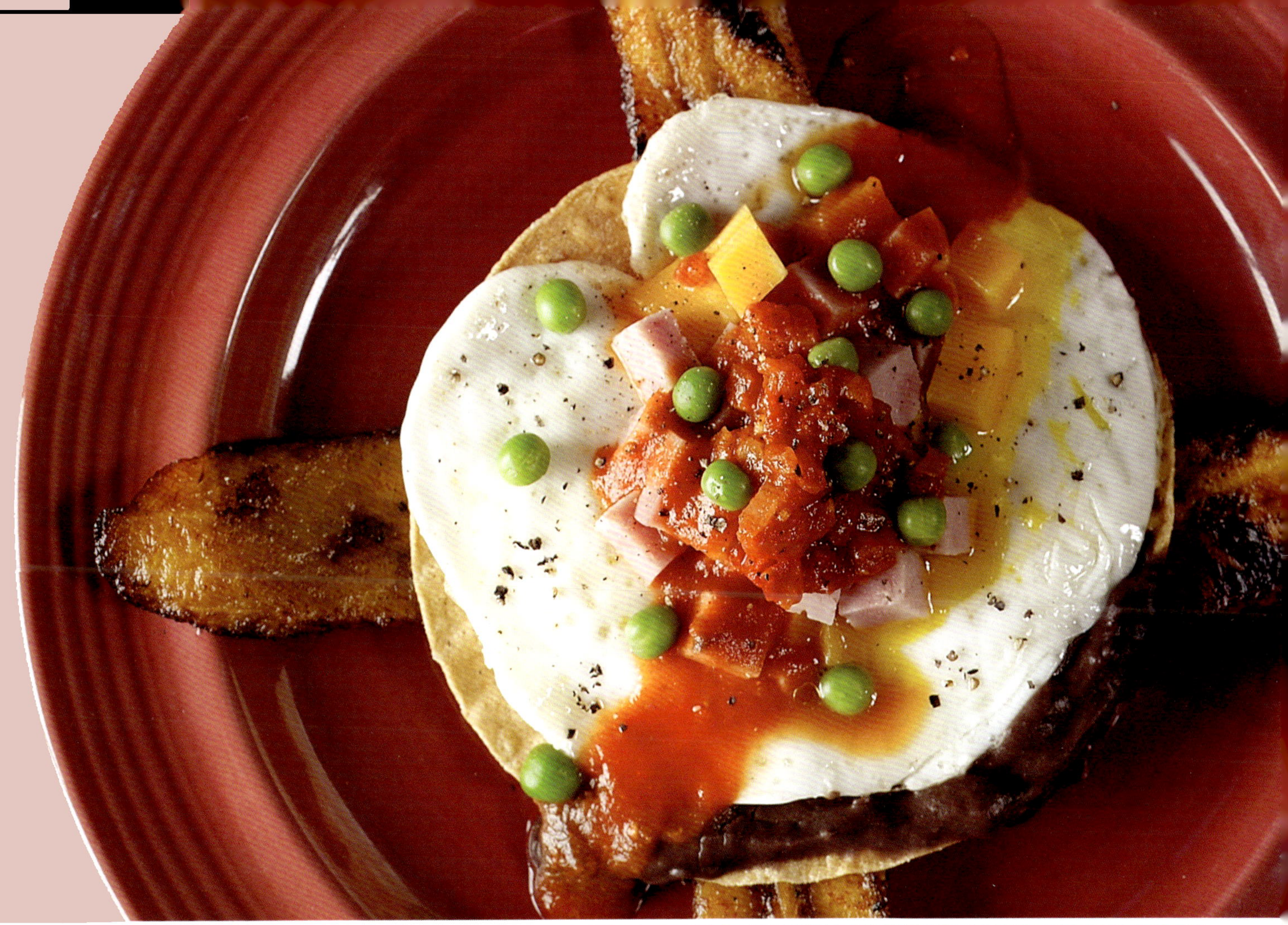

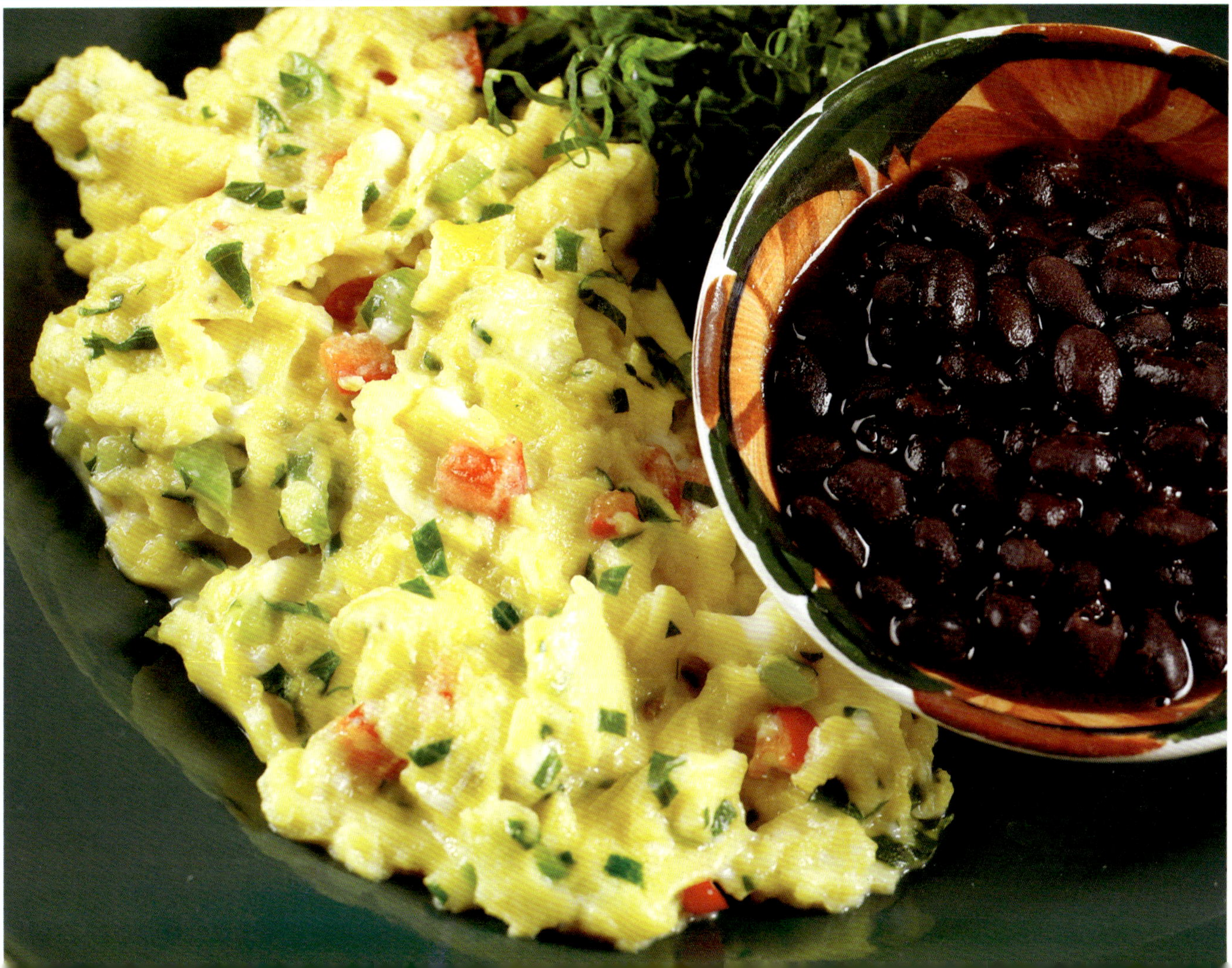

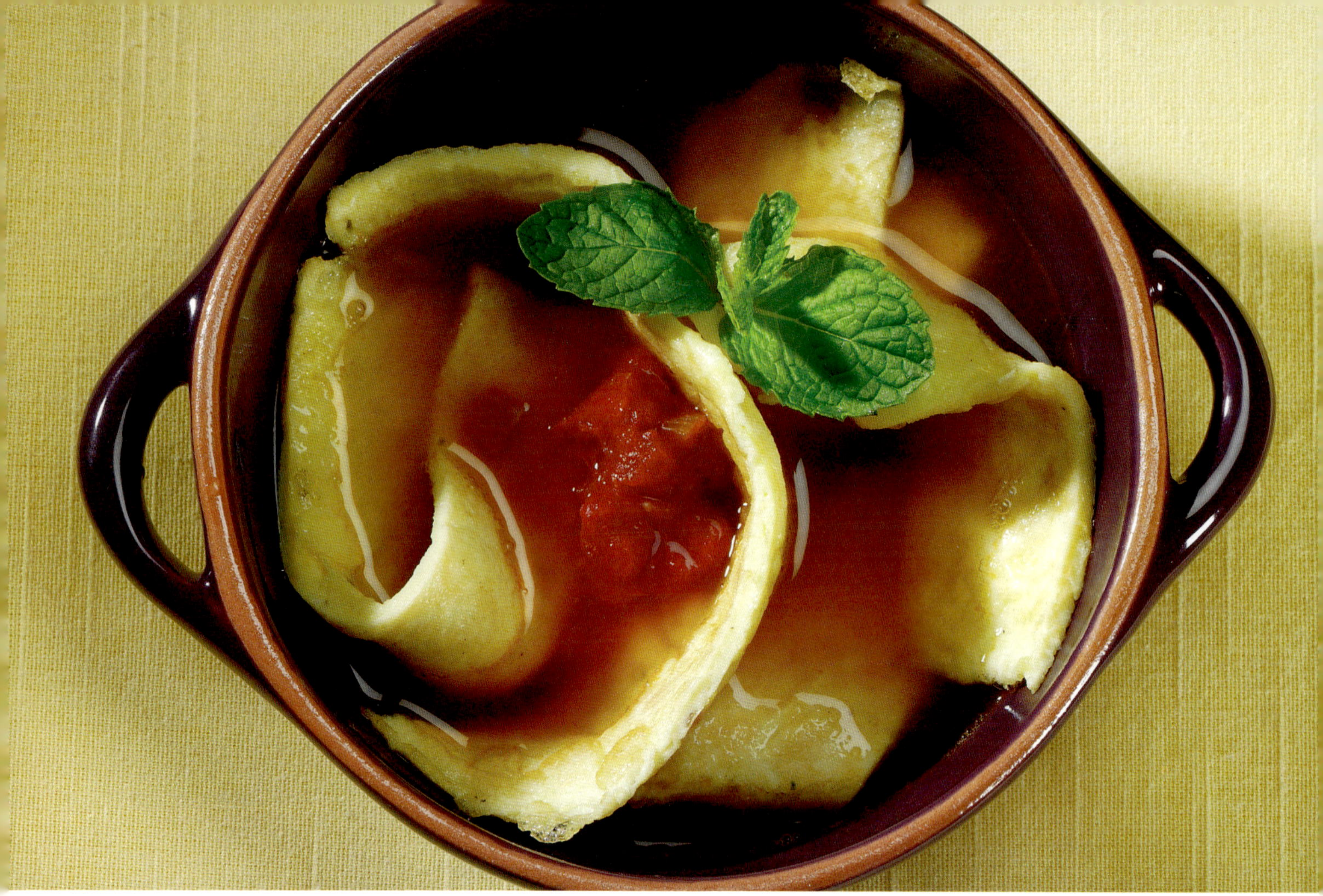

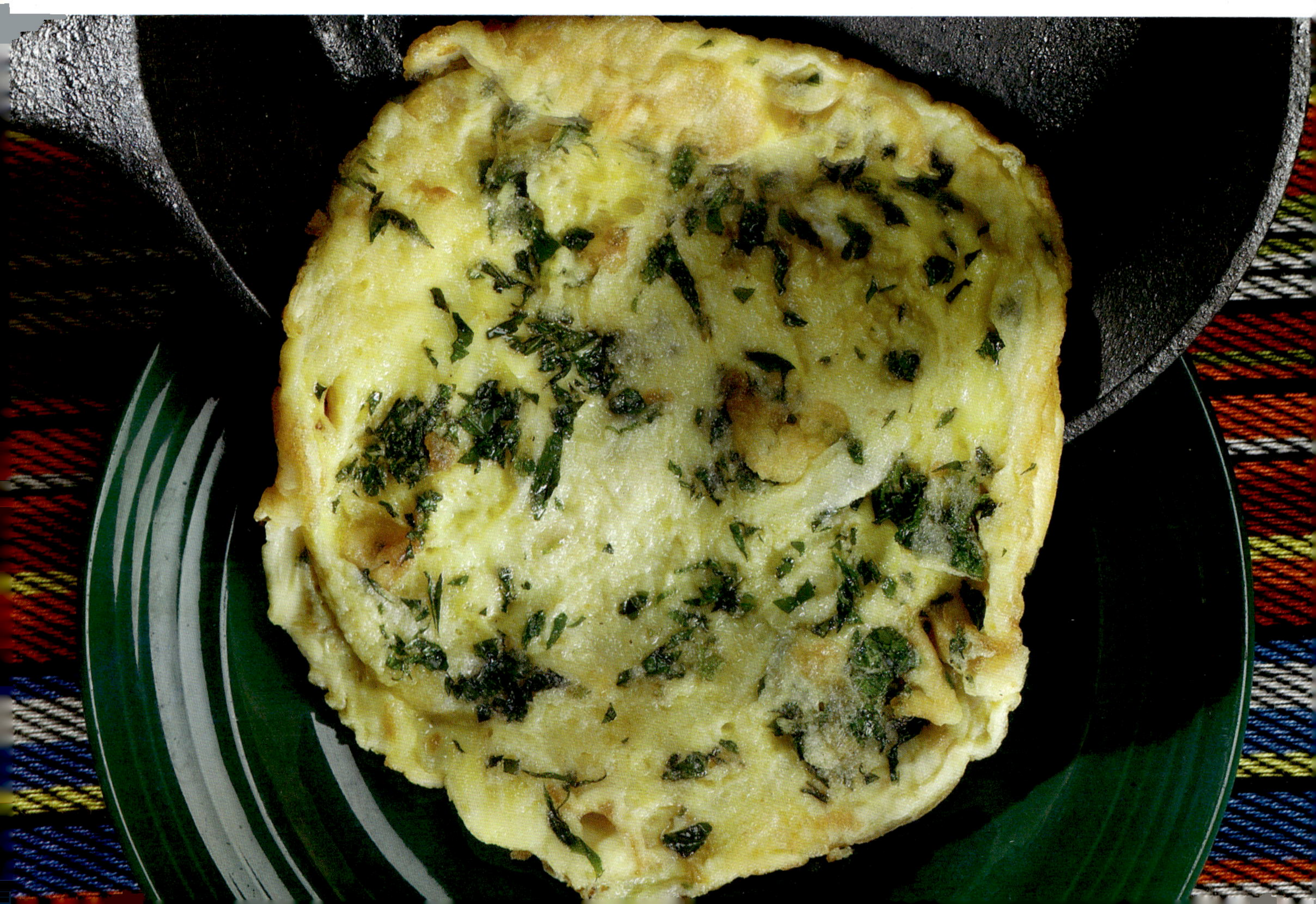

Caldillo de Huevo

Omelet Soup with Achiote Sauce

Serves about 6–8 (top in photo at left)

Caldillo de huevo may seem a little counter intuitive. Make an omelet and then cook again in stock? Well, yes. But the stock is flavored with *recado rojo* and topped with savory *sofrito de tomate*. What you get is a delicious omelet soup. How's that for a light meal? Actually, this dish is popular during Lent in the Yucatán.

1. Break the eggs into a bowl with the salt and mint. Whisk lightly.

2. Heat the oil in a 10-inch frying pan, pour in the beaten eggs. Do not stir but let set over medium heat.

3. Slice the omelet like a pizza into 6 sections.

4. Arrange the slices in a pot and pour enough stock in until you almost cover the omelet.

5. Dilute the *recado rojo* in about 1/4 cup stock and strain into the pot. Cover and simmer for 15 minutes.

To serve: Serve in deep bowls topped with *sofrito de tomate* and accompanied by corn tortillas.

Ingredients

12 eggs

1 teaspoon salt

1–2 sprigs fresh mint, minced

2 tablespoons vegetable oil

2–3 cups chicken stock

1/2 teaspoon *recado rojo* (see recipe)

Garnish

Sofrito de tomate (see recipe)

Torta de Huevo con Hierbabuena

Mint Omelet

Serves 6 (bottom in photo at left)

If you thought *caldillo con huevo* (see recipe) was unique, you might think the same thing about this omelet. The mint leaves add a fresh note. Don't let the word "torta" confuse you. This is not a sandwich . . . it's more in the tradition of a Spanish "tortilla." Make each serving one at a time.

1. For one omelet, whisk 2 eggs in a bowl with a pinch salt and 6–7 mint leaves.

2. Heat 1–2 tablespoons vegetable oil in a small frying pan and add the eggs. Do not stir. Let cook for 2–3 minutes and fold in half and remove.

3. Top with *cebolla para panuchos*. Repeat until six omelets are made

To serve: Accompany with *frijoles negros guisados* (see recipe), *salsa de chile habanero* and corn tortillas.

Ingredients

12 eggs

Salt

Vegetable oil

1 bunch fresh mint, leaves only

Garnishes

Cebolla para panuchos (see recipe)

Salsa de chile habanero (optional) (see recipe)

Moncho

Egg, Ham and Cheese Sandwich

Makes 6 sandwiches

Ingredients

6 *barras de francés* (or French rolls or *bolillos*) (see Glossary)

Mayonnaise

Vegetable oil

6 eggs

6 thick slices smoked ham

6 thick slices cheddar cheese (or *queso chihuahua*)

Jalapeño chiles, sliced (optional)

An egg, ham and cheese sandwich may not sound exotic, but this one has a tale that adds to its appeal. There was this guy named Ramón who had a restaurant in the Mercado García Rejón in Mérida, Yucatán, for many, many years. He served this sandwich all day long. Since "Moncho" is a nickname for Ramón, it didn't take too long before this *torta* became known as a "moncho." Moncho's Restaurant is still in the *mercado* but, now, more than 50 years later, it serves a *super moncho especial* with roasted pork meat added. Make each sandwich one at a time.

1. Slice a roll in half lengthwise and lightly toast in the oven. Remove and spread mayonnaise on both halves.

2. Heat 1–2 tablespoons vegetable oil in a small frying pan. Add 1 egg and fry over easy until yolk is firm or set. Slice in half.

3. Top the bottom half of the the roll with the 2 slices of egg, a slice of ham and cheese, a couple of jalapeño chile slices and top with the other half of the roll. Repeat until all 6 eggs are fried and each *moncho* is assembled.

To serve: Serve the *monchos* with fresh fruit or *ensalada de papa* (see recipe).

Notes: What is a "*barra de francés*"? What is the difference between a French roll and a *bolillo*? What do they prefer to use in the Yucatán? For answers, see Glossary.

"**Donde se compone el mundo**" Putting things to right takes on a congenial tone in Mérida, Yucatán. There are a handful of restaurants in Mérida that have been around for a very long time. Over the years, regular customers who are the owners of nearby businesses come to sit and discuss all the troubles of the world and resolve business and personal matters. They also "*cuidan sus negocios desde el restaurante.*" That is, they keep an eye on their businesses from the restaurant. Semi-retirees and retirees also make up this group of problem solvers. It just so happens that Moncho's Restaurant is one of these meeting spots.

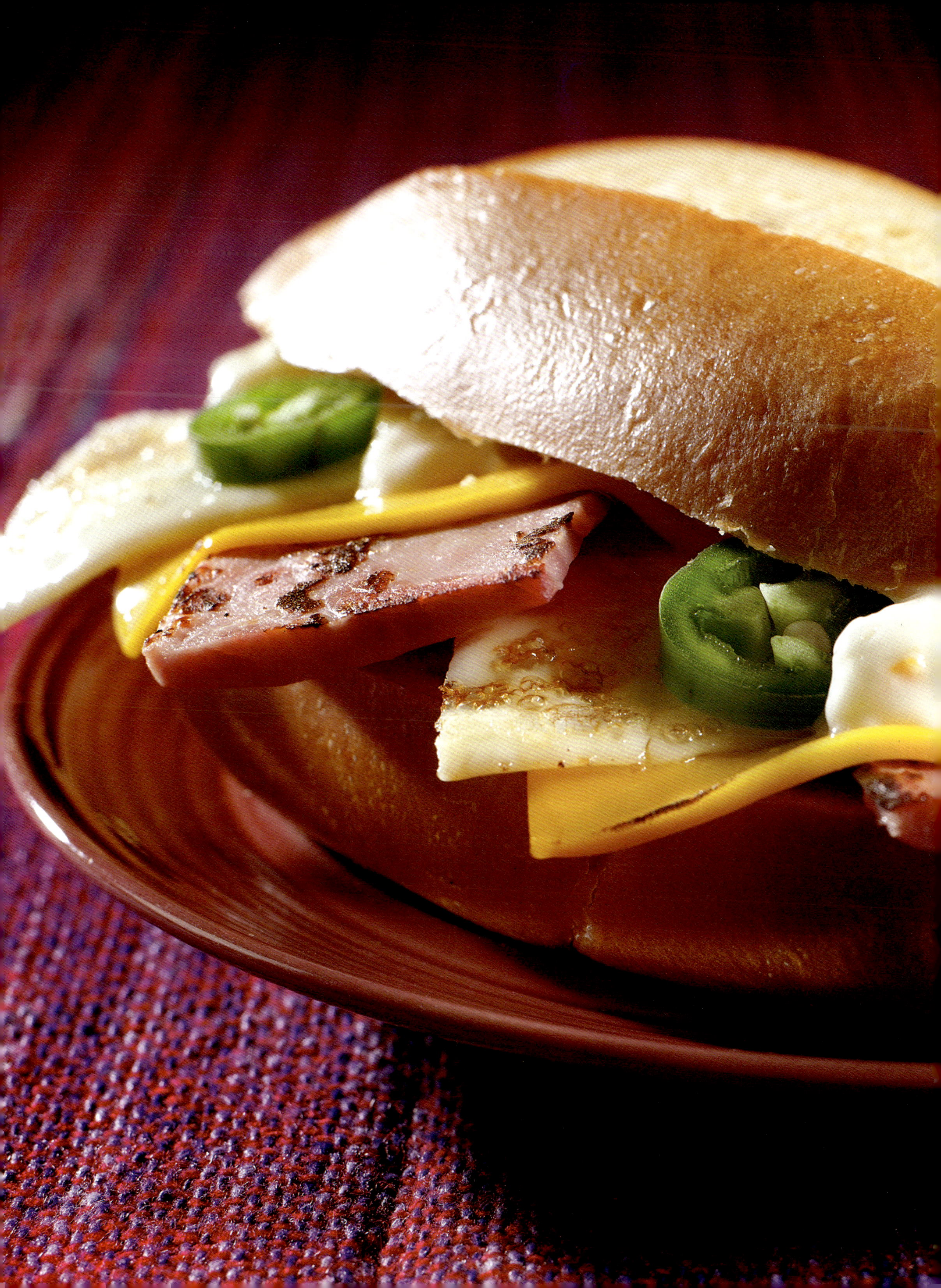

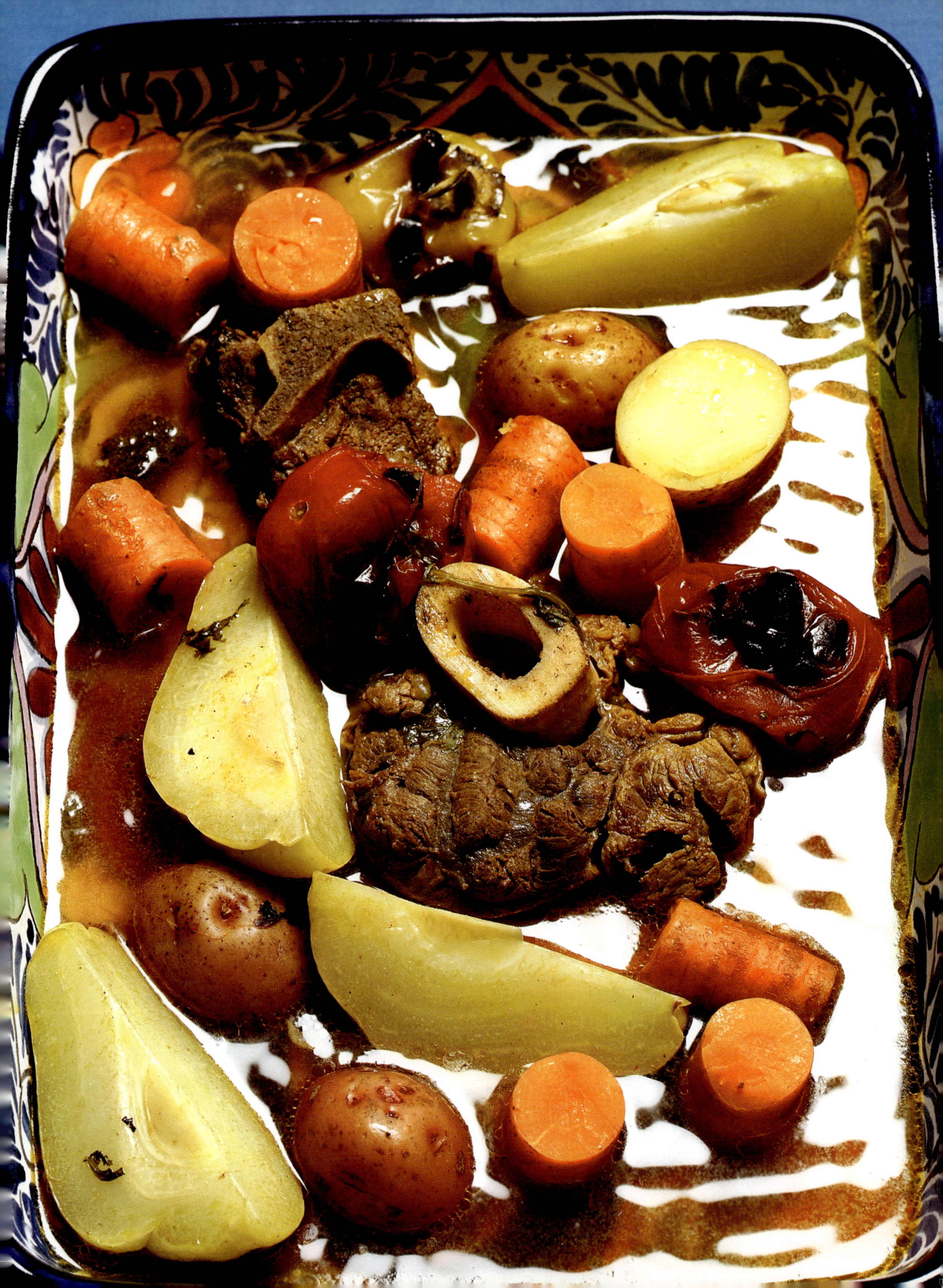

CHAPTER 4

Soups & Stews . . .
Sopas y guisos

Every culture has its comfort foods, and it's not surprising that many are slow-cooked soups and stews that simmer and bubble on stovetops with aromas that make stomachs growl.

In the Yucatán, soups and stews can be light or hardy. Some can start a meal; others make a whole meal. Many resemble familiar dishes, but invariably there is an ingredient or cooking technique that has Yucatán written all over it. Perhaps it's the use of *lima agria* or *chaya*, or the roasting of onions and garlic. Or it could be the *sofrito* that adds loads of flavor.

Some of the recipes in this chapter are good for everyday meals while others are for weekends or special occasions. Regardless, you will be adding new comfort foods to your culinary repertoire.

Make sure to check out other recipes in the chapters on pork, chicken and beef because there are a few dishes that have all the characteristics of stews. They are all one big pot of goodness.

Opposite page: Kabic de res *(page 58).*

Right, from top: Plum tomatoes with a smile; the Mayan ruins of Chichén Itzá, Yucatán; and cut up vegetables ready for soups and stews in the market.

CONSOMÉ DE PAVO

TURKEY STOCK

Makes about 1 gallon

INGREDIENTS

15-pound turkey (including neck and giblets)

4 gallons water

1/2 teaspoon dried oregano

2 sprigs fresh mint (or 20 leaves)

8 sprigs fresh cilantro

1 garlic head, roasted

1 large red onion, roasted

2 teaspoons ground black pepper

2 tablespoons salt

The stock you make serves as a base for *caldo de pavo*, *sopa de lima* and *sopa de pasta* (see recipes). The turkey, however, requires one more step before its meat is used in these and several other dishes. The turkey must be rubbed with *recado rojo* and grilled or roasted (see recipe for *pavo asado*). You will use the meat of the *pavo asado* in the soups and for *panuchos, salbutes, pavo en escabeche* and *sah kol de pavo*.

1. Put water to boil in a 10-gallon stockpot. Carefully lower the turkey into the boiling water. Before it returns to a boil, skim the foam that rises to the top with a slotted spoon and discard. Once clean, add the rest of the ingredients.

2. Lower the heat to medium and simmer, uncovered, for 1 1/2 to 1 3/4 hours. When the turkey is done, carefully remove it from the water. Breast temperature should reach 160°F.

3. Strain the stock through a fine strainer. Reserve at least 1 gallon stock.

Notes: Don't forget to roast the garlic and onion.

CALDO DE PAVO

TURKEY SOUP

Serves about 6–8

PREPARED TURKEY STOCK

2 tablespoons vegetable oil

2 plum tomatoes, chopped

1/2 white onion, chopped

1/2 green bell pepper, chopped

1/2 red bell pepper, chopped

1 gallon *consomé de pavo* (turkey stock, see recipe)

1/2 teaspoon salt, or to taste

1/2 teaspoon pepper, or to taste

GARNISHES

Curtido de repollo (see recipe)

Pavo asado, shredded (see recipe)

Cebolla para panuchos (see recipe)

Lime wedges

Tortilla chips (see Techniques)

The stock from the recipe for *consomé de pavo* is the base for this tasty soup. Its flavor gets a boost from a *sofrito* (sautéed vegetables) and the great toppings and accompaniments when served.

1. Heat the oil in a skillet over medium heat and add the tomatoes, onion, green and red bell peppers, salt and pepper. Sauté until cooked but chunky.

2. Heat the turkey stock and bring to a simmer. Add the sautéed vegetables and simmer for 5 more minutes. Adjust salt and pepper.

To serve: Serve up each deep bowl of turkey soup by first placing a bit of *curtido de repollo, pavo asado, cebolla para panuchos* and a squeeze of lime wedge in the bowl. To this, add a ladle of prepared turkey stock. As a final touch, break up some tortilla chips on top of the soup.

Notes: Be careful with the salt and pepper. Since the turkey stock already has both, you may find you don't need to add any more. This is true with all recipes calling for stock or broth that already have salt and pepper.

More notes: For tortilla strips, see notes following *sopa de lima* or Techniques.

Sopa de Lima

Lime Soup

Serves about 6-8

Sopa de lima is one of the signature dishes of the Yucatán region. Just about every restaurant will feature it on its menu. It is light and filling at the same time.

1. Heat the oil in a skillet over medium heat and add the tomatoes, onion, green and red bell peppers, salt and pepper. Sauté until cooked but chunky.

2. Heat the turkey stock and bring to a simmer. Add the sautéed vegetables and *lima agria* juice (or lime juice) and simmer for 5 more minutes. Adjust salt and pepper.

To serve: In an individual bowl, place a small handful of tortilla strips and shredded *pavo asado*. Ladle prepared turkey stock into the bowl. Garnish with one slice of *lima agria* (or lime) slightly squeezed and twisted.

Notes: It's easy to make your own tortilla strips. Just slice 6–7 corn tortillas into 1/4-inch strips about 2 inches long. Heat the vegetable oil in a frying pan and add tortilla strips. Fry until golden and crispy like a tortilla chip. Remove to a paper towel to drain.

Prepared turkey stock

2 tablespoons vegetable oil

2 plum tomatoes, chopped

1/2 white onion, chopped

1/2 green bell pepper, chopped

1/2 red bell pepper, chopped

1/2 teaspoon salt, or to taste

1/2 teaspoon pepper, or to taste

1 gallon *consomé de pavo* (see recipe)

Juice of 1 *lima agria* (or lime)

Garnishes

Tortilla strips

Pavo asado, shredded (see recipe)

Slices of *lima agria* (or limes)

Sopa de tortilla estilo Quintana Roo

Tortilla Soup Quintana Roo Style

Serves about 6–8

Prepared turkey stock

2 tablespoons vegetable oil

2 plum tomatoes, chopped

1/2 white onion, chopped

1/2 green bell pepper, chopped

1/2 red bell pepper, chopped

1/2 teaspoon salt, or to taste

1/2 teaspoon pepper, or to taste

1 *consomé de pavo* (see recipe)

Garnishes

Tortilla strips

Cheddar cheese, diced

Tortilla soup is a popular item on menus of many Mexican restaurants. But, of course, this version has a twist. It's base is the delicious *consomé de pavo* (turkey stock, see recipe). In fact, it starts like *caldo de pavo* (see recipe).

1. Heat the oil in a skillet over medium heat and add the tomatoes, onion, green and red bell peppers, and salt and pepper. Sauté until cooked but chunky.

2. Heat the turkey stock and bring to a simmer. Add the sautéed vegetables and simmer for 5 more minutes. Adjust salt.

To serve: For each serving, in a deep bowl, place a handful of tortilla strips and chunks of diced cheddar cheese followed by the prepared turkey stock.

Notes: For tortilla strips, see notes following *sopa de lima* or Techniques.

Caldo de pollo

Chicken Stock

Makes about 1 gallon stock

Ingredients

1 1/2 gallon water

6 chicken legs and 6 chicken thighs (with skin and bones) (about 4–6 pounds)

1 head garlic, roasted

1/2 onion, roasted

1/2 teaspoon whole black peppercorns (or 1/3 teaspoon ground black pepper)

1 pinch dried oregano

1 sprig fresh cilantro

1 sprig fresh mint

1–2 tablespoons salt

This soup or stock is not so much a stand-alone dish, but one that will come in handy if you prefer to make your own chicken stock, and you will need it to make *pollo asado* and *salsa de achiote para tamales* (see recipes) for the fillings for some of the tamales in Chapter 9. The sauce goes with the shredded chicken meat used to stuff the tamales.

1. Bring the water to a boil and add the chicken. As it returns to a boil, skim the foam that rises to the top with a slotted spoon and discard.

2. Add the garlic, onion, peppercorns, oregano, cilantro, mint and salt and lower heat to medium and simmer for 30–45 minutes or until the chicken is tender. Remove the chicken and cool.

3. Strain the chicken stock, reserving it and the meat for other uses.

Notes: The garlic and onion are roasted. Don't forget!

Crema de Chaya

Cream of Chaya Soup

Serves about 8–10

The deep green leaves from the *chaya* bush (see Glossary) are one of those ingredients unique to the cuisine of the Yucatán. It is used in tamales, added to meat dishes or stirred into scrambled eggs. In fact, it is used much as you would spinach, which makes an adequate substitute, fresh or frozen.

1. In a large stockpot, heat the oil and add the tomatoes, onion, bell pepper and garlic. Sauté until cooked but chunky.

2. Add the *chaya* (or spinach) and the chicken stock. Cook until the *chaya* is tender, about 15 minutes if the *chaya* fresh. Let cool.

3. Blend the soup in a blender until the mixture is a smooth puree.

4. Place the purée in a clean pot and re-heat over medium heat.

5. In a bowl, mix the flour, milk and *crema media* and whisk until the flour is incorporated. Stir slowly into the puree over medium heat until heated and slightly thickened. If it is too thick, add more milk; if it is too watery, add more flour.

6. Adjust the salt and turn off heat. Add the black pepper (now or upon serving).

To serve: Ladle soup into a bowl. Top with a dollop of *sofrito de tomate* and croutons. If you have not already added the black pepper, sprinkle a pinch over the *crema de chaya*. Best served piping hot.

Notes: You can also drop Galletas Globitos (pictured above and on page 178) on top of the soup instead of croutons. This is a popular cracker in the Yucatán that you might be able to find in specialty shops. If not, buy some on your next trip to the Yucatán.

Ingredients

2 tablespoons olive oil

3 plum tomatoes, chopped

1/2 white onion, chopped

1/2 green bell pepper, chopped

1 clove garlic, minced

1 pound chopped *chaya* leaves (or spinach), fresh or frozen

1/2 gallon chicken stock

1/2–2/3 cup all-purpose flour

1 cup whole milk

1 can (7.6 ounces) *media crema* or 3/4 cup heavy cream

1/2 teaspoon salt, or to taste

1/4 teaspoon ground black pepper

Garnishes

Sofrito de tomate (see recipe)

Croutons (or mini cracker rounds or Galletas Globitos, see Glossary)

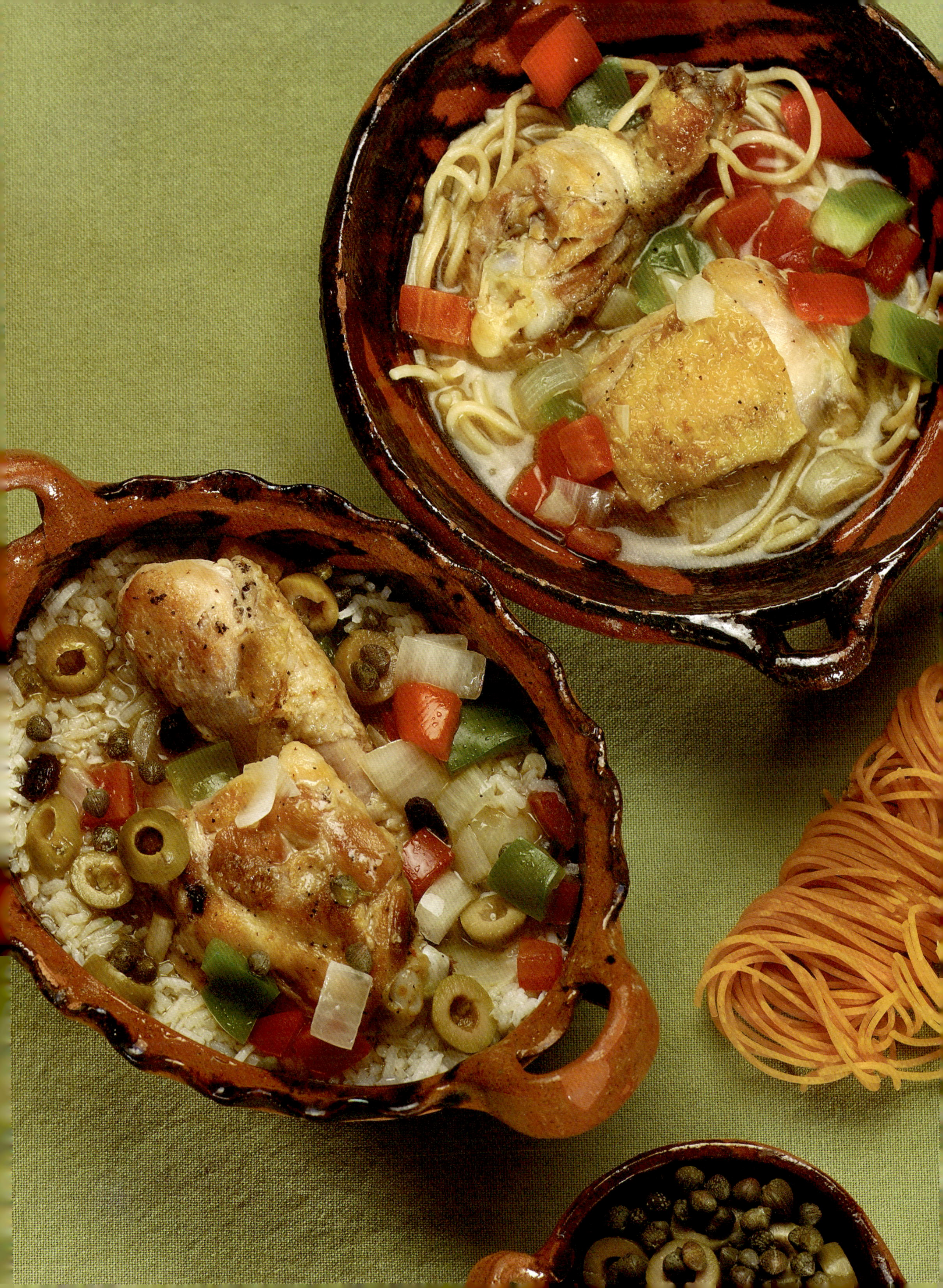

POLLO CON FIDEOS
Chicken Soup with Pasta

Serves about 6–8

Pollo con fideos is more like a stew—you need a fork to eat it—and a meal in itself. In the Yucatán, this dish is also called "*comida de enfermos*" ("food for sick folk") because that's for whom it is most often prepared. As delicious as it is, if you request it, someone will invariably ask if you are under the weather.

1. Salt and pepper both sides of the chicken pieces.

2. Heat the oil in a frying pan over medium heat and brown the chicken on both sides. Drain on paper towels.

3. In the pan drippings, add the tomatoes, onion, and green and red bell peppers, and sauté until cooked through but chunky. Add more vegetable oil if needed.

4. In another deep pot, place chicken and add water or chicken stock and sautéed vegetables. Cover and simmer for 30 minutes.

5. Add the *fideos*, cover and cook over low heat for 15 minutes or until the chicken is tender. Adjust salt.

To serve: Simply dish up in large bowls and make sure to provide knives and forks too.

Notes: In the Yucatán, folks like their pasta nice and tender—OK, a bit overcooked. If you like your pasta more al dente, add the *fideos* 10 minutes before the cooking time is complete and chicken is tender. Some of you might remember thin *fideos* similar to vermicelli. The *fideos* used here are thicker, resembling spaghetti, which makes an adequate substitute.

More notes: Note that the tomatoes, onion and bell peppers are sliced, not chopped. Cut your vegetables lengthwise and then slice across as thinly as you can. It's all about aesthetics.

Ingredients

Salt

Ground black pepper

3 tablespoons vegetable oil

6 chicken legs and 6 chicken thighs, with skin and bones

2 plum tomatoes, thinly sliced

1/2 white onion, thinly sliced

1/2 green bell pepper, thinly sliced

1/2 red bell pepper, thinly sliced

6 cups water (or chicken or turkey stock)

1 package (8 ounces) *fideos* (or vermicelli or spaghetti) (see Glossary)

Opposite page, from top: Pollo con fideos *and* pollo alcaparrado *(page 65).*

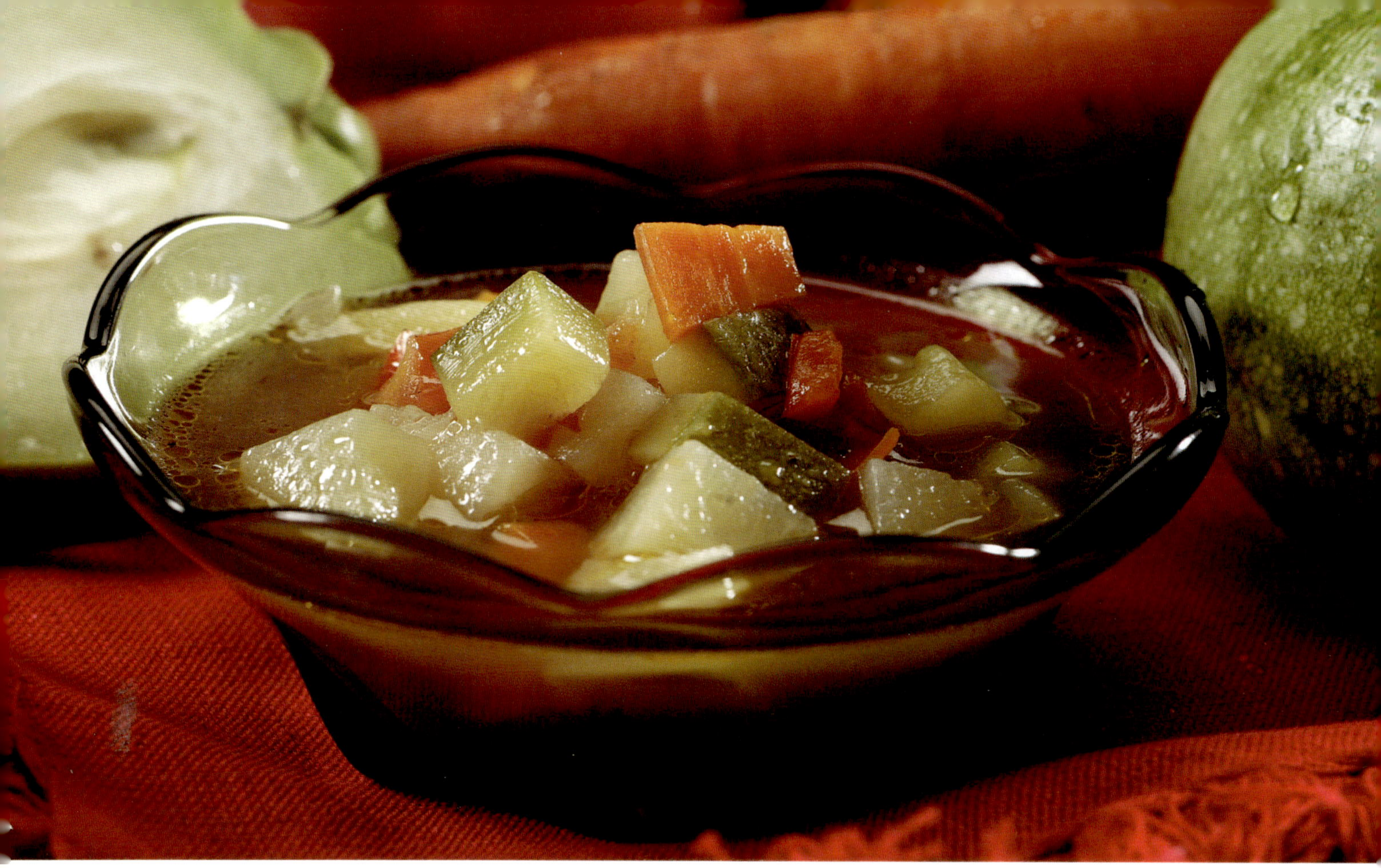

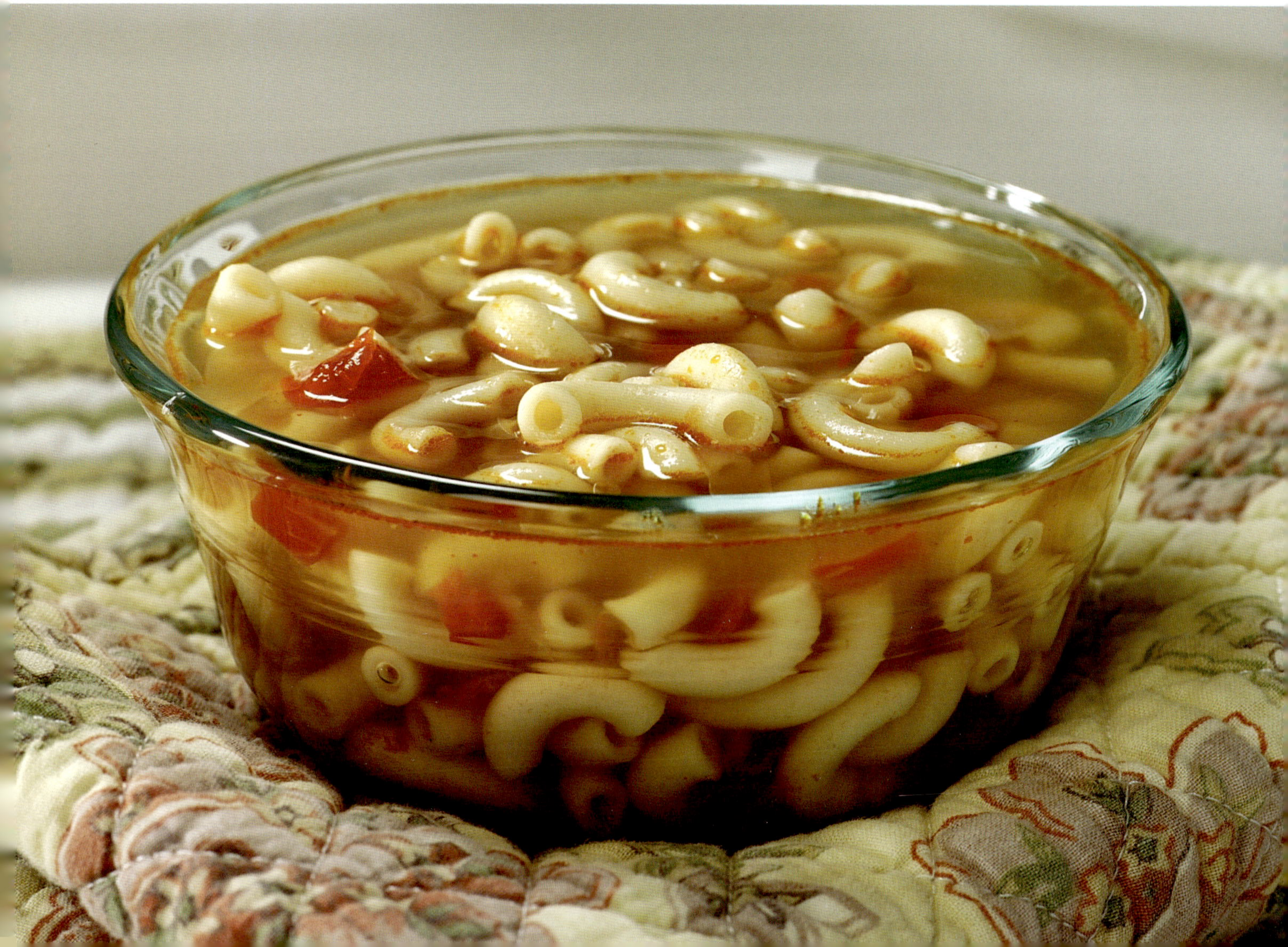

Sopa de Verduras
Vegetable Soup

Serves about 6–8 (top in photo at left)

A tasty vegetable soup is always good to have in your culinary repertoire. The Yucatecan twists that go into this basic soup are the *sofrito* (sautéed vegetables) and chayote. Chayote is a squash also known as a vegetable pear or *christophene,* among other names. Look for those with a smooth skin, not spiny. The soup is a great starter to just about any meal.

1. Heat the vegetable oil in a skillet over medium heat and add the tomatoes, onions, and green and red bell peppers. Sauté until cooked but chunky, about 6–8 minutes. Set aside.

2. Wipe the skillet and then wipe with a paper towel dipped in vegetable oil. Add the carrots and cook for 2 minutes, add the potatoes for another 2 minutes, and finally the chayote and zucchini for about 4 more minutes. Do not burn or overcook the vegetables.

3. Add the sautéed vegetables and the other vegetables to a large stockpot. Pour in the chicken stock and heat over a medium heat. Adjust salt.

To serve: Simply ladle into soup bowls.

Notes: Chop your carrots, potato, chayote and zucchini into uniform-sized cubes for a nice looking soup. Either 1/4-inch or 1/2-inch cubes will do. If you prefer, you can peel the vegetables.

Ingredients

2 tablespoons vegetable oil

2 plum tomatoes, chopped

1/4 white onion, chopped

1/4 green bell pepper, chopped

1/4 red bell pepper, chopped

2 carrots, peeled and diced

1 medium Russet potato, diced

1 chayote, diced

1 zucchini, diced

6 cups chicken stock

1/2 teaspoon salt, or to taste

1/4 teaspoon pepper, or to taste

Sopa de Pasta
Pasta Soup

Serves about 6–8 (bottom in photo at left)

This is comfort food with a *yucatecan* accent and is most often followed by *pavo* or *pollo asado* (see recipes). Your whole family is sure to take a liking to this.

1. Heat the oil in a skillet over medium heat and add the pasta and lightly toast.

2. Add the tomatoes, onion and green and red bell peppers. Sauté until cooked but chunky, about 6–8 minutes.

3. Add to the chicken stock.

4. Bring the stock to boil over a high heat. After it starts to boil, lower heat to low. Simmer partially covered until the pasta is done, about 8 minutes. Adjust salt and pepper.

To serve: This is a simple soup to serve. Just ladle with plenty of pasta into a bowl. Top with a sprinkle of baby Edam cheese if desired.

Notes: Remember the turkey and all its parts that you boiled for the *consomé de pavo*? Well, chop the gizzard, liver and heart and add with the stock. Many *yucatecan* families like those tasty tidbits added to their *sopa de pasta*.

Ingredients

3 tablespoons vegetable oil

1 package (8 ounces) elbow macaroni

2 plum tomatoes, chopped

1/2 white onion, chopped

1/2 green bell pepper, chopped

1/2 red bell pepper, chopped

10 cups chicken stock (or vegetable stock)

Salt, to taste

Pepper, to taste

Baby Edam cheese, shredded

POTAJE DE LENTEJAS

LENTIL STEW

Serves about 6-8

INGREDIENTS

1 gallon water

1 pound pork meat (pork loin, pork butt, cushion or boneless pork shoulder), cut into 1-inch cubes

1/2 pound dried green lentils (or 1 cup)

1 medium carrot, cut into 1/2-inch rounds

2 teaspoon salt

6 strips bacon, diced

3 plum tomatoes, diced

1/2 white onion, diced

1/2 green bell pepper, diced

1/2 green red bell pepper, diced

1 generous teaspoon *recado rojo* (see recipe)

2 tablespoons white vinegar

1/2 pound smoked ham, cut into 3/4-inch cubes

4 ounces *longaniza tipo Valladolid*, cut into 1-inch slices (or chorizo) (see Glossary)

1 chayote, cut into 1/2-inch cubes

2 Mexican squash (or zucchini), cut into 1/2-inch rounds (see Glossary)

1 Russet potato, cut into 1/2-inch cubes

1 plantain, sliced into 1-inch pieces, skin on

1/4 cabbage, chopped into large pieces (remove core)

6-8 eggs

This is a Cetina family favorite. In fact, we have a special salsa we make to accompany it that I will share below. While lentils are used in this preparation, other legumes can be used, such as garbanzos, *frijol colorado* (red bean) and *frijol canario* (Canary bean). However, cooking times will not be the same. "*Potaje*," by the way, comes from Old French "*potage*" or "*pottage*," which means "potted dish." This dish is similar to *mondongo a la andaluza* (see recipe).

1. Bring the water to a boil and add the pork meat (but not the bacon or ham). Before it returns to a boil, skim the foam that rises to the top with a slotted spoon and discard. Lower the heat and simmer for 20 minutes.

2. Add the lentils, carrots and salt to the pot and simmer for 10 minutes.

3. In a large frying pan over low heat, add the bacon. As it starts to cook, raise the heat and fry until crispy.

4. Add the tomatoes, onion, and green and red bell peppers and sauté for 3–5 minutes until limp. Add to the pot with the lentils and pork meat.

5. Mix the *recado rojo* and vinegar, and strain into the pot.

6. Add the ham, *longaniza* to the pot, and simmer for 5 minutes. Then add the chayote, Mexican squash, potato, plantain and cabbage.

7. Continue to simmer covered until the meat is tender and vegetables are al dente. Adjust salt.

8. Right after you turn off the heat, break the eggs into the *potaje*, replace cover and let them poach.

To serve: Simple, just ladle into a bowl and serve with hot corn tortillas. Don't forget to snag a poached egg for each serving. If you want to enjoy it the way our family does, then you need to top it with *cebolla picante de los Cetina*—a family secret until now.

CEBOLLA PICANTE DE LOS CETINA

20 *chiles de árbol*, roasted with stem removed (see Glossary)

1/3 cup white vinegar

1 teaspoon salt

2–3 tablespoons vegetable oil

2 medium red onions, sliced

1. Purée the chiles, vinegar and salt in a blender or use a mortar and pestle. It should be on the chunky side rather than a smooth puree. Set aside.

2. Heat the oil in a frying pan and add the onions. Stir until the onions are coated with the oil. Add the puréed chiles. Sauté over medium heat until the onions are translucent. Adjust salt.

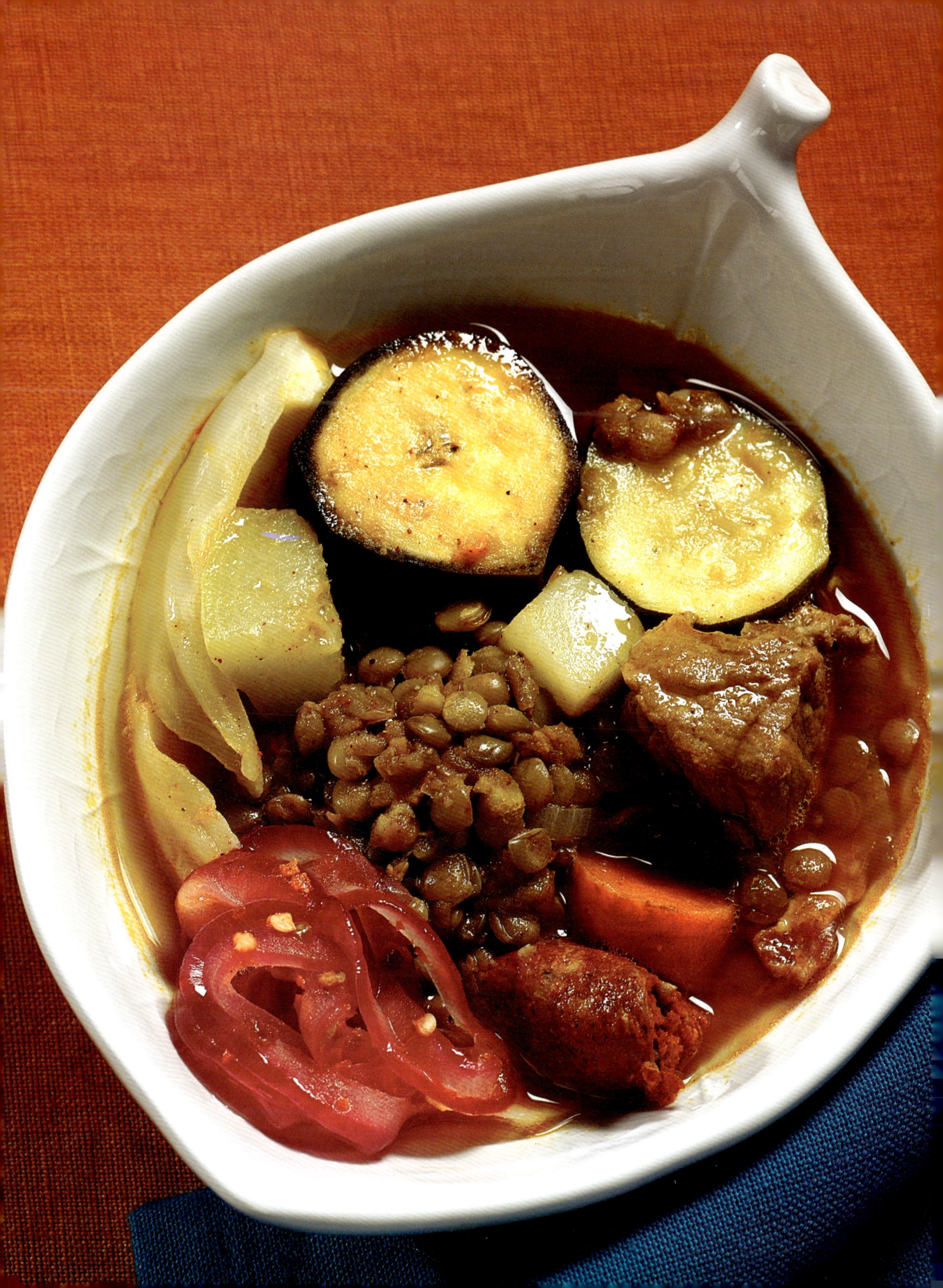

Puchero de Tres Carnes

Three-meat Stew

Serves about 8

Part 1: The Stock

2 gallons water

1 pound sirloin, cut into 1-inch cubes

1 pound beef neck bones

2–3 tablespoons salt

1 pound pork meat (cushion pork, butt, shoulder), cut into 1-inch cubes

8 chicken thighs, with skin and bones

1 tablespoon *recado para puchero* (see recipe)

1/2 cup water

1 head garlic, roasted

1 cinnamon stick

4 small pinches saffron

2 *limas agrias,* halved (or limes)

The first thing you might notice about this dish is that is requires many steps to prepare and serve. As such, it shares much in common with typical Spanish *cocidos*. A calendar dish, this hearty stew is typically served on Sundays and is a meal all by itself. You will note that my approach is rather mathematical. I just want to make sure that all eight servings have something of everything. My servings are generous; you might find this recipe serves more than eight people.

Part 1: Preparing the Stock:

1. Bring the water to a boil. Add the sirloin and beef neck bones and salt. As the water returns to a boil, skim the foam that rises to the top with a slotted spoon and discard. Boil for 10 more minutes.

2. Add the pork, and before the water begins to boil again, skim the foam that rises to the top with a slotted spoon and discard.

3. Add the chicken and before the water begins to boil again, skim the foam that rises to the top with a slotted spoon and discard.

4. Mix the *recado para puchero* and the water and add to the pot followed by the roasted garlic, cinnamon and saffron. Boil for 15–20 more minutes or until the chicken is cooked.

5. Squeeze the *limas agrias* into the stock and add the peel (no seeds). Leave the peel in for 2 minutes and remove and discard.

6. Once all the meats are cooked and tender (may require another 15 minutes of cooking), remove the meats, cover and keep warm.

7. Remove the cinnamon stick from the stock and discard.

Part 2: Preparing the vegetables:

1. Bring the stock back to a boil.

2. Cut the vegetables into 8 pieces or slices (except cabbage). Add the carrots and cook for 6–8 minutes; add the chayote, plantain, yams and cook another 6–8 minutes; and add the Mexican squash and cabbage and cook another 5–6 minutes. The vegetables should be tender.

2. Remove vegetables to a separate bowl, cover and keep warm.

3. Reserve 2–3 cups of the stock for the *fideos* and *sofrito* and set aside.

Part 3: Preparing the rice and garbanzos:

1. Add rice, garbanzos and pinch of saffron to the stockpot. Cover and let simmer. It will take about 15–20 minutes for the rice to cook.

Part 4: Preparing the fideos and sofrito:

1. Heat the oil in a deep skillet over medium heat and add the tomatoes, onion, and green and red bell peppers. Cook for 5–7 minutes.

2. Break up the *fideos* into the sautéed vegetables and stir for another 3–5 minutes. Add 2–3 cups of reserved stock, pinch of saffron and 3–4 thin slices of *lima agria* and cook until the *fideos* are tender.

3. Once the *fideos* are tender, remove the *lima agria* slices and discard.

Part 5: Preparing the "salpicón":

1. In a separate bowl, toss the radish, cilantro, lime juice and salt.

CONGRATULATIONS! You are now ready to assemble your *puchero*.

To serve: For individual servings, place about a 1/2 cup of *fideos* in the center of a large plate. On top of the *fideos*, place 1 piece of chicken and pieces of sirloin and pork. Then place at least one piece of each vegetable around this mound of *fideos* and meat. Top this mound with *salpicón*. In a bowl, ladle about a cup of the *caldo* (stock) reaching deep into the pot to make sure you get rice and garbanzos. Top this with more *salpicón* and garnish with a slice of *lima agria*. Serve the bowl of soup alongside the plate of *fideos*, meats and vegetables with warm corn tortillas. (Normally, the neck bones are not served, but there are those who love to gnaw on them, so don't be in a hurry to discard them.)

Notes: It is curious that the *fideos*, meats and vegetables are served separately from the stock. This makes it similar to the famous *cocido madrileño*, which is served in much the same way. Another interesting point is that in Spain, the clay pots in which *cocidos* are cooked are called "*pucheros*."

More notes: If you dine among *yucatecos* eating *puchero*, you might hear the telltale clack of fork and knife against plate as they meticulously cut up and mix together the *fideos*, meats and vegetables. The resulting mix is called "*puch*."

Part 2: The Vegetables

Cut the vegetables, except the cabbage, into 8 pieces or slices.

2 carrots

1 chayote

1 plantain, sliced, skin on (yellow, but not overripe)

2 yams

2–3 Mexican squash (or zucchini, see Glossary)

1 medium green cabbage, quartered

Part 3: The Rice and Garbanzos

1/2 cup short-grain white rice (or Rose rice)

1 can (15 ounces) garbanzos, drained

1 pinch saffron

Part 4: The Fideos and Sofrito

3 tablespoons vegetable oil

2 plum tomatoes, chopped

1/2 white onion, chopped

1/2 green bell pepper, chopped

1/2 red bell pepper, chopped

1 bag (8 ounces) *fideos* (or vermicelli or spaghetti)

2–3 cups reserved stock

1 pinch saffron

1 *lima agria*, thinly sliced (or limes)

Part 5: The "Salpicón"

5 radishes, minced

3/4 bunch fresh cilantro, finely chopped

Juice of 2 limes

1/2 teaspoon salt

Garnish

Limas agrias, sliced

Mondongo Kabic

Tripe Soup

Serves about 8–10

Ingredients

2 gallons water

2 tablespoons salt

1 cow's foot (*pata*) without skin, cut into 8 pieces (slice lengthwise and then quarter—or ask your butcher to do it)

1 head garlic, roasted whole

1 white or yellow onion, roasted whole

8 pounds beef honeycomb tripe (fresh and clean), cut into 1-inch cubes

2 limes

7–8 dry *chiles guajillos* (see Glossary)

6 ounces (1/2 cup) *recado rojo* (see recipe)

5 plum tomatoes, quartered

1 cup *naranja agria* juice (or lime juice)

Toppings

Chives, chopped

Lime wedges

Call it the *menudo* of the Yucatán, if you will. This eye-opening stew is a great way to start the day. Especially if you've done a little too much partying the night before, this is a remedy for hangovers. Or as a *yucateco* might say, "*Es bueno para la cruda de los domingos.*" It does take a lot of cooking time, so you might want to make it a day ahead to have it ready to clear heads the following morning. By the way, you will need to make *mondongo kabic* in order to prepare *mondongo a la andaluza,* which follows.

1. Bring the water to a boil, and add salt. Add the pieces of cow's *pata* and simmer for 1 hour covered. Occasionally skim the foam that rises to the top with a slotted spoon and discard.

2. Add the garlic and onion, cover and return to high simmer.

3. In a separate bowl, add the cut-up honeycomb tripe and squeeze the juice of the 2 limes into the tripe. Add the rinds and toss. This bleaches the tripe slightly to make it whiter. Leave for 10–20 minutes and drain the juice and remove th rinds.

4. Rinse the chiles and remove the stems. Place in a pot and add water to barely cover. Bring the water to a boil and then simmer the chiles for 10–15 minutes to soften them. Purée the chiles, with the water, in a blender. Set aside.

5. Dilute the *recado rojo* in the *naranja agria* juice (or lime juice), and set aside.

6. At the 2-hour mark, add the honeycomb tripe into the pot with the *patas*. Follow that by straining the puréed chiles and *recado rojo* into the pot. Add the tomatoes.

7. Return cover and cook the *mondongo kabic* for about 6 more hours. The tomatoes should have broken apart completely; and the tripe should be very, very tender. As to the cow's feet, the meat from the *patas* should have fallen off the bone; the tendons "melted" into the *mondongo*.

8. Adjust the salt and the acidity or tanginess of the stock. It should have a definite tang from the *naranja agria* juice (or lime juice). If not, add more juice. Remove the *pata* bones.

To serve: Ladle stock into a bowl with pieces of tripe and *pata* meat. Top with chopped chives and serve with a wedge of lime. Serve with *barras de francés* (French rolls) or *bolillos* or corn tortillas.

Notes: In the Yucatán, they prefer their tripe *very* tender. You may have had a bowl of menudo with chewy tripe. That's not what the *yucatecos* are after. They are looking for the melt-in-the mouth effect.

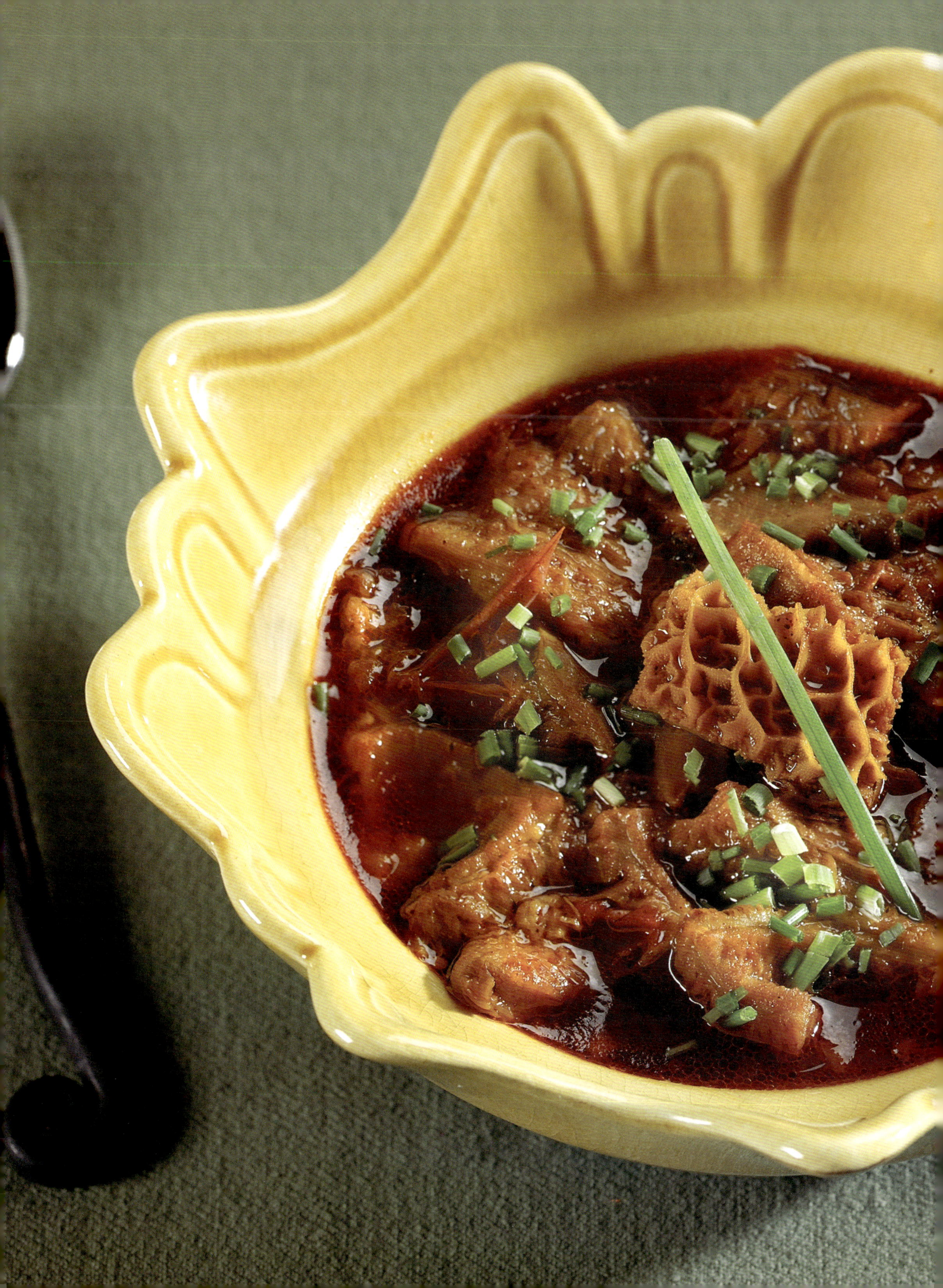

Mondongo a la Andaluza

Andalusian-style Tripe Soup

Serves about 6

Ingredients

6 ounces bacon, roughly chopped

3 plum tomatoes, diced

1 medium white onion, diced

1/2 green bell pepper, diced

1/2 red bell pepper, diced

6 ounces smoked ham, cut into 1/4-inch cubes

6 cups *mondongo kabic* (see recipe)

1 can (8 ounces) garbanzo beans, drained

1/2 pound *longaniza tipo* Valladolid, cut in 3/4- to 1-inch slices (or chorizo, see Glossary)

3 medium Russet potatoes, cut into 1/4-inch cubes

Garnishes

Chives, chopped

Lime wedges

Chile habanero, chopped (optional)

Another hearty stew, this one is also served traditionally on Sundays. Think of this as a greatly enhanced *mondongo kabic* (see recipe) as you will have had to make a pot of that to complete this dish. So consider all your time well spent. I almost always drink an orange-flavored drink with this version of *mondongo*. I just like the way it tastes with the stew's flavors.

1. Over a low heat, add the bacon to a wide frying pan. Once it starts to cook, raise the heat and fry until crispy, being careful not to burn, about 6-8 minutes.

2. Add the tomatoes, onion, and green and red bell peppers. Sauté about 5 minutes.

3. Add the ham and cook another 2–3 minutes.

4. Add the *mondongo kabic* (tripe and meat with the stock) and bring to a boil.

5. Add the garbanzos, *longaniza* and potatoes. Lower the heat and cook until the potatoes are just tender to the fork.

To serve: Ladle into a bowl, top with chopped chives and serve with a wedge of lime and *chile habanero*. Serve with French rolls or *bolillos* or corn tortillas.

Kabic de Res

Beef Soup

Serves about 6–8 (photo on page 44)

Frequent visitors to Mexican restaurants might recognize this soup as falling into the *caldo de res* (beef soup) category. Another way to look at it is as a simpler *puchero* (see recipe). It is a meal in itself. An important step, and one that adds a distinctive smoky taste to this soup, is the roasting of the tomatoes, onion, garlic and chiles.

1. Bring the water to a boil. Add the salt and beef neck bones. As the water returns to a boil, skim the foam that rises to the top with a slotted spoon and discard. Boil for 10 more minutes.

2. Add th sirloin, and as the water returns to a boil, again skim the foam that rises to the top with a slotted spoon and discard. Boil for 10 more minutes.

3. Mix the *recado rojo* and the *naranja agria* juice (or lime juice) and strain into the pot.

4. Add the tomatoes, onion, garlic, and *chiles güeritos*. Simmer for 45 minutes until the meat is tender.

5. Add the carrots and simmer for 5–10 minutes.

6. Add the potatoes, chayote and zucchini and simmer for another 15 minutes or until the vegetables are tender. Adjust salt.

7. To make the *salpicón*, toss the radishes, cilantro, *naranja agria* (or lime juice) and salt. Set aside.

To serve: Ladle meat, vegetables and broth into large, individual bowls. Top with *salpicón* and serve with corn tortillas.

Ingredients

1 gallon water

1 tablespoon salt

1 pounds beef neck bones

3 pounds beef sirloin, cut in 1-inch cubes

1 tablespoon *recado rojo* (see recipe)

1/3 cup *naranja agria* juice (or lime juice)

3 plum tomatoes, roasted whole

1/2 white onion, roasted whole

1 head garlic, roasted

2 *chiles güeritos*, roasted

3 medium carrots, cut in 1-inch slices

3–4 sprigs fresh cilantro

6 small red potatoes, whole

1 chayote, cut into 6 slices lengthwise

2 zucchinis, each cut into 3–4 pieces

"Salpicón" Topping

5 radishes, minced

3/4 bunch fresh cilantro, finely chopped

1/3 cup *naranja agria* juice (or lime juice)

1/2 teaspoon salt

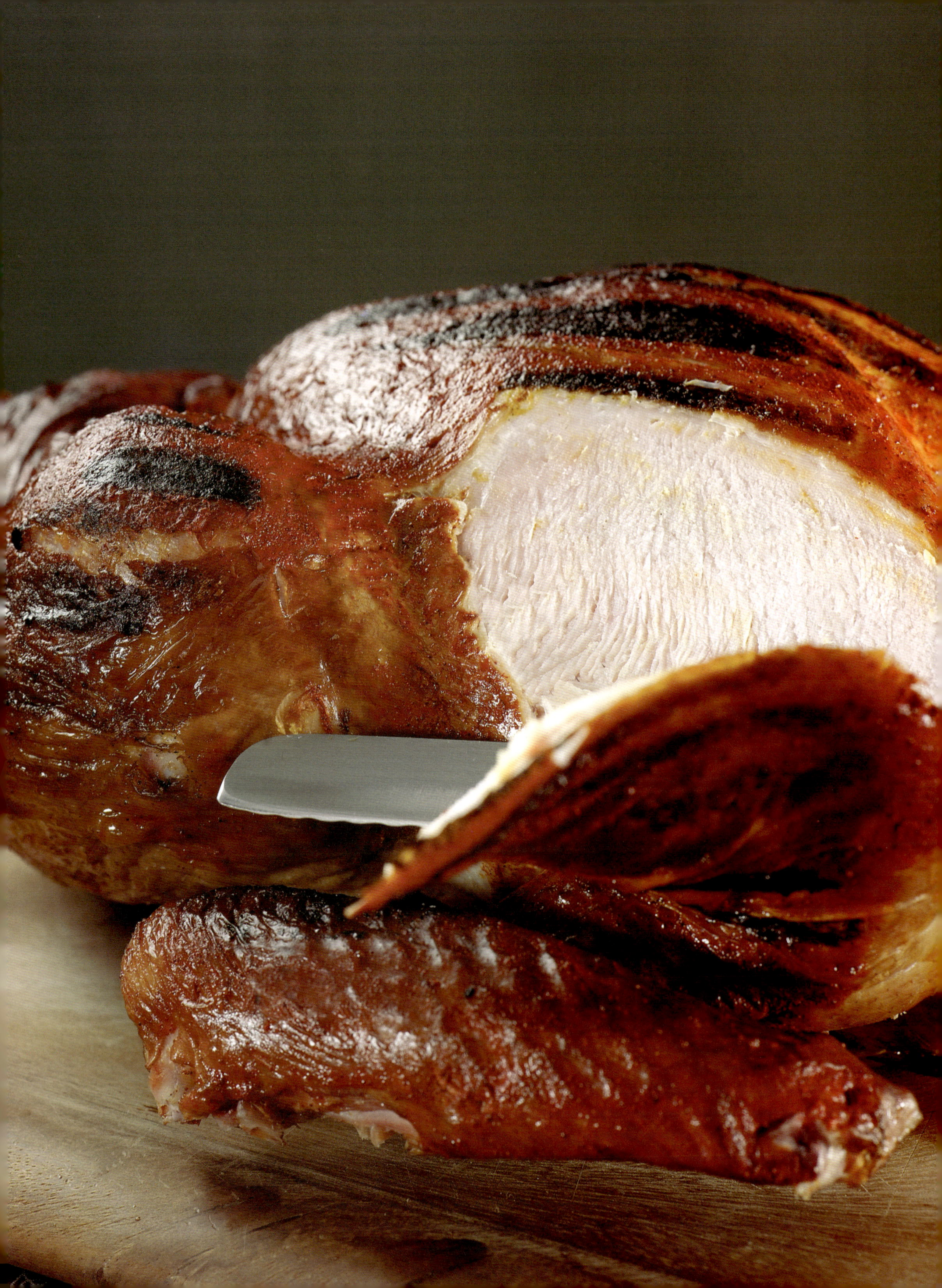

CHAPTER 5

POULTRY...
AVES

Chickens were among the many foodstuffs that the Spanish brought with them to the New World. The Maya certainly took to them for their meat and eggs. Today, *yucatecos* enjoy preparing chicken in many different ways. You'll find that some dishes in this chapter fall into the comfort-food category so plan on adding them as regular meal choices

Turkey is a particularly interesting fowl because it comes from the New World. It was introduced to the Spanish who found it a nice change from the biggest fowls they knew—geese and peacocks. That they called turkey "Indian fowl" reflects the confusion that took some time to sort out. The bird was from a "new" continent but not from India.

The Maya and Aztecs raised turkeys and highly valued them for their meat, eggs and feathers. They were also linked to deities and religious ceremonies.

We can thank these ancient peoples for giving us our centerpiece for a very special meal enjoyed every November in the United States. What would a Thanksgiving meal be without a roasted turkey? (For more on turkey, see the Glossary.)

(For egg-based recipes, see Chapter 3.)

Opposite page: Pavo asado *(page 74).*

Right, from top: Turkeys awaiting their fate in the market, a traditional Mayan home in Campeche, and a turkeys-for-sale sign in the market points the way.

CHAPTER 5: POULTRY/AVES 63

POLLO TICULEÑO
Ticul-style Chicken

Serves 6

Ingredients

1 1/2 tablespoons *recado para bistec* (1 ounce) (see recipe)

1/2 cup lime juice $–5 limes)

1 teaspoon salt

2 pounds chicken breasts, skinned and boned

1 to 2 cups flour

2 eggs, slightly beaten

2 cups crushed *galletas Mariá* (see Glossary) (or Panco crumbs)

3–4 tablespoons vegetable oil

24 slices of plantains (cut on a slant into 1/4-inch slices) (about 2 plantains, not overly ripe)

12 corn tostadas, whole (see Techniques)

Toppings

1–1 1/2 cups *frijol colado* (see recipe)

Peas, drained if canned, thawed if frozen

Cubed smoked ham, cut in 1/4-inch cubes

Cubed cheddar cheese, cut in 1/4-inch cubes

1–1 1/2 cups *salsa de tomate* (see recipe)

1/2 cup *sofrito de tomate* (see recipe)

Pimento slices (canned or jarred)

If you've already prepared *puerco empanizado* (see recipe), you know about the marinade and secret breading; if you've made *huevos motuleños* (see recipe), you already know how to construct this dish. However, here chicken breast meat takes center stage. The dish is named after Ticul, the name of the municipality and municipal seat some 60 to 90 minutes south of Mérida Yucatán. The city of Ticul is known as "*la Perla del Sur*," the "Pearl of the South."

1. Make a marinade by blending the *recado para bistec*, lime juice and salt in a nonreactive bowl.

2. Slice the chicken breasts lengthwise into 1/8-inch-thick slices. Add to the marinade for up to 30 minutes. Do not marinate too long as the chicken will become too acidic. Pat meat slices dry with paper towels. Discard marinade.

3. Dredge the chicken slices lightly into flour; don't press. Dip in the beaten eggs and press into the crushed *galletas María*.

4. Fry the chicken "steaks" in about 2–3 tablespoons vegetable oil in a frying pan over medium-high heat until golden, about 2 minutes on each side. Set aside and cover to keep warm.

5. Heat more vegetable oil in the skillet and fry the plantain slices until golden on both sides. Drain on paper towels.

6. To assemble each plate, place 4 slices of fried plantains spaced on a plate to serve as a base or supporting posts for the tostadas (refer to photo below). Place tostadas, slightly overlapping, on top of the plantains, smear generously with *frijol colado*, followed by a piece of chicken. Top with a generous spoonful of *sofrito de tomate* and surround it with *salsa de tomate*. Then finish with the ham, cheese, peas and pimentos.

POLLO ALCAPARRADO

Chicken and Capers

Serves about 6–8 (photo on page 50)

This everyday dish falls into a group of stew-like dishes that uses capers, olives and raisins to give a dish a sweet and sour flavor. They are an example of how foodstuffs from the Old World influenced New World cooking, including that of the Yucatán.

1. Mix the *recado para bistec* and the vinegar to make a marinade in a nonreactive bowl.

2. Add the chicken pieces to the marinade for up to 30 minutes. Do not marinate too long as the chicken will become too acidic.

3. In a large skillet, heat the oil and brown the chicken pieces on both sides. Drain on paper towels.

4. In the same skillet in which you browned the chicken, add the tomatoes, onion, and green and red bell peppers, and sauté for 6–8 minutes.

5. In a large stock pot (6–8 quarts capacity) over medium heat, add the chicken pieces, sautéed vegetables, water, garlic, capers, olives, raisins and *chiles güeritos*.

6. Lower heat to low, cover and simmer for 30–45 minutes or until the chicken is tender. Adjust salt.

To serve: Plate the *pollo alcaparrado* over *arroz blanco* (see recipe) or with the rice on the side. And don't forget the corn tortillas.

Ingredients

1 teaspoon *recado para bistec* (see recipe)

2 tablespoons white vinegar

6 chicken legs and 6 chicken thighs (with skin and bones)

4 tablespoons vegetable oil

4 plum tomatoes, sliced

1 small white onion, sliced

1/2 green bell pepper, sliced

1/2 red bell pepper, sliced

2 cups water

1 head garlic, roasted

2 tablespoons capers

2–3 tablespoons green olives, chopped or whole (if not pitted, advise your guests)

2 tablespoons raisins

2 *chiles güeritos*, roasted whole (see Glossary)

Pollo en Escabeche Oriental

Valladolid-style Marinated Chicken

Serves about 6–8

The marinade

1 tablespoon *recado para escabeche* (see recipe)

1 cup white vinegar

2 red onions, sliced

1 head garlic, roasted

6 *chiles güeritos,* roasted

1 tablespoon salt

4 bay leaves

The chicken

2 gallons water

1 tablespoon salt

1 chicken (4–5 pounds), cut into pieces

1 head garlic, roasted

1/2 teaspoon dry oregano

1 teaspoon ground black pepper

2 sprigs fresh mint

2 sprigs fresh cilantro

There are two kinds of escabeche in Yucatán. Oriental style is from Valladolid ("*la Sultana del Oriente*") and is a bit more sophisticated. The other is a more simplified one, fondly referred to as the "*escabeche del pueblo*" or "of the people." This recipe represents the "*estilo oriental*" from Valladolid and, like all escabeches, is tangy, tangy, tangy with a bit of a bite. Valladolid, the municipality and city, are located in the eastern part of the state of Yucatán.

Preparing the marinade

1. Make a marinade by dissolving the *recado para escabeche* in the vinegar in a nonreactive bowl. Add the red onions, garlic, *chiles güerito,* salt and bay leaves. Mix and set aside.

Preparing the chicken

1. Bring the water to a boil with the salt. Then add the chicken, garlic, oregano, black pepper, mint and cilantro. Bring back to boil and skim the foam that rises to the top with a slotted spoon and discard.

3. Lower the heat and simmer for 30–45 minutes.

4. Remove the chicken, and set aside to cool. Once cool, place the chicken pieces in the marinade for up to 1 hour.

5. Remove the chicken from the marinade, reserving the marinade, and roast on the stovetop or in the oven at 350°F until golden, between 15–30 minutes.

6. Strain one gallon of chicken stock into a separate stockpot on the stove. Add the chicken pieces, and return to a boil for another 5 minutes.

7. Add the marinade (with the onions, garlic chiles, bay leaves). Let this return to boil for about 1–2 more minutes, cover, and turn off the heat. The chicken should be so tender it easily falls off the bone. Adjust salt.

To serve: Ladle the soup into a bowl without forgetting to make sure each bowl has a piece of chicken, some onions, garlic cloves, chiles, etc. Serve with corn tortillas.

Escabeche: Nice and Tangy Escabeche refers to dishes in which foods are marinated in an acidic marinade. In the Yucatán this can be a marinade made with the juice from any number of citrus fruits—*lima, lima agria, naranja agria*—or vinegar. This kind of preparation comes from Persia and the term *al-sikbaj*. *Sik* meant "vinegar" and *ba* meant "food" referring to meat dishes that were cooked in vinegar and something sweet like honey or date molasses. The Moors picked this up from their conquest of Persia and introduced it to the Iberian Peninsula during their mandate. This style of dish is common in Spain and Portugal and throughout most of Latin America.

Opposite page, from top: Pollo en escabeche oriental *(recipe this page)* and pollo con papas *(page 69).*

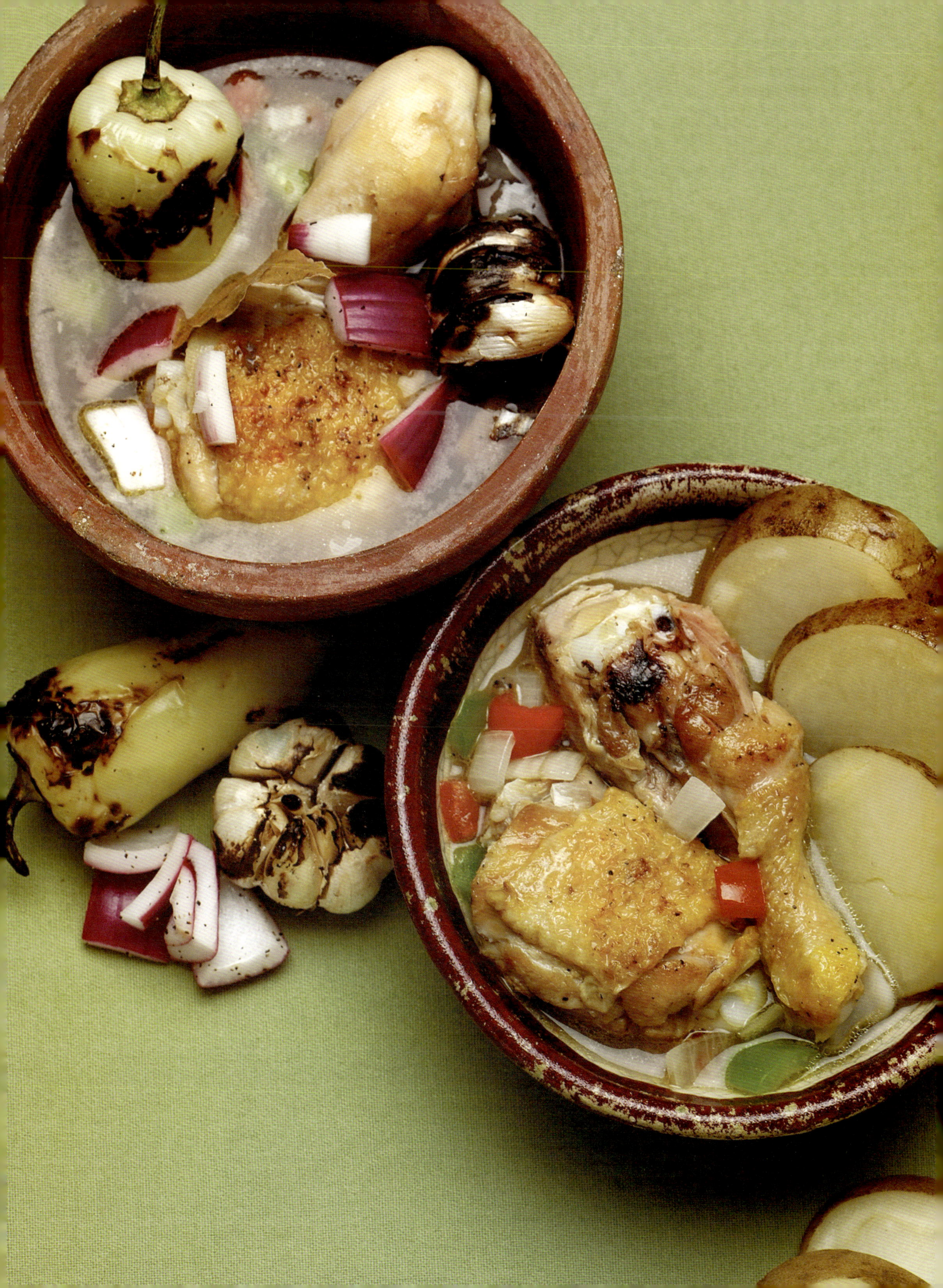

Pollo en Pipián

Chicken in Pumpkin Seed Sauce

Serves about 6–8

Ingredients

1 gallon water

1 tablespoon salt

6 chicken legs and 6 chicken thighs (with skin and bones)

6 plum tomatoes, quartered

3–4 cups ground *pepitas de calabaza tostadas sin cáscara* (ground, toasted, pumpkin seeds, see recipe)

1 sprig fresh epazote

1 *chile serrano*

1 cup *masa harina*

1 cup warm water (or chicken, beef or pork stock)

Garnishes

Plum tomatoes, chopped

Whole pumpkin seeds, toasted

Fresh epazote sprigs

You'll notice the similarities to *costillas en pipián* (see recipe). This time it is chicken that is smothered in pumpkin seed sauce. The word *"pipián"* gives it away that pumpkin seeds are involved. For the early Maya, pumpkin seeds were an important source of protein. Back then, other proteins would have come from such animals as deer, fowl, peccary, etc.

1. Bring the water to boil with salt in a large pot. Add the chicken and bring to a boil again. Skim the foam that rises to top with a slotted spoon and disgard.

2. Add the tomatoes, ground pumpkin seed, epazote and *chile serrano*. Cover and cook over medium heat for 30 minutes or until the meat is cooked. (Use the tortilla test, see Techniques.)

3. Remove the chicken from the pot and place in a covered bowl to keep warm. Remove all stray bones too.

4. To make the sauce, liquefy the contents of the pot in a blender or with a handheld emulsion blender.

5. In a separate bowl, mix the *masa harina* and warm water or stock until well blended. Add this slowly to the pot, stirring until the sauce thickens as desired. If the sauce is still a bit grainy, liquefy again until smooth; if too thick, add more water or stock.

6. Return the chicken to the sauce and heat for 5 minutes. Adjust salt.

To serve: Spoon the *pollo en pipián* over *arroz blanco* (see recipe), and top with chopped tomatoes, pumpkin seeds and epazote sprigs. Serve with corn tortillas.

Pollo con Papas

Chicken and Potatoes

Serves about 6–8 (photo on page 67)

The name tells you this is comfort food. How more basic can you get by matching chicken with potatoes? Another everyday dish, it gets an extra punch from a *sofrito* of sautéed vegetables and the roasted garlic and chiles.

1. Salt and pepper both sides of each piece of chicken.

2. In a wide skillet, heat the vegetable oil and brown the chicken on both sides. Drain on paper towels.

3. In the same skillet in which you browned the chicken, add the sliced tomatoes, onion, and green and red bell peppers. Sauté for 6–8 minutes.

3. In a large stockpot (6–8 quarts capacity) over medium heat, add the chicken, sautéed vegetables, water, garlic, and *chiles güeritos*.

4. Lower heat to low, cover and simmer for 30 minutes or until the chicken is tender. Bring back to a boil and add the potatoes. Simmer for another 10–15 minutes or until the potatoes are tender. Adjust salt.

To serve: Nothing tricky here. Just serve up in a bowl accompanied by *arroz blanco* (see recipe) and corn tortillas.

Ingredients

6 chicken legs and 6 chicken thighs (with skin and bones)

Salt

Pepper

3–4 tablespoons vegetable oil

4 plum tomatoes, sliced

1 small white onion, sliced

1/2 green bell pepper, sliced

1/2 red bell pepper, sliced

2–3 cups water (or chicken stock)

1 head garlic, roasted

2 *chiles güeritos*, roasted

2 Russet potatoes, unpeeled and sliced into 1/2-inch slices (or 5–6 small red potatoes)

The "Bell Pepper" Story Green and red bell peppers are some of the ingredients called for to make the *sofrito* (sautéed bell peppers, onion and garlic) that adds flavor to many recipes in this book. However, they are not used in the Yucatán. Instead a kind of bell pepper called "*chile dulce*" is used. While it resembles a green bell pepper, its flavor is milder and sweeter. While green and red bell peppers are used as substitutes, use with restraint as their flavors can be domineering. (See photo of *chile dulce* on page 81 and in the Glossary.)

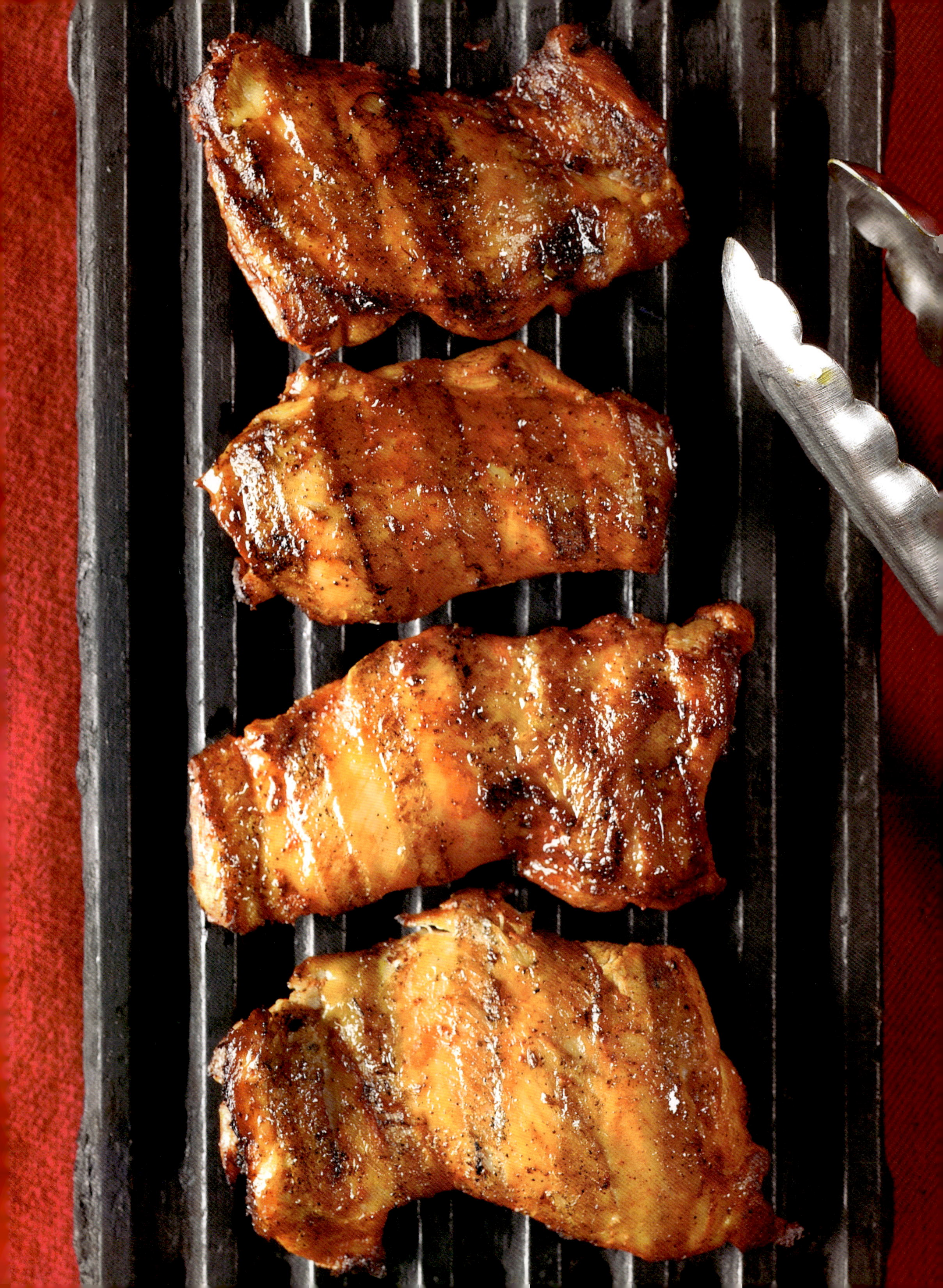

Pollo Asado

Grilled Chicken

Serves about 6–8

Obviously a relative of *pavo asado* (see recipe), it is one of the most common dishes in the Yucatán. It falls more into the everyday category, while *pavo asado* is more for festive occasions. It gets its color and punch from a nice *recado rojo* marinade. This recipe will come in handy when you get to the tamales in Chapter 9.

1. Prepare the recipe for *caldo de pollo*. Remove the chicken and allow to cool. (Strain and reserve the stock for other purposes.)

2. Make a marinade by mixing the *recado rojo,* vinegar and oil in a nonreactive bowl.

3. Add the chicken pieces to the marinade and marinate for 30 minutes to 1 hour.

4. Grill the chicken pieces on a stovetop grill for 6–7 minutes on each side (or outside barbecue). The skin will glisten because of the oil-based marinade. It will turn opaque when thoroughly roasted.

To serve: It is traditionally served with *sopa de pasta* (see recipe). But don't forget the *cebolla para panuchos*, the corn tortillas or the *salsa de chile habanero* on the side. I also like to add a flourish with a radish flower.

Notes: As an option, you can roast the chicken in the oven instead of grilling it. Simply place the chicken in an oven and roast for about 30 minutes at 375°–400°F.

Ingredients

1 recipe *caldo de pollo* (chicken stock, see recipe)

2 tablespoons *recado rojo*

4 tablespoons white vinegar

2 tablespoons vegetable oil

Garnishes

Green leaf lettuce

Cebolla para panuchos (see recipe)

Radish flowers (my personal touch) (optional)

Salsa de chile habanero (see recipe)

On the Grill: *Pollo asado* on the grill at Chichén Itzá Restaurant.

Pollo Pibil
Achiote-rubbed Chicken Baked in Banana Leaves

Serves about 6–8

Ingredients

1 1/2 tablespoons (1 ounce) *recado rojo* (see recipe)

1 1/2 cup *naranja agria* juice (about 10–12 oranges) (or lime juice)

3 whole chickens (2 1/2–3 pounds each), cut into pieces

Banana leaves, thawed if frozen, prepared if fresh (see Techniques and Glossary)

Garnishes

Cebolla para panuchos (see recipe)

Whole *chiles habaneros* (optional)

If you've mastered the classic *cochinita pibil* (see recipe), you won't have much trouble making succulent *pollo pibil*. Just note that the difference is in the marinating and baking time. So please adjust your preparation as noted. And make sure your guests are hungry because servings are generous.

1. Make a marinade by mixing the *recado rojo, naranja agria* juice and salt until well blended in a nonreactive bowl.

2. Marinate the chicken pieces in the *recado rojo* marinade. For best flavor, refrigerate at least three hours or overnight, turning at least once.

3. Line a Dutch oven or casserole with the banana leaves, overlapping the leaves slightly and covering bottom and sides of the baking dish.

4. Place the marinated chicken halves in the banana-leaf-lined pan. Pour the remaining marinade over the meat and fold the banana leaves so that the meat is completely covered.

5. Cover and seal the baking dish with aluminum foil, heavy preferred.

6. Place foil-covered baking dish in a 350°F preheated oven. Bake for 2 hours or until the meat is tender to the point of falling off the bone (or passes my tortilla test, see Techniques).

To serve: As a main dish, serve a portion of chicken with *frijoles negros guisados* (see recipe), *arroz blanco* (see recipe) and corn tortillas. Oh, and the garnishes of *cebolla para panuchos* and *chiles habaneros*. The meat, shredded, can also be used for *salbutes* (see recipe) or *tortas* (sandwiches). I like to eat it with *curtido de repollo* (see recipe), even though *cebolla para panuchos* is the more traditional garnish.

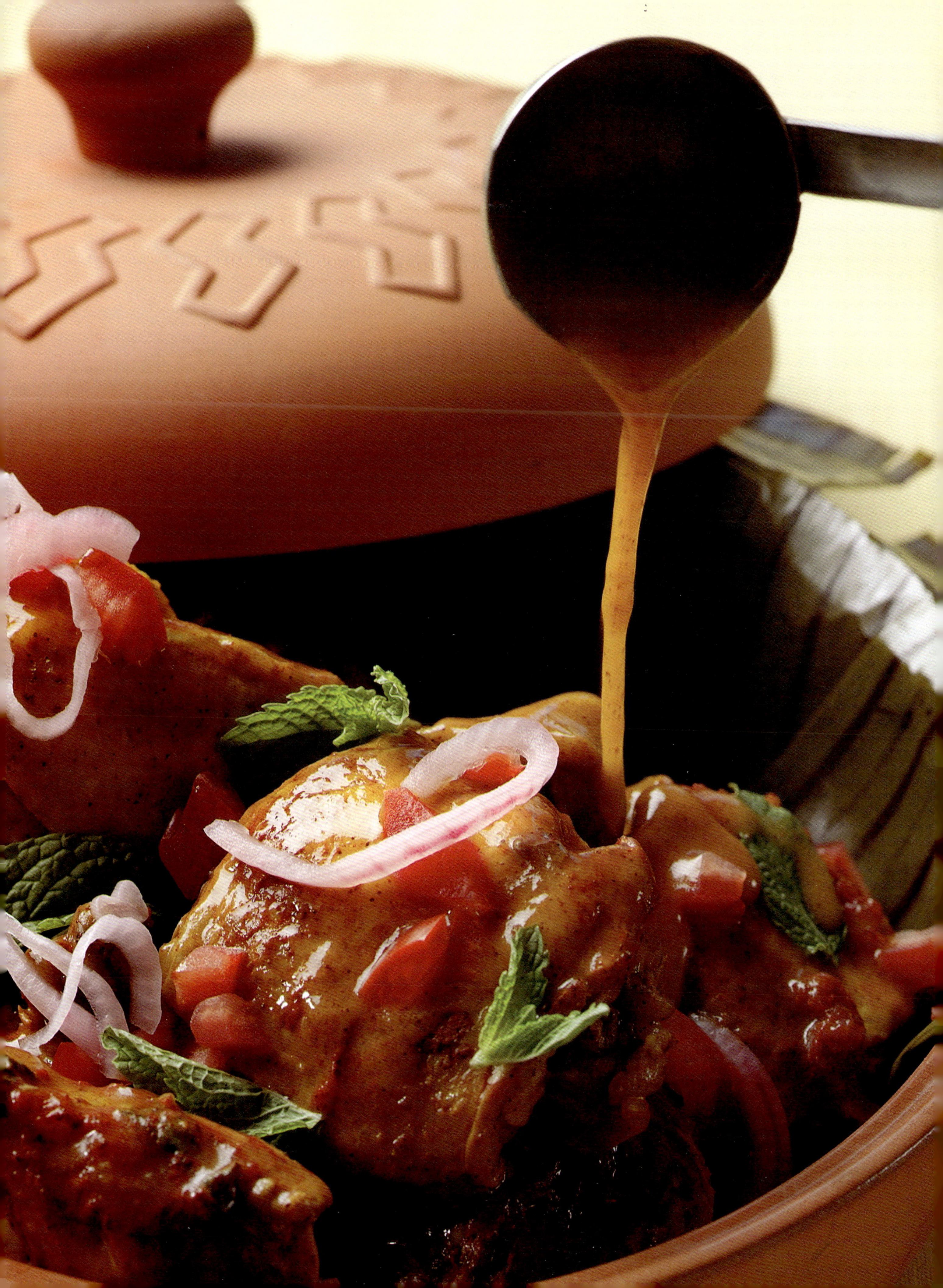

Pavo Asado
Roasted Turkey

Serves about 10–15 (photo on page 62)

Ingredients

4 tablespoons (about 2.6 ounces) *recado rojo* (see recipe)

3 1/2 tablepoons white vinegar

1 teaspoon salt

1 1/2 tablespoons vegetable oil

1 prepared 15-pound turkey (see recipe for *consomé de pavo*)

Making a succulent *pavo asado* is something to master as the meat is a key ingredient in many classic dishes. It requires multiple steps, but they are well worth the effort. To arrive at the point at which this recipe starts, you must have already boiled the turkey as explained in the recipe for *consomé de pavo* (turkey stock, see recipe).

1. Mix the *recado rojo,* vinegar, salt and vegetable oil in a nonreactive bowl to make a moist rub.

2. Rub this liberally all over the prepared turkey. Wear plastic gloves to avoid staining your hands with the *recado rojo*.

3. Grill the turkey on an outside barbecue over a high heat for about 5–8 minutes on each side until the turkey takes on a burnt red color. You can achieve the same effect using a stovetop grill or baking in a hot oven at 375°F for 20–30 minutes. Split the turkey if you roast it in an oven.

To serve: Carve the turkey for individual servings. Or shred the meat to use in *caldo de pavo* and *sopa de lima* (see recipes) or as toppings for *panuchos* and *salbutes* (see recipes). It is also needed for *pavo en escabeche* and *sah kol de pavo* (see recipes).

Notes: If you roast the turkey over too low a heat, it will take longer to achieve the desired effect and the meat will get dry. Remember, the turkey is already cooked. This final grilling or roasting is designed to add more complex flavors to the turkey, bringing out the flavor of the *recado rojo* rub and the seasonings that were used when the turkey was boiled.

Turkey: America's Bird Turkey stars in many Yucatecan dishes and not surprisingly so since they are native to the Americas. Folks in the Yucatán continue to raise them at home. In fact, if they know they have a big party ahead, like a wedding, families will carefully inventory and care for their poultry to make sure they will have what they need when the time for the big party arrives. They'll say, "These turkeys are for when my daughter gets married." And *pavo asado* takes center stage on Christmas Eve across the Yucatán. (See below and Glossary for more on turkeys.)

Menu para Nochebuena During the holidays, the whole, roasted turkey is the centerpiece of the Christmas Eve meal. The family gathers after *Misa de Gallo* (Midnight Mass) to indulge. Traditional side dishes include *sopa de pasta, ensalada de verduras* and *queso napolitano*. Leftovers make for great sandwiches for Christmas Day or New Year's Day. Don't be shocked to find out that *yucatecos* like to use *pan de sanwich* (white bread) for their sandwiches. But French rolls (*barras de francés*) or *bolillos* will work too. What about *teleras*? Not so much a Yucatecan thing, but they'll do as well. See Glossary for more information about your bread choices.

Sah Kol de Pavo

Roasted Turkey with White Sauce

Serves about 6

This dish was created when someone thought of something delicious to do with leftover *pavo asado* (see recipe). It's a great excuse to make sure that you do, in fact, have some leftover *pavo asado*. *Sah kol* means *salsa blanca* (white sauce).

1. Sauté the tomatoes, onion, and green and red bell peppers over a medium-high heat in the vegetable oil until the onion is translucent.

2. Add the *pavo asado* and incorporate it into the sautéed vegetables.

To serve: For each serving of *sah kol de pavo,* place about 1/4–1/3 cup of *sah kol* (*salsa blanca*) into a deep or wide soup bowl. Top with about 1 cup of the turkey-vegetable mix. Serve with corn tortillas.

Notes: Leftovers take on real significance in the Yucatán. This dish is just one example. Leftovers from *puchero* and *caldo de res* also find new life. The vegetables are puréed for baby food and the meat is used to make *trapo viejo* (known as *ropa vieja,* or "old clothes," in other parts of the Caribbean) or *machaca con huevo* (scrambled eggs with meat). Lunch can foretell dinner. For example, if you have *pan de cazón* for lunch, there's a good chance that you'll have *empanadas de cazón* for dinner.

Ingredients

3 plum tomatoes, chopped

1/2 white onion, chopped

1/3 green bell pepper, chopped

1/3 red bell pepper, chopped

2 tablespoons vegetable oil

6 cups chunks *pavo asado* with skin (see recipe)

2 cups *sah kol* (see recipe)

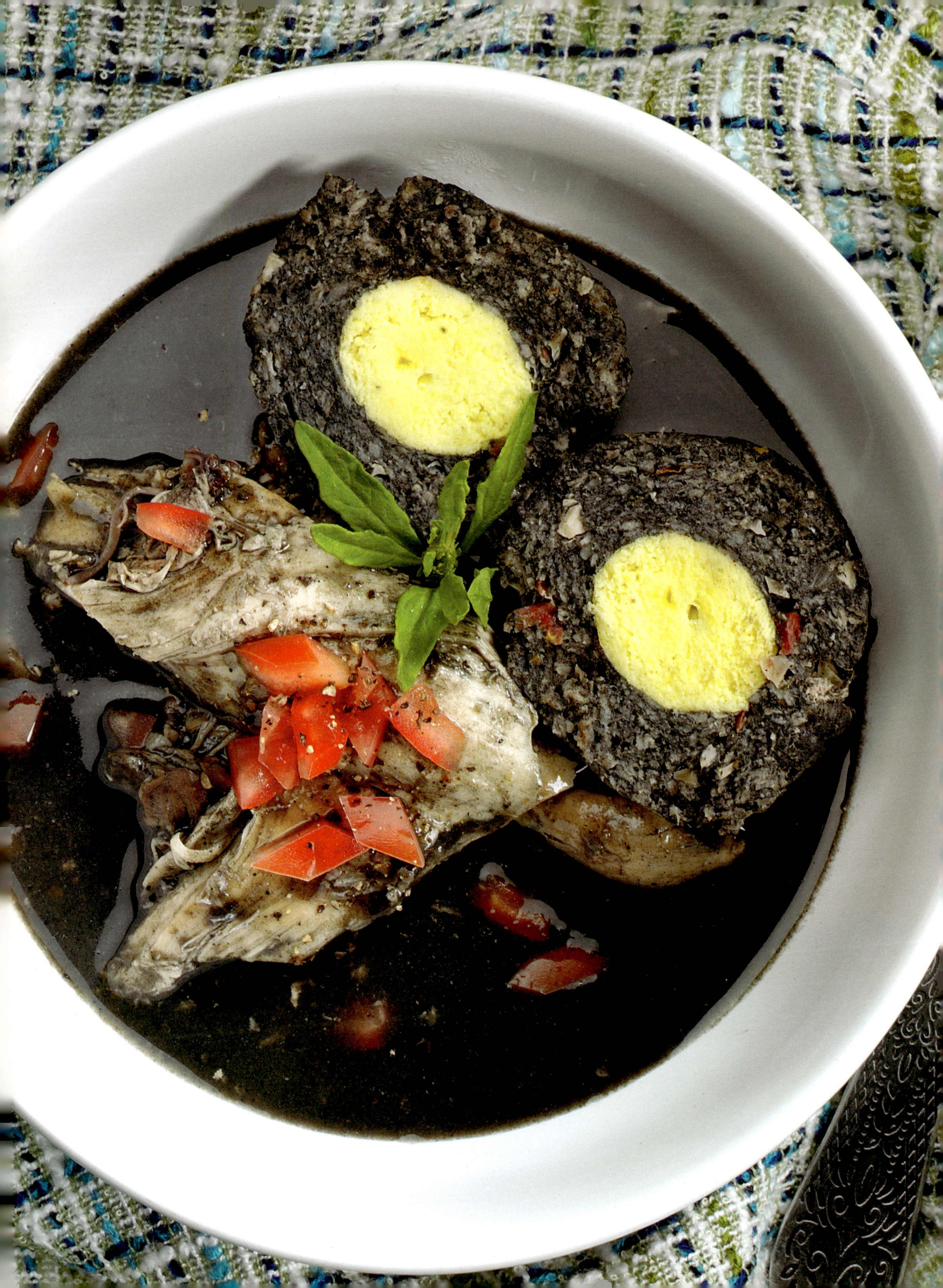

PAVO EN RELLENO NEGRO
Roasted Turkey with Pork Meatballs in Recado Negro

Serves 20

This traditional *guiso* is a popular dish for weddings, festivals and other important occasions, especially in rural communities. This black-and-white mosaic (you'll see when you slice open a meatball) with its multiple layers of flavors is something you will come to crave. And so will your family or guests. It is a bit labor intensive, but well worth the effort. You'll discover that the English translation of the name doesn't do the dish justice.

To make the caldo (soup)

1. In a large, 8-gallon pot, bring the water and salt to a boil, add the pork neck bones and the turkey. As it returns to a boil, skim the foam that rises to the top with a slotted spoon and discard.

2. Dissolve the *recado negro* into 1/2 cup of the boiling water and strain back into the pot.

3. Add the roughly chopped tomatoes and epazote, and lower the heat to medium. Simmer, uncovered, for 2 hours. Adjust salt.

4. Remove the neck bones, but don't discard because someone will surely want to gnaw on them. Remove the turkey and, as soon as you can handle it, debone and tear the meat into chunks. Set aside and keep warm.

To make the albóndigas (meatballs or "relleno"):

1. Take the hard-cooked eggs and separate the egg yolks from the egg whites being careful not to tear or break the egg yolks. Set the whole yolks aside; chop the egg whites.

2. In a large bowl, mix the ground pork, the finely chopped tomatoes, epazote, chopped egg whites and salt.

3. Blend the *recado negro* with the 2 raw eggs and add to the ground pork mixture. (Use the third egg if the meat mixture appears too dry.) Mix well, and divide the ground meat mixture into 20 portions.

4. To form the *albóndigas,* (meatballs or "*relleno*") take one portion of the ground meat mixture and pat into a slightly flattened "patty" in your palm with an indent in the middle. Place one egg yolk in the indent in the meat "patty" and carefully and completely enclose the egg yolk in the center of the meatball. It is a large meatball. Repeat until all 20 meatballs are formed.

5. Bring the *caldo* back to a boil and carefully place the *albóndigas* into the pot. Reduce the heat and let simmer over medium heat for about 20–30 minutes.

6. If you feel the *caldo* is too watery, remove the turkey, neck bones and *albóndigas* (keeping them warm). Mix the cornstarch in 4–5 tablespoons of water (not the warm *caldo*), and stir slowly into the *caldo* and let it thicken slightly.

To serve: Place a handful of turkey chunks in a deep or wide soup bowl. Add one *albóndiga*, sliced open (to reveal the black and white mosaic and surprise yolk), and ladle the *caldo* over this. Serve with corn tortillas.

The caldo

2 gallons water

1 tablespoon salt

2 pounds pork neck bones

1 whole turkey (about 15 pounds), cut into serving pieces

4 ounces (a bit more than 1/3 cup *recado negro* (see recipe)

4 plum tomatoes, roughly chopped;

1/2 bunch fresh epazote

2 tablespoons cornstarch (optional)

The albóndigas (meatballs or "relleno"):

20 hard-cooked eggs

5 pounds ground pork

4 plum tomatoes, finely chopped

1/2 bunch fresh epazote, leaves only, minced

2 tablespoons salt

4 ounces (a bit more than 1/3 cup *recado negro* (see recipe)

2–3 raw eggs

RECADO TIPS When you dissolve *recados* into a liquid, it is important to strain it. It is possible, for example, that the hard achiote seeds that go into *recado rojo* may still leave a gritty residue no matter how finely they appear to be ground. In addition, store-bought *recados* may have fillers, such as flour or ground corn, and straining them ensures better results. Take the surprise out of the equation and make your own *recados*. (See Chapter 1.)

Pavo en relleno blanco

Roasted Turkey with Pork Meatballs in Recado Blanco

Serves about 20

The caldo

2 gallons water

2 pounds pork neck bones

1 whole turkey (about 15 pounds), cut into serving pieces

1 tablespoon salt

3 tablespoons (2 ounces) *recado para bistec* (see recipe)

2 tablespoons white vinegar

1 head garlic, roasted

2 tablespoons cornstarch (optional)

The albóndigas (meatballs or "relleno")

20 hard-cooked eggs

2 ounces *recado blanco*

2 tablespoons white vinegar

5 pounds ground pork meat

20 green olives, minced

20 capers (about 1–2 tablespoons)

1 cup raisins

1/2 cup finely diced white onion

1/2 cup finely diced green bell pepper

1/2 cup finely diced red bell pepper

2 tablespoons salt

2–3 raw eggs

The brother to *pavo en relleno negro* (see recipe), this dish is surprisingly similar yet strikingly distinct. Like its darker-hued relative, *pavo en relleno blanco* is generally reserved for special occasions. Don't let the color fool you; white is as complex as black.

To make the caldo

1. In a large, 8-gallon pot, bring the water to a boil and add the pork neck bones, turkey and salt. As it returns to a boil, skim the foam that rises to the top with a slotted spoon and discard.

2. Dissolve the *recado par bistec* into the vinegar and pour into the pot. Add the garlic, and lower the heat to medium. Simmer, uncovered, for about 2 hours.

4. Remove the neck bones, but don't discard because someone might like to gnaw on them. Remove the turkey and, as soon as you can handle it, debone and tear the meat into chunks. Set aside and keep warm.

To make the albóndigas (meatballs or "relleno")

1. Take the hard-cooked eggs and separate the egg yolks from the egg whites being careful not to tear or break the egg yolks. Set aside the whole yolks; chop the egg whites.

2. Dissolve the *recado para bistec* in the vinegar and, in a large bowl, strain into the ground pork meat.

3. Then add the chopped egg whites, olives, capers, raisins, onion, red and green bell peppers, and salt to the ground meat mixture. Mix well, and divide the ground meat mixture into 20 portions.

4. To form the *albóndigas* (meatballs or "*relleno*"), take one portion of the ground meat mixture and pat into a slightly flattened "patty" in your palm with an indent in the middle. Place one egg yolk in the indent in the meat "patty" and carefully and completely enclose the egg yolk in the center of the meatball. It is a large meatball. Repeat until all 20 meatballs are formed.

5. Bring the *caldo* back to a boil and carefully place the *albóndigas* into the pot. Reduce the heat and simmer over medium heat for about 20–30 minutes.

6. If you feel the *caldo* is too watery, remove the turkey, neck bones and meatballs (keeping them warm). Mix the cornstarch in 3–4 tablespoons of water (not the warm caldo), and stir slowly into *caldo* and let it thicken slightly.

To serve: Place a handful of turkey chunks in a deep or wide soup bowl. Add one *albóndiga*, sliced open (to reveal the black and white mosaic and surprise yolk), and ladle the *caldo* over this. Serve with corn tortillas.

Notes: For both *pavo en relleno negro* and *pavo en relleno blanco*, chicken can be substituted for turkey. Just adjust cooking times, as chicken requires less time to cook. By the way, meatballs are called "*relleno*" (stuffing) because sometimes the seasoned meat is used to stuff a whole turkey.

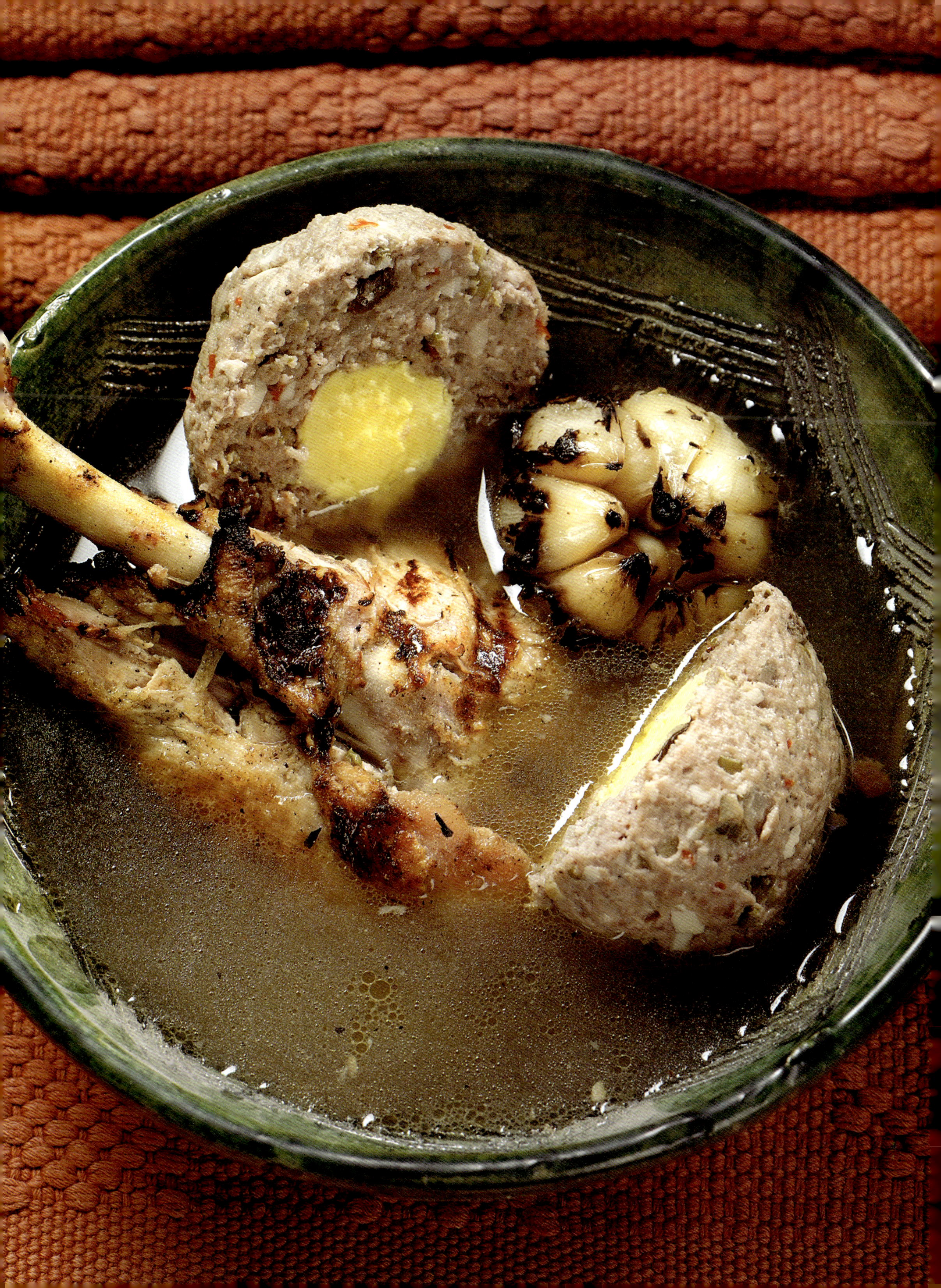

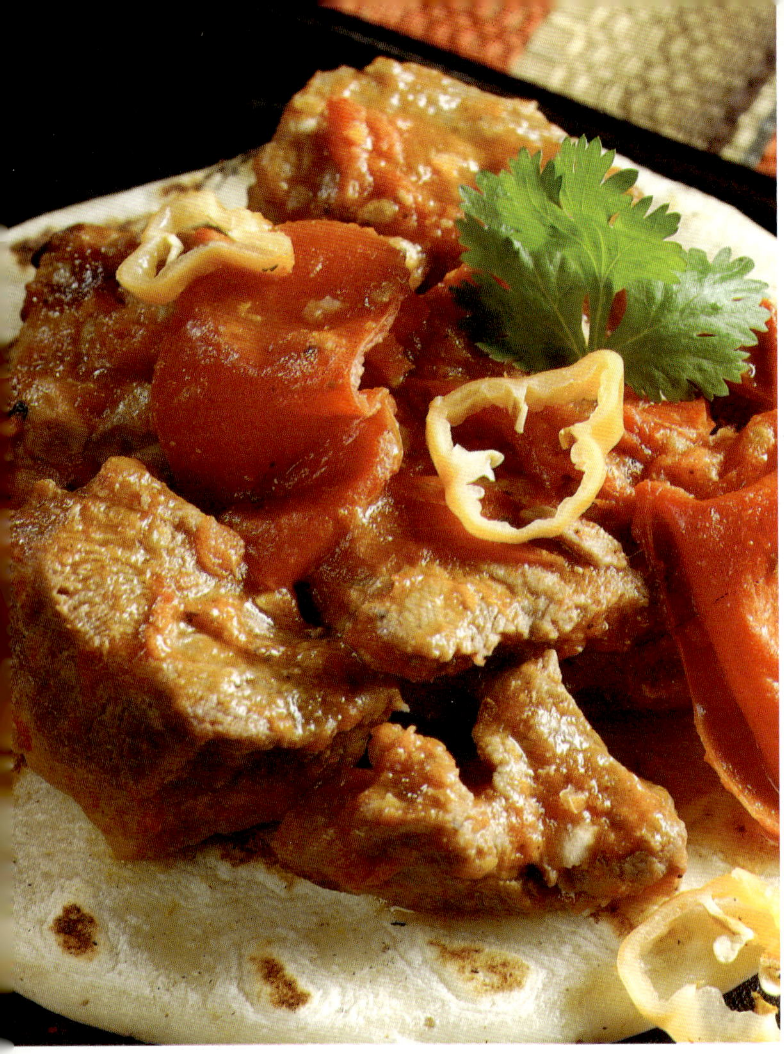
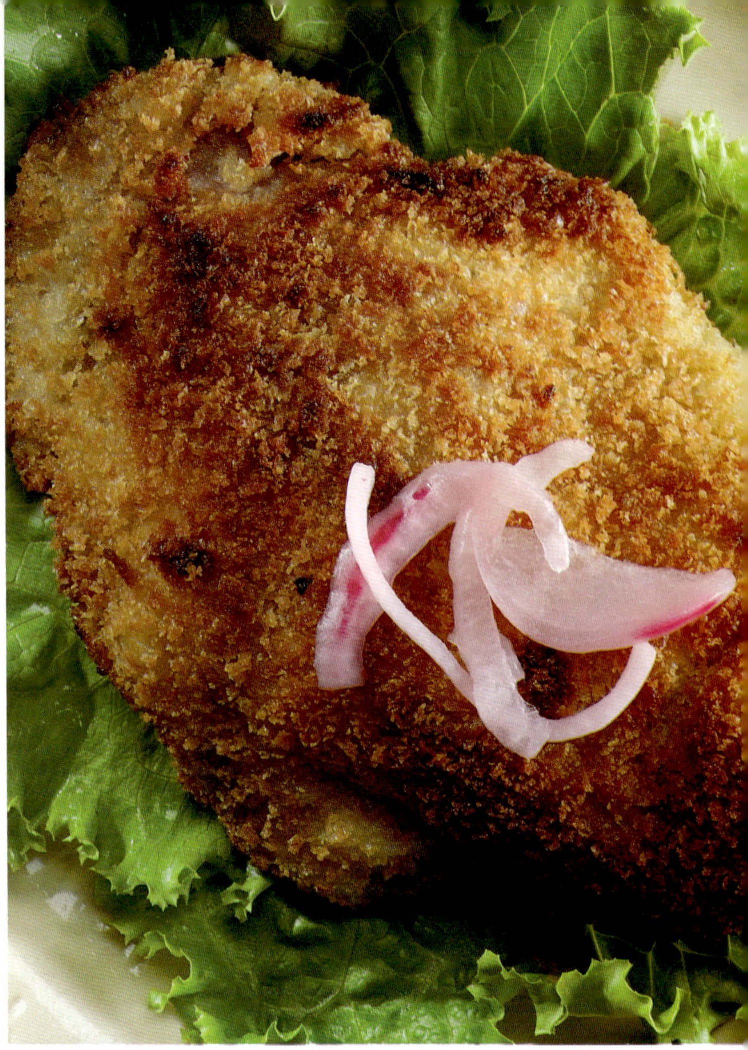
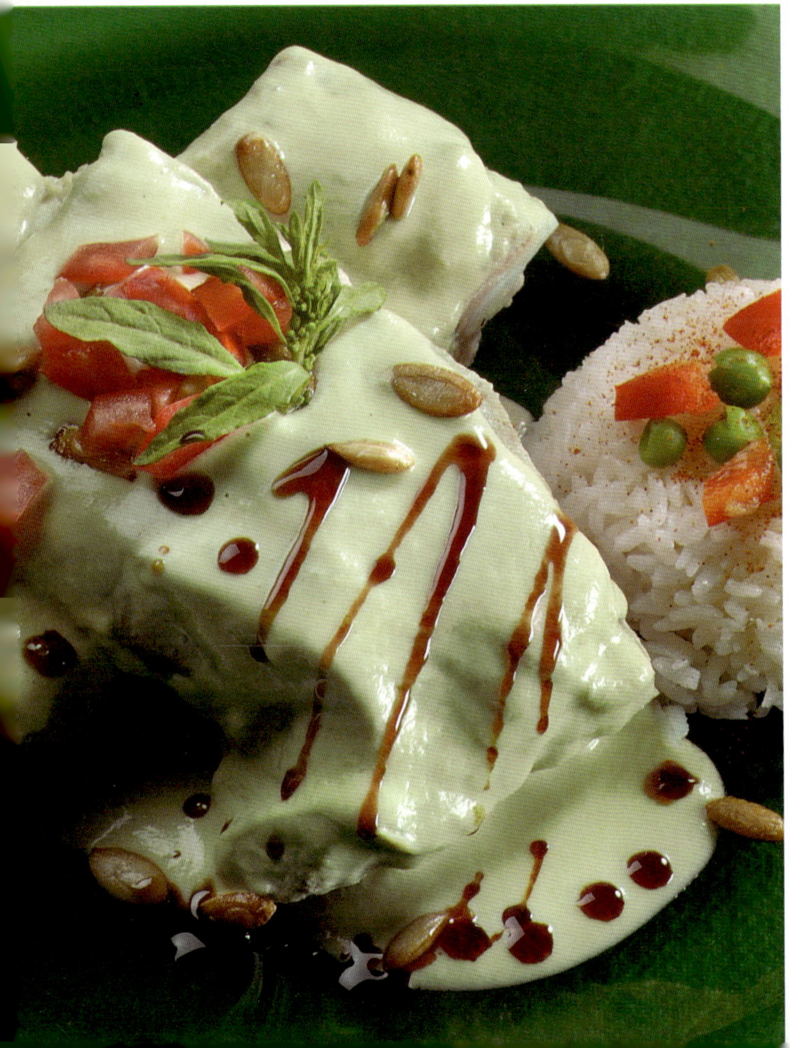
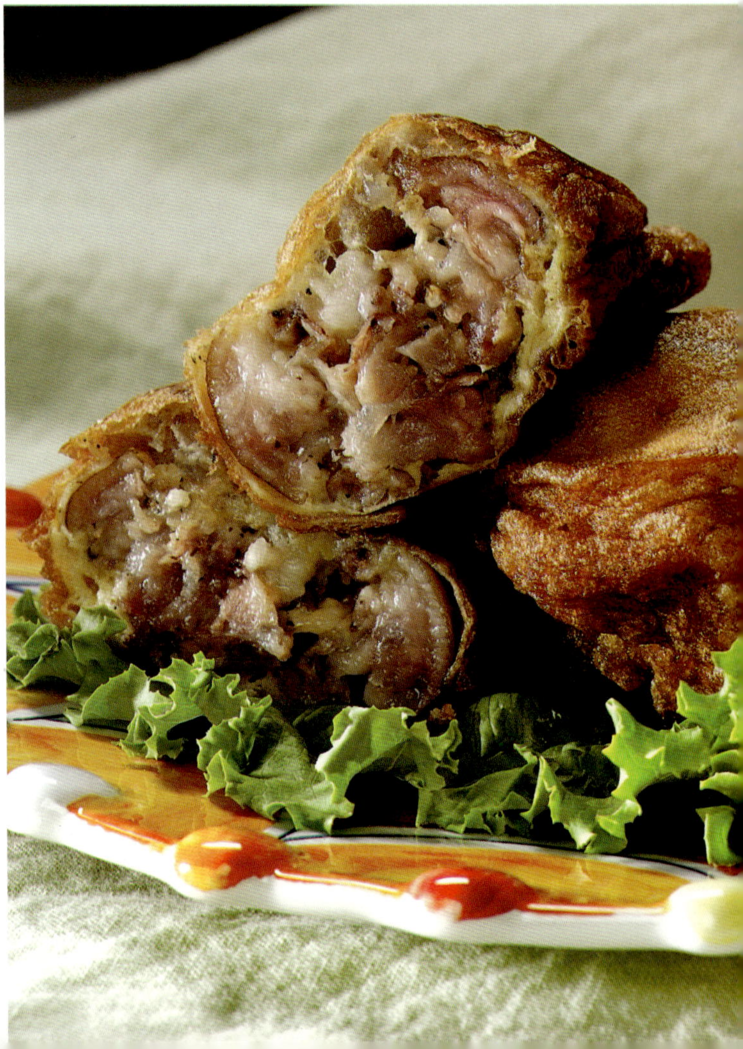

CHAPTER 6

PORK...
PUERCO

It is so hard to imagine a world without pork. But such was the New World before the Conquest. Sure, ancient cultures, including the Maya, had their peccary, but does it really compare to a nicely fattened pig?

After the Spanish brought pigs to the New World, they were quick to be appreciated and were turned into many delicacies that would become typical. The Maya found many delicious things to do with pork, and they learned to appreciate all parts of the animal, including the tasty lard rendered from its fat. *Yucatecos* continue to savor pork today.

Perhaps the most famous Yucatecan dish represents a direct link to the ancient Maya and how they prepared meat using a traditional method of cooking (see side bar on "*pibil*"). The dish is *cochinita pibil*, a tribute to the succulence of pork and local ingenuity.

Pork shanks and pigs' feet are the more uncommon cuts of pork used in a couple of the recipes in this chapter. That's not to say that *yucatecos* don't like fried pig skin (*chicharrones*), pigs' ears, heads, etc., etc....

Opposite page, clockwise from top right: Puerco entomatado *on a* pime *(page 92)*, puerco empanizado *(page 90)*, pezuñas rebosadas *(page 92) and* costillas en pipián *(page 87)*.

Right, from top: The more mild chile dulce *is used instead of green bell peppers in the Yucatán, market restaurants ready for business, and* recados *packaged for sale.*

CHAPTER 6: PORK/PUERCO 81

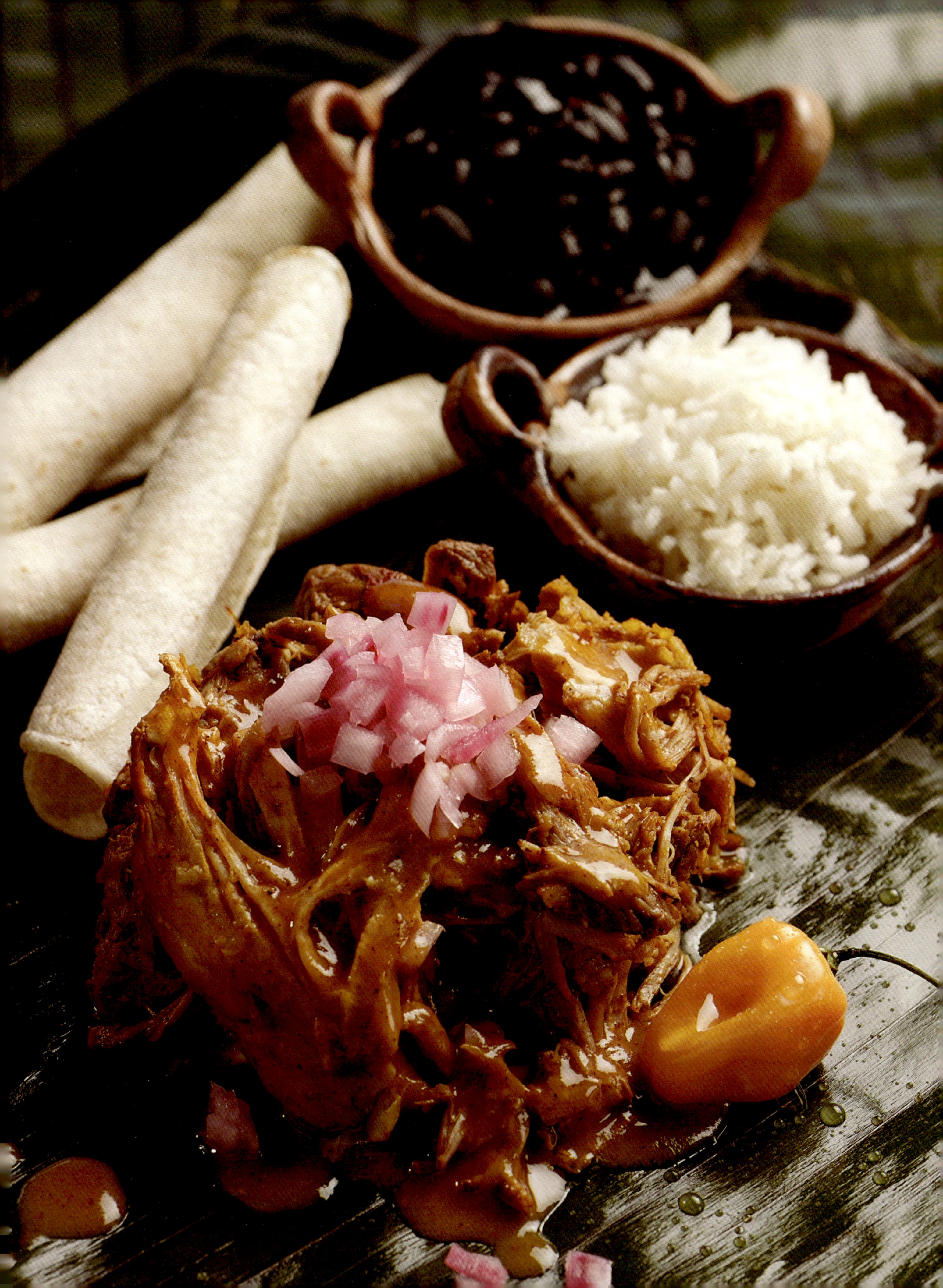

COCHINITA PIBIL

Achiote-marinated Pork Baked in Banana Leaves

Serves about 8–10

Yucatán's signature dish is seeped in tradition as well as chilies and spices. "*Pibil*" refers to the way the Maya cooked meat in pits on site after a hunt to preserve it. (See side bar below and Glossary.) It is also a popular dish to eat out because it is often made in large quantities. Today, *cochinita pibil* has been adapted for the home kitchen without losing any of its succulence. The dish gets it flavors from a complex, yet easy-to-make, marinade, Its tenderness comes from slow cooking folded in banana leaves that impart their unique, earthy flavor and aroma. This dish is great for serving a large crowd or for providing plenty of leftovers for next-day eating.

1. Make a marinade by mixing the *recado rojo, naranja agria* juice (or lime juice) and salt until well blended.

2. In a large, nonreactive bowl, marinate the pork meat in the *recado rojo* marinade.

3. Line a Dutch oven or casserole with banana leaves, overlapping the leaves and covering the bottom and sides of the baking dish well.

4. Place the marinated pork meat in the banana-leaf-lined pan. Pour the remaining marinade over the meat and fold the banana leaves so that the meat is completely covered.

5. Cover and seal the baking dish with aluminum foil, heavy preferred.

6. Place foil-covered baking dish in a 350°F preheated oven. Bake for 3 1/2 to 4 hours or until the meat is tender to the point of falling apart with a fork (or passes my tortilla method, see Techniques).

To serve: As a main dish, serve with *frijoles negros guisados* (see recipe), *arroz blanco* (see recipe) and corn tortillas. Don't forget the garnishes of *cebolla para cochinita pibil* and *chiles habaneros*.

Notes: The meat can be cooked right away, but for the best flavor, let it marinate for at least three hours or overnight. The meat, shredded, can also be used for *salbutes* (see recipe). *Yucatecos* really like in it tacos and *tortas*.

INGREDIENTS

2 1/2 tablespoons (about 1.6 ounces) *recado rojo* (see recipe)

1 1/2 cups *naranja agria* juice (or lime juice)

1 tablespoon salt

5 pounds pork meat (pork loin, pork butt, cushion or boneless pork shoulder)

Banana leaves, thawed if frozen or prepared if fresh (see Techniques and Glossary)

Garnishes

Cebolla para cochinita pibil (see recipe)

Whole *chiles habaneros* (optional)

Opposite page: Cochinita pibil *is pictured with* frijoles de la olla *(page 143),* arroz blanco *(page 146), and topped with* cebolla para cochinita pibil *(page 142).*

PIBIL: A WAY OF COOKING

When hunting for wild animals was more common, Mayan hunters adapted a way of cooking the meat on site, a technique still used today. This preserved the meat until they were able to return to their families. Once game was caught, skinned and butchered, the Maya would dig deep pits in the ground and line them with aromatic woods and small, limestone rocks. After lighting the wood, they would wait until the wood was smoldering and the rocks red hot. They then crisscrossed these with the stripped veins from the leaves of a native palm tree—the guano palm. Next came a thick layer of avocado leaves—or later banana leaves. On top of this went the meat that was covered by more leaves. Then went a final layer of dirt or sod so that no heat would escape. The meat would be allowed to bake overnight or even up to two or three days, delivering the hunters a tasty meal whenever needed. Yucatán's signature dish, *cochinita pibil* (see recipe), evolved this way. Luckily, this method of cooking has been highly adapted, making the dish practical to make at home. By the way, "*pibil*" means "buried" in Mayan.

AKAT DE CODILLOS
ACHIOTE-MARINATED PORK SHANKS IN BANANA LEAVES

Serves about 8–10

INGREDIENTS

2 1/2 tablespoons (about 1.6 ounces) *recado rojo* (see recipe)

1 cup *naranja agria* juice (or lime juice)

1 tablespoon salt

5 pounds pork shanks

Banana leaves, thawed if frozen or prepared if fresh (see Techniques and Glossary)

Garnishes

Cebolla para cochinita pibil (see recipe)

Whole *chiles habaneros* (optional)

If you've prepared *cochinita pibil,* you will immediately see the similarities between that dish and this one. However, *akat de codillos* is not as succulent or tender as *cochinita pibil,* so take care not to overcook as it will become dry. Yucatecan families frequently eat this dish because it is so economical and good.

1. Make a marinade by mixing the *recado rojo, naranja agria* juice (or lime juice) and salt until well blended in a nonreactive bowl.

2. Marinate the pork hocks in the marinade.

3. Line a stockpot with the banana leaves, overlapping the leaves slightly and covering the bottom and sides of the baking dish well.

4. Place the marinated pork hocks in the banana-leaf-lined pot. Pour the remaining marinade over the meat, and fold the banana leaves over to completely cover the pork hocks. Cover the stockpot.

5. Cook over a medium heat for 1 1/2 hours or until the meat is tender to the point of falling apart with a fork or passes my tortilla method.

To serve: Serve with the same garnishes and sides that accompany *cochinita pibil.*

Notes: Refer to Techniques for preparing fresh banana leaves.

ACHIOTE: THE COLOR OF THE YUCATÁN
A typical ingredient in the Yucatecan kitchen is achiote or annatto seed from the fruit pods of a bush-sized tree (*Bixa orellana*). The seeds are a rich, deep, chestnut color. When used in cooking, they deliver a beautiful color and earthy flavor to food. Typically, the seeds are ground and mixed with garlic, black pepper, allspice and oregano. To make a paste, this spice mix is moistened with vinegar or citrus juice. Toasting the paste gives its flavor extra depth. This *recado rojo* (also called *recado colorado,* achiote paste or *pasta de achiote*) can then used to rub on meats before cooking, or, as in *cochinita pibil, akat de codillos* and *pollo pibil,* used as a marinade. *Recado rojo* can be found in grocery stores that cater to Latinos or ordered on-line. You can make your own from scratch starting with the whole or ground achiote seeds (see recipe). I recommend working with ground achiote because the seeds are very hard to grind to a powder. You can guess why it's called the "poor man's saffron." But can you guess why it's also called the "lipstick tree"? The name comes from "*achiotl*" meaning "shrub" in Nahuatl. See Glossary for more information about achiote. (Photo by S. López/I. Escovedo)

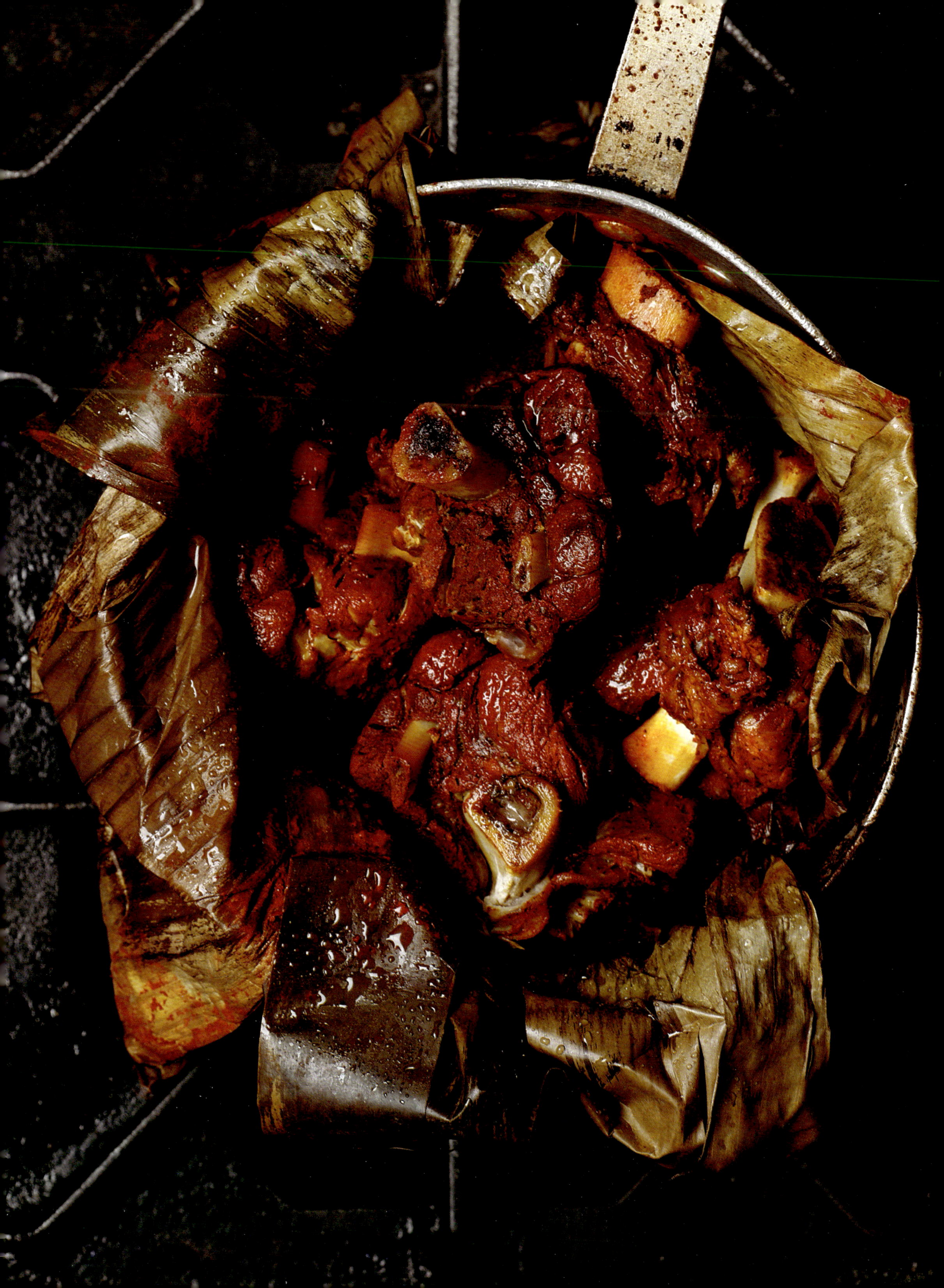

Frijol con puerco

Black Beans and Pork

Serves about 8–10

Ingredients

1 1/2 gallons water

2 tablespoons salt

1 pound pork neck bones

1 1/2 pound dried black beans (cleaned and sorted)

3 pounds pork meat (pork butt, shoulder or cushion), cut into 1-inch cubes

1/2 bunch fresh epazote, roughly chopped (discard thick part of stem)

1/2 bunch fresh cilantro, roughly chopped

Garnishes

Red onion, chopped

Radishes, chopped

Fresh cilantro, chopped

Avocado, sliced

Chiltomate (see recipe)

Lime wedges

Whole *chiles habaneros* (optional)

After a party-heavy weekend, a common saying in Yucatán is: "*Me voy a curar con mi frijol con puerco.*" So popular is this dish as an antidote for a hangover that it has become a dish traditionally served on Mondays. Some revelers even miss work to have their *frijol con puerco* or rush home early for the cure. But you don't have to save this dish for that kind of situation; any time you want a hearty meal will do.

1. Bring the water to a boil with salt. When boiling, add the neck bones. Cover and lower heat to high simmer for 45 minutes until the meat is tender and releases its gelatin (collagen). Skim the foam that rises to the top with a slotted spoon and discard.

2. Add the black beans, cover and leave at slow boil until the beans begin to open, about 30 minutes.

3. Then add the cubed pork. Cover and simmer for an hour or until the pork is cooked and tender. But, about five minutes before that, add epazote and cilantro. Adjust salt.

4. Before serving, remove neck bones, which have served their flavoring purposes (but don't discard them because, meatier on this side of the border, they are finger-licking good too). Adjust salt.

To serve: Plate the meat in deep dishes and sprinkle with chopped onion, radish and cilantro, which you can toss together beforehand if you like. Add slices of avocado, dollops of *chiltomate*, and top with the *chile habanero*. Alongside, serve bowls of beans with broth with a dollop of *chiltomate,* a squeeze of lime and its own sprinkle of chopped onions, radish and cilantro. Serve with corn tortillas, *bolillos* or *barras de francés* (French rolls). Also good with *arroz blanco* (see recipe).

COSTILLAS EN PIPIÁN
Baby Back Ribs in Pumpkin Seed Sauce

Serves about 6–8 (photo on page 80)

The use of pumpkin seeds in this dish links it to pre-Columbian times. It was an ingredient commonly used long ago. Remember, the Americas gave the world squashes. Before the Spanish arrived, a version of this dish would have been served with deer or rabbit.

1. Bring the water to a boil with salt in a large pot. Add the neck bones and lower the heat to medium low. Cook covered for 15 minutes, adding more water if the level drops. Skim the foam that rises to the top with a slotted spoon and discard.

2. Add the baby back ribs. As it returns to a boil, skim the foam that rises to top with a slotted spoon and discard.

3. Add the tomatoes, ground pumpkin seeds, epazote and *chile serrano*. Cover and cook over high simmer for 1 hour or until the meat falls off the neck bones and the ribs are tender.

4. Remove the meat from the pot, debone and place the meat in a covered bowl to keep warm.

5. To make the sauce, liquefy the contents of the pot in a blender or with a handheld emulsion blender. (Make sure there are no bones left in the pot.)

6. In a separate bowl, mix the *masa harina* and warm water or stock until well blended. Add this slowly to the pot, stirring until the sauce thickens as desired. If the sauce is still a bit grainy, liquefy again until smooth; if too thick, add more water or stock.

7. Return the baby back ribs to the sauce and heat for 5 minutes. Adjust salt. Don't stir too much as to cause the meat to break apart. (Remember, don't discard the neck bones.)

To serve: Spoon the *costillas en pipián* over *arroz blanco* (see recipe) and top with chopped tomatoes, pumpkin seeds, and epazote sprigs. Serve with corn tortillas.

INGREDIENTS

1 gallon water

1 tablespoon salt

1 pound pork neck bones

3-3 1/2 pounds baby back ribs

6 plum tomatoes, quartered (about 1 1/2 pounds)

3 cups *pepitas de calabaza tostadas sin cáscara* (see recipe)

1 sprig fresh epazote

1 *chile serrano*

1 cup *masa harina* (see Glossary)

1 cup warm water (or chicken, beef or pork stock)

GARNISHES

Plum tomatoes, chopped

Whole pumpkin seeds, toasted

Fresh epazote sprigs

Poc chuc

Charcoaled Pork

Serves about 6–8

Ingredients

3 pounds pork loin, sliced into 1/4-inch diagonal slices

Salt

Vegetable oil

Garnishes (depending on how it is to be served)

Naranja agria wedges (or lime wedges)

Chiltomate (see recipe)

Cebolla para poc chuc (see recipe)

Sliced avocado

Sliced tomatoes

Green leaf lettuce

Whole *chiles habaneros* (optional)

Frijoles de la olla or *frijoles colados* (see recipes)

Longaniza (or chorizo, see Glossary) (optional)

This dish's history is linked to that of the men who worked the *caoba* (cedar) and other precious hardwood in the Yucatán; and the *chicleros,* those who collected *chicle* or the gummy sap from the *zapote* tree (and still do). As they would blaze trails farther and farther into the forest, they would get too far from home to return for meals. So they came up with a way to prepare or preserve meat for up to two weeks at a time. Basically, they cured pork in wood boxes by layering meat, salt, fat and skin. To eat, they would soak the meat in water to get rid of the salt and grill it over charcoal and eat it simply with juice of *naranja agria* and corn tortillas. Fortunately, this dish has been adapted for the home kitchen.

1. Lightly salt both sides of the pork slices.

2. Place the meat on a hot grill over charcoal and grill about 5 minutes, turning once. You can also prepare in a lightly oiled frying pan or on a stovetop grill.

To serve: There are three popular ways to eat *poc chuc*. As a main course, plate slices of meat with *frijoles de la olla* or *frijoles colados, cebolla para poc chuc, chiltomate,* sliced avocado and maybe even a *longaniza*. Make a *torta* by slicing a *barra de francés* (French roll) or *bolillo* and smearing each half with *frijoles colados*. Build the sandwich with the *poc chuc,* sliced tomatoes, lettuce, *chiltomate* and *cebolla para poc chuc*. Or use the meat—chopped roughly—to build tasty tacos with warmed corn tortillas, *frijoles colados,* lettuce, *chiltomate* and *cebolla para poc chuc*. Don't forget the *chiles habaneros* if you like heat.

Notes: In the Yucatán, beans are always black beans and tortillas are always corn (see Glossary).

These sides are pictured here with the poc chuc: Chiltomate *(page 16),* cebolla para poc chuc *(page 142), and* longaniza *(Yucatán-style* chorizo, see Glossary*)*.

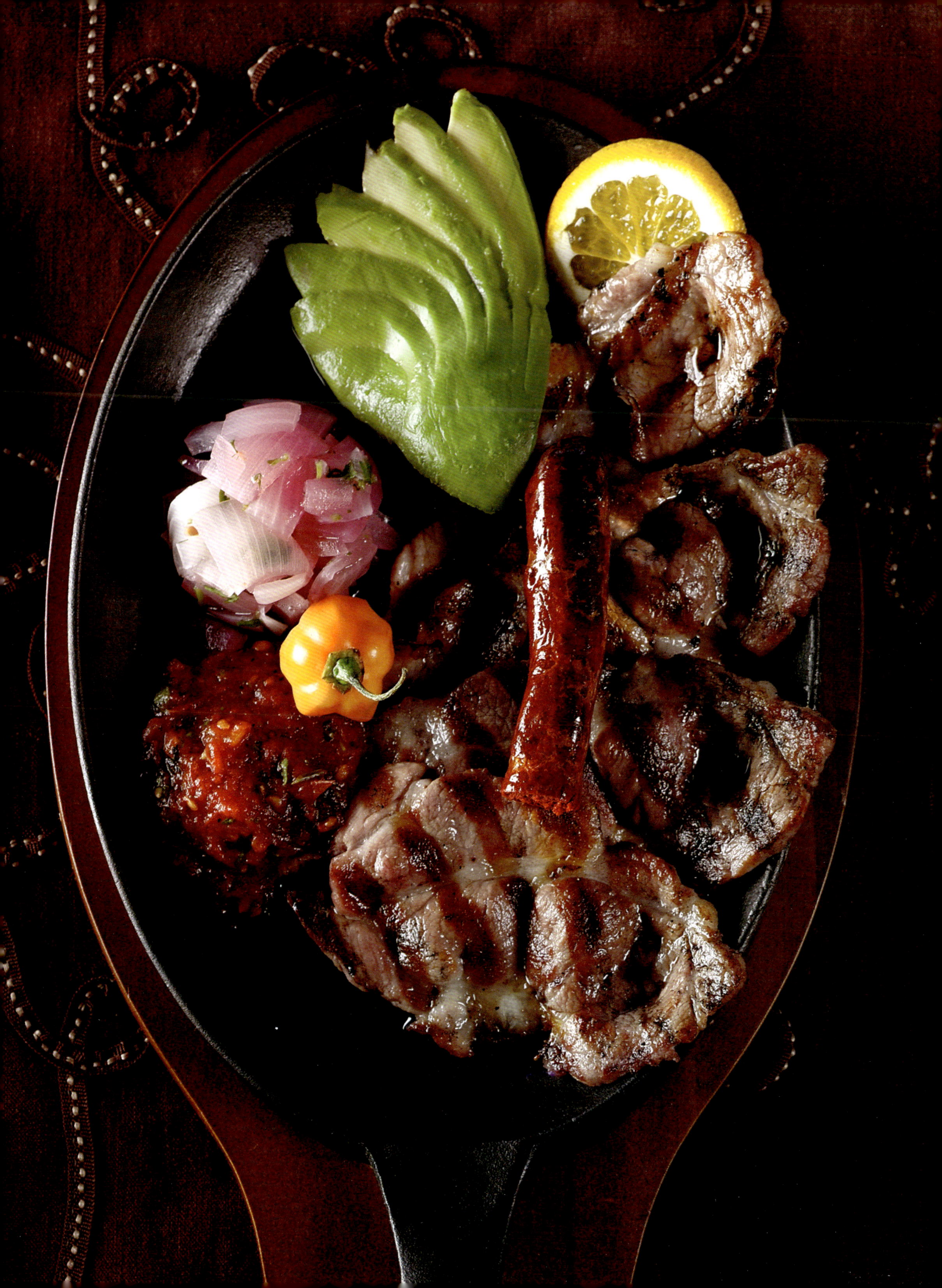

PUERCO EMPANIZADO
Pork Milanesa Yucatán Style

Serves about 6–8 (photo on page 80)

Ingredients

1 1/2 tablespoons *recado para bistec* (see recipe)

1/2 cup lime juice

1/2 teaspoon salt

2 pounds pork loin, sliced into 1/8-inch thick slices

1 cup flour

2 eggs, slightly beaten

2 cups crushed *galletas María* (or Panko crumbs, see notes and Glossary)

1/2 cup vegetable oil

Cebolla para panuchos (see recipe)

Here's another popular, everyday dish that's great as an entrée or in tacos or *tortas*. It is very similar to an Italian-style *milanesa* but with a Yucatecan twist.

1. To make a marinade, blend the *recado para bistec*, lime juice and salt in a nonreactive bowl.

2. Marinate the meat for 30 minutes. Do not marinate too long as the meat will taste acidic.

3. Drain the liquid and drain and pat meat slices on paper towels.

4. Dip both sides lightly into flour; don't press. Dip in beaten eggs and press into crushed *galletas María*.

5. Heat vegetable oil in a frying pan and fry meat over medium heat until golden, about 2 minutes on each side.

To serve: To serve family style, line a platter with green leaf lettuce and place the *milanesas* on top and garnish with *cebolla para panuchos*. Serve with *arroz con azafrán* (see recipe), *frijoles de la olla* or *frijoles colados* (see recipes). Don't forget the corn tortillas.

Notes: *Galletas María* are popular and inexpensive cookies that are enjoyed throughout Latin America, and they are easy to find in most markets in the United States. Sometimes they have different names, but are all pretty much the same. You can use Panko crumbs as a substitute, but why? The *galletas* are not overly sweet and add another layer of flavor.

CHILMOLE DE PUERCO
Pork in Recado Negro Sauce

Serves about 6–8 (photo at right)

Ingredients

1 gallon water

1 pound pork neck bones

2 pounds pork cushion, cut into 1-inch cubes

3 tablespoons (2 ounces) *recado negro* (see recipe)

1 tablespoon salt

6 plum tomatoes, diced

Consider this a more casual version of *pavo en relleno negro* (see recipe). What it's missing is the *relleno* (or meatballs or *albóndigas*). What it's not missing is the earthy *recado negro*. It colors the dish and gives it its intense, smokey flavors. A nice touch is poaching eggs in the *caldo* (soup) just before serving.

1. Bring the water to a boil in a large stockpot. Add neck bones and cubed pork meat. Bring back to a boil, but *antes que rompa el hervor* (before it breaks into a boil), skim the foam that rises to the top with a slotted spoon and discard. Cook for 15 minutes. Separate 2 cups of broth.

2. Mix the *recado negro* and 1 cup of the warm broth (from step #1) in a blender. Pour through a sieve into the stockpot with the meat. Add the salt, diced tomatoes and epazote. Bring to a boil again, then lower to simmer and partially cover. Simmer for 1 to 1 1/4 hours.

3. Just before the hour is up, mix the remaining 1 cup of broth (from step #1) and *masa harina* in a blender. Add slowly to the stock to thicken. Stir until it reaches desired consistency of a thick sauce. Adjust salt.

4. Break 6 raw eggs, one by one, into the sauce to poach. Then add *ciruelas*, turn off the heat. Once the eggs are cooked, it's ready.

To serve: Dish up *chilmole de puerco* in bowls and serve with corn tortillas, French rolls or *bolillos*. This dish is not served with beans or rice. If you choose not to poach the eggs in the sauce, top with sliced hard-cooked eggs, but always top with diced tomatoes and epazote.

Notes: *Ciruelas (Spondias mombin)*, are a very sour fruit that will be difficult to find. They are not used by everyone in the Yucatán, but my family likes the acidity it adds to the dish. *Ciruelas* might remind you of small plums. They are related to *jocotes*, from the cashew family. In English, they are knows as yellow mombins or Spanish plums. As a substitute, you can use *tomatillos milperos*, a very small *tomatillo*, also hard to find stateside. If you can't find either, don't worry, your *chilmole de puerco* will taste just fine.

2 sprigs of fresh epazote (discard thick part of stem)

1/2 cup *masa harina*

6 eggs

20 *ciruelas* (optional) (see notes)

GARNISHES

Hard-cooked eggs, peeled and sliced (optional, see serving instructions)

Plum tomatoes, diced

Fresh epazote, roughly chopped

PUERCO ENTOMATADO
PORK SMOTHERED IN TOMATOES

Serves about 6–8 (photo on page 80)

INGREDIENTS

4 pounds pork meat (pork butt, pork shoulder, cushion, pork loin or tenderloin), cut into 1-inch cubes

Water

1 1/2 teaspoons salt

1 teaspoon ground black pepper

2 pounds plum tomatoes, quartered

This dish, which originated in Valladolid, the former capital of the state of Yucatán, is cousin to the dish *lomitos de Valladolid*. The difference is the use of pork meat versus organ meats. Either way, *puerco entomatado* is so easy to make that cooks around the Yucatán often have it simmering on their stoves to satisfy the appetites of their families at a moment's notice.

1. Place the cubed pork in a large skillet. Pour enough water in until you almost cover the meat. Add salt and pepper.

2. Cover the meat with the quartered tomatoes. Cover the skillet and, starting at a high heat, cook for 4 to 5 minutes. Then lower heat and simmer for 1 1/2 to 2 hours until meat is tender.

3. Stir to break up the tomatoes and mix with meat. Adjust salt.

To serve: Accompany with *frijoles de la olla* (see recipe) and plenty of corn tortillas. It's as simple as that.

PEZUÑAS REBOSADAS
BATTERED PIG'S FEET

Serves about 8 to 10 (photo on page 80)

INGREDIENTS

1 gallon water

10 medium-sized pig's feet (about 12 ounces each), cut in half lengthwise

1 head garlic, roasted

2 teaspoons salt

1 teaspoon ground black pepper

1/2 teaspoon dried oregano

6 eggs

1 cup flour

Vegetable oil

GARNISH

Cebolla para panuchos (see recipe)

Pig's feet (*pezuñas*, *patas* or trotters) have regained popularity among chefs, gourmets and gourmands. This dish is finger licking good, so grab a stack of napkins and dig in.

1. In a large pot, bring the water to a boil.

2. Add the pig's feet, garlic, salt, pepper and oregano, and bring back to a boil. Then lower heat and simmer, partially covered, for 2–2 1/4 hours. The *patas* should be so tender that the tendons want to fall away from the bones.

3. Remove the *patas* carefully and pat dry with paper towels. (See notes below for boning, optional.)

4. Beat eggs until they are foamy.

5. Heat vegetable oil, about 1-inch deep, in a frying pan over medium-high heat.

6. Dredge the *patas* in the flour and then in the eggs and place in the frying pan. Fry on both sides until golden. Remove and drain on paper towels. (You can deep fry as well at 375°F.)

To serve: Top the *pezuñas* with *cebolla para panuchos* and serve with corn tortillas and *frijoles de la olla* (see recipe). I love eating them in tacos too.

Notes: The new fangled way of preparing *pezuñas rebosadas* is to debone them after they have been cooked. To do this, cool the *patas* and, wearing gloves (they are sticky), ease your fingers in to pop out the bones and cartilage trying to keep each *pezuña* in one piece. Then move on to step 6.

QUESO RELLENO
STUFFED BABY EDAM CHEESE

Serves about 12

Balls of baby Edam cheese are very popular in the Yucatán. This dates back to early sea trade with the Dutch and pirates who plied the waters off the Caribbean. Seafarers could take their time hollowing out the balls of cheese on their long voyages. Eventually the cheese found its way into the state of Quintana Roo and worked its way to the state of Yucatán. However, not just any ball of baby Edam cheese will do. A Dutch brand by the name of Gallo Azul is made and marketed exclusively in this area of Mexico—especially for making *queso relleno*. This dish has several steps, so you might want to read the recipe through before starting.

PREPARING THE MEAT FILLING

1. Put 1 cup water, salt, pepper, vinegar, tomatoes, onion, green and red bell peppers, and garlic in a food processor. Process until it's like a chunky salsa.

2. In a large pot, add ground pork meat and the processed "salsa" (from step above). Cook over medium heat, stirring to break up the meat until there are no clumps, about 45 minutes.

3. Once the meat is partially cooked, add the olives, capers, raisins and almonds. Cook another 15–20 minutes.

4. Add the chopped, hard-cooked egg whites and continue cooking until all of the moisture has evaporated, another 30-45 minutes. Adjust salt.

INGREDIENTS

1 ball of baby Edam cheese (about 3 pounds)

MEAT FILLING

1–2 cups water

2 1/2 teaspoons salt

3 teaspoons ground black pepper

1/8 cup white vinegar

8 small plum tomatoes

1 medium white onion, chopped

1 medium to large green bell pepper, chopped

1 medium to large red bell pepper, chopped

2 garlic cloves, peeled and finely chopped

5 pounds lean ground pork

30 pitted green olives, sliced

2 teaspoons capers

1/2 cup raisins

2 teaspoon sliced, blanched almonds

6 hard-cooked eggs (separate the yolks and egg whites; chop the egg whites, but leave the yolks whole)

Salsa blanca para queso relleno

6–7 tablespoons margarine

1 1/2 tablespoons minced white onion

1 1/2 tablespoons minced green bell peppers

1 1/2 tablespoons minced red bell peppers

2 cloves garlic, peeled and minced

4 cups chicken stock

8 to 10 threads saffron

3–4 tablespoons flour

1 1/2 teaspoons capers, minced

Salt, to taste

Ground black pepper, to taste

Sofrito para queso relleno

2 tablespoons olive oil

8 small plum tomatoes, cut in half lengthwise and thinly sliced

1 white onion, thinly sliced

2 cloves garlic, peeled and chopped

1 *chile x'catic* (*chile güerito* or blond chile), thinly sliced (see Glossary)

1 teaspoon salt

1/4–1/2 cup chicken stock, if needed (or *salsa de tomate,* see instructions)

Garnish

Chiles habaneros, salsa de chile habanero or *chile kut* (see recipes) (optional)

Preparing and Stuffing the Cheese Ball

1. With the ball of baby Edam cheese ball at room temperature, remove the plastic wrapping.

2. Score the outside of the cheese ball into four sections and remove both layers of wax; the thicker, outer, red layer and the thinner, yellow one. These wax layers are not that thick so score carefully.

3. With a small knife, score a 1 1/2-inch square on the top center of the ball of cheese. Holding the knife at a slant facing the heart of the cheese, cut deeply along all four sides of the hole in order to remove a pyramid-shaped wedge of cheese. Then cut the tip off of the "pyramid" to create a "plug." Save.

4. With a spoon (such as an iced tea spoon), scoop out cheese until the ball is hollow, leaving a 1/2- to 3/4-inch thick wall all the way around. (See notes.)

5. Fill half of the ball with the meat filling, packed tightly.

6. Nestle the 6 hard-cooked yolks gently—but not deeply—into the meat filling.

7. Fill with more meat to the top, packed tightly. Place "plug" over the opening. You will have plenty of meat filling left over to use for the plating.

8. Wrap the filled ball of cheese tightly in a couple layers of aluminum foil.

9. Place the wrapped and stuffed ball of cheese in a heatproof glass bowl as close to the diameter of the ball as possible so it fits snugly. Place in a double boiler (bain-marie) over boiling water, cover with aluminum foil or lid and steam for 45 minutes. (This is a good time to make the *salsa blanca para queso relleno* and "*sofrito.*"

10. Remove from the double boiler and let the ball rest for at least 30 minutes. Remove foil just prior to serving.

Preparing the salsa blanca

1. Melt the margarine in a saucepan over low to medium heat. Add the onion, green and red bell peppers, and garlic and sauté until limp.

2. In a separate pot, bring the stock to a boil and add the sautéed vegetables and saffron.

3. Dissolve the flour in a bit of stock and pour into the pot to thicken it. the stock should be thick enough to coat a spoon without dripping.

3. Add the capers and stir until well blended.

4. Add salt and pepper to taste.

Preparing the "sofrito"

1. In a frying pan, heat olive oil. Add tomatoes, onion, garlic, chile and salt. Sauté over low heat for about 10 minutes. The *sofrito* should not be watery, but if it's too dry, add 1/4–1/2 cup chicken stock or salsa de tomate. Adjust salt.

To serve

Place a 1-inch wedge of the *queso relleno* on a plate on top of a few spoonfuls of excess meat filling and spoon the *salsa blanca* and *sofrito* for the *queso relleno* on top. Serve with corn tortillas, French rolls or *bolillos* and the chiles or chile sauce of your choice.

Notes: It might take a Yucatecan family a week or longer to hollow out a ball of cheese because they scoop out pieces to eat and enjoy until it is hollow and ready to make into *queso relleno*. Once the ball has been steamed and unwrapped, the whole ball is presented on a platter at the dinner table with the extra meat filling, *salsa blanca* and *sofrito para queso relleno* on the side for each person to serve his or her own slice. Other kinds of ground meat can be used even though pork is most commonly used. You don't need to be told to save the cheese you've scooped out for other purposes.

More notes: If you place the opening of the ball on the bottom in the tight-fitting bowl, it seals itself. If the bowl you use to steam the cheese ball is larger than the ball, it will expand and slightly flatten.

Below: Yucatán's favorite brand of baby Edam cheese—Gallo Azul—is perfect for a delicious queso relleno.

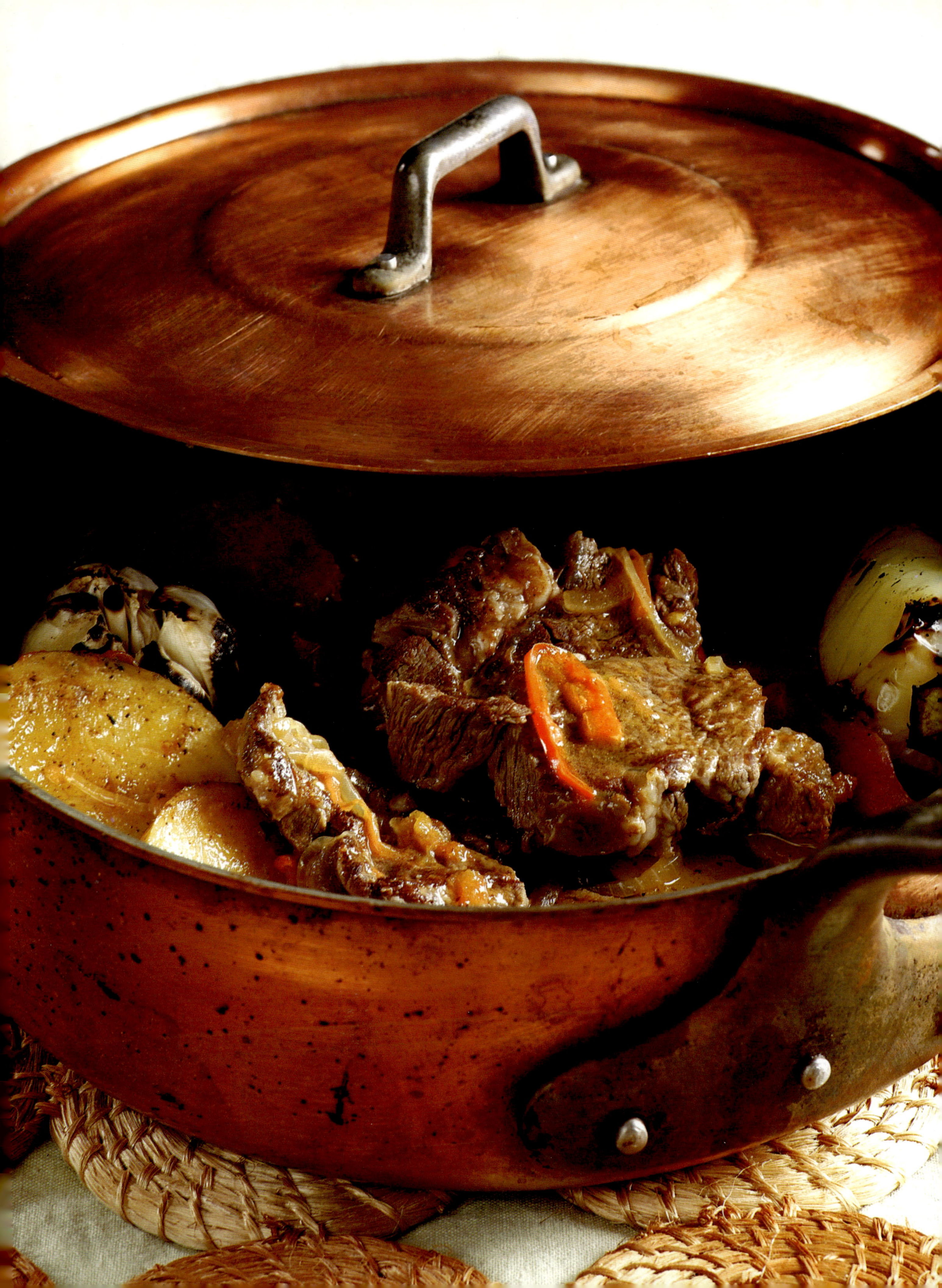

CHAPTER 7

BEEF & VENISON...
CARNE DE RES Y DE VENADO

We have to credit Cristopher Columbus for bringing the first cattle to the New World on his second voyage to the New World in 1494. The Spanish continued to bring cattle across the Atlantic, and by the 1520s there were a reported 8,000 head of cattle in what is now Mexico. In fact, it was from Mexico that cattle were driven north to what would become the United States and south to the grasslands of South America.

For our purposes we are talking about cows, calves and bulls and not other bovine animals. Although it was easier to adapt to pigs and chickens, beef must have been appreciated as a major source of readily available protein.

But, we must also remember that with cattle came milk and from milk came cheese and other dairy products. Cattle represented a boon to the diets of the Maya and, over time, home cooks and culinary professionals developed many innovative dishes that blended New and Old World foods.

Every part of the cow—from head to tail—finds a place on the dinner table. However, only the recipe for *chocolomo* (see recipe) creatively uses such cuts as liver, kidney, heart, and marrow bones or tail.

ON THE WILD SIDE

The Maya took advantage of the bounty that nature offered them. They did not have cattle until after the Conquest, but they knew what to do with wild deer. In the Yucatán this included the white-tailed and brocket deer. Unfortunately, populations of these species have been greatly reduced in the Yucatán due to overhunting and destruction of their habitat.

The good news is that venison is readily available from commercial deer farms so that you can still prepare dishes that are closely linked to the early Maya. If you can't find venison in a market near you, check on-line sources. And if you've mastered their beef or pork equivalents, you'll have an easy time preparing the venison dishes presented here.

For more on game meats, see Glossary.

Opposite page: Bistec de cazuela *(page 98).*

Above, from top: Market vendors (she is wearing a traditional huipil); a selection of palm-woven gifts for sale in Becal, Campeche; green *chiles habaneros.*

Bistec de Cazuela

Beef in a Pot

Serves about 6 (photo on page 96)

Ingredients

2 pounds top sirloin, sliced into 1/2-inch slices

Juice from 3–4 *naranjas agrias* (or limes) (about 1/3 cup juice)

1 tablespoon *recado para bistec* (see recipe)

1 teaspoon salt

2–3 tablespoons vegetable oil

4 plum tomatoes, halved lengthwise and thinly sliced

1/2 medium white onion, sliced

1 head garlic, roasted

1/2 green bell pepper, sliced

1/2 red bell pepper, sliced

2 *chiles güeritos,* roasted

2–3 cups water

2 medium Russet potatoes, unpeeled, sliced into 1/4- to 1/2-inch rounds

Like *bistec de vuelta y vuelta* (see recipe), this dish gets an extra layer of flavor by marinating the meat in *recado para bistec*. But it's the slow braising in a pot that makes the meat extra tender and tasty. The familiar *sofrito* of sautéed vegetables adds another layer of great taste.

1. Dilute the *recado para bistec* in *naranja agria* juice (or lime juice) and salt in a nonreactive bowl to make a marinade.

2. Add the meat to the marinade and marinate for up to 30 minutes.

3. Heat the vegetable oil in a hot frying pan, and quickly fry each slice of meat for about 30 seconds on each side to brown. Set aside, keeping them warm and covered.

4. In the same pan in which you fried the meat, add the tomatoes, onion, garlic, green and red bell peppers and *chiles güeritos* (with or without seeds) and any marinade that was left. Sauté until the onions become translucent.

5. Place the browned meat slices and the sautéed vegetables in a pot and add enough water until you almost cover the meat and vegetables. Cover the pot and let cook over low to medium heat until the meat is tender, about 45 minutes.

6. Arrange the potato slices on top of the meat, cover and simmer for another 5 minutes. Then flip the potato slices over, return cover, turn off the heat and let sit for another 5 minutes or until the potatoes are tender. Adjust salt.

To serve: Serve with *arroz blanco* (see recipe), *frijoles de la olla* (see recipe) and corn tortillas. Make sure everyone gets some potatoes.

Bistec de Vuelta y Vuelta

Yucatán-style Steak

Serves about 6 (pictured at right)

Bistec and onions

Juice from 3–4 *naranjas agrias* (or limes) (about 1/3 cup juice)

1 tablespoon *recado para bistec* (see recipe)

1 teaspoon salt

2 pounds beef tenderloin or top sirloin, sliced into 1/4-inch medallions

This dish is not often made at home because some think it's a bit complicated. But it really isn't and is worth the effort. It is the extra jolt of flavor it gets from marinating the meat in *recado para bistec* that makes it special. The equivalents in other parts of Latin America might be the Cuban *lomo encebollado* or Peruvian *lomo saltado*.

To prepare meat

1. Dilute the *recado para bistec* in *naranja agria* juice (or lime juice) and salt in a nonreactive bowl to make a marinade.

2. Pound the beef medallions into thin, 1/8-inch cutlets (see notes). Add to the marinade and marinate for up to 30 minutes.

3. Heat the vegetable oil in a hot frying pan. (If the heat is too low you end up steaming the meat.) Quickly fry each cutlet about 30 seconds on each side to brown. Set aside, keeping them warm and covered.

4. In the same pan in which you fried the meat, add the onions, and any marinade that was left. Sauté until the onions are caramelized. Set aside, keeping warm and covered.

TO PREPARE POTATOES

1. Soak the potato slices in water with salt for 1 hour.

2. Pat dry with paper towels.

3. Fry over a medium heat in vegetable oil until cooked through and golden brown on the outside.

To serve: Place a slice of meat on a leaf of green leaf lettuce and accompany with caramelized onions, potatoes, and slices of *plátanos fritos* along with *pico de gallo* and radish garnishes. *Arroz blanco* (see recipe), *frijoles colados* (see recipe) and corn tortillas round out this hearty meal.

Notes: To pound the meat, place each piece between 2 sheets of plastic wrap, and pound with the flat side of a meat mallet or a small, heavy skillet until it is the size and thickness you want—in this case about 1/8-inch thick.

2 tablespoons vegetable oil

2 medium red onions, thinly sliced

POTATOES

2 Russet potatoes, peeled and sliced into 1/8-inch rounds

Water

1 teaspoon salt

2 tablespoons vegetable oil

GARNISHES

Green leaf lettuce leaves

Plátanos fritos (see recipe)

Pico de gallo, (see recipe)

Radishes to make decorative garnishes (optional)

Salpicón de Res

Shredded Beef Salad

Seves about 6

Ingredients

2 pounds flank steak or brisket (see notes)

1/2 gallon water

1 head garlic, roasted

1/2 teaspoon dried oregano

1 tablespoon salt

1/2 teaspoon ground black pepper

2 sprigs of fresh cilantro

1 recipe *salpicón* (see recipe)

Garnishes

Chiltomate (see recipe)

Chiles habaneros, whole (optional)

This dish is relatively low fat and refreshing. Nothing is fried; flavors come from the fresh, basic ingredients used throughout the Yucatán Peninsula. This dish is best served and eaten immediately after preparing. I can barely restrain myself from making a taco once the *salpicón* is tossed.

1. Add the meat, water, garlic, oregano, salt, pepper and cilantro to a large pot and bring to a boil. Skim the foam that rises to the top with a slotted spoon and discard. Lower to simmer, cover and cook until the meat is tender and breaks apart easily, about 1–1 1/2 hours. (There's always the tortilla test too, see Techniques.)

2. Remove the meat and let cool. Then finely shred the meat, removing tendons.

3. In a large bowl add the shredded meat and the *salpicón*. Toss until well mixed. Adjust salt.

To serve: Serve family style in a large bowl with *chiltomate* and whole *chiles habanero* as garnishes. Complete with the *frijoles colados* (see recipe) and corn tortillas.

Notes: In many markets catering to a Latino clientele, you will see meat labeled "*carne para deshebrar*" ("meat for shredding"). This could be flank steak or brisket and either is fine for this recipe. See photograph for *salpicón de venado,* page 111, as reference.

Chocolomo

Mixed-meats Beef Soup

Serves about 6 (pictured at right)

Ingredients

1 gallon water

2 pounds beef neck bones

1 tablespoon salt

2 pounds beef sirloin, cut into 1-inch cubes

1/2 pound beef heart, cut into 1-inch cubes

1/2 pound beef liver, cut into 1-inch cubes

1/2 pound kidney, cut into 1-inch cubes

Chocolomo is the Yucatecan equivalent of another dish popular throughout Mexico—*cocido de res* (beef soup). As expected, this dish has its unique twists. It uses organ meats and the onion and garlic are roasted. The dish evolved from the use of the meat of the unfortunate bulls that lost the battle in so-called "bullfights" in small towns around the Yucatán. These "bullfights," called "*charlotadas*," were often part of the festivities that were held to honor the patron saint of a town. It is a safe guess that many of the bullfighters-for-the-day had probably had one too many . . .

1. In a large pot, bring the water to a boil. Add the neck bones and salt. Lower the heat, cover and cook for 30 minutes at high simmer. Occasionally skim the foam that rises to the top with a slotted spoon and discard.

2. Add the sirloin, heart, liver, kidney and marrow bones (or beef tails), as well as the onion, garlic, peppercorns and oregano. Cover and cook over low heat for another 45 minutes to an hour or until the meats are tender. (Watch water level, and add more if needed to keep water level above meats by 1/2–1 inch.) Adjust salt.

To serve: Just dish the *chocolomo* into deep bowls with *salpicón* (pictured above) as the classic topping along with plenty of corn tortillas.

Notes: You can substitute beef marrow bones with beef tails, which you will find surprisingly meaty and tender. And as always, save those neck bones because their meat will be tender and tasty too.

1/2 pound beef marrow bones (or beef tails)

1 white onion, roasted and quartered

1 head garlic, roasted

1 teaspoon whole peppercorns

1/2 teaspoon dried oregano

Garnish

Salpicón (see recipe)

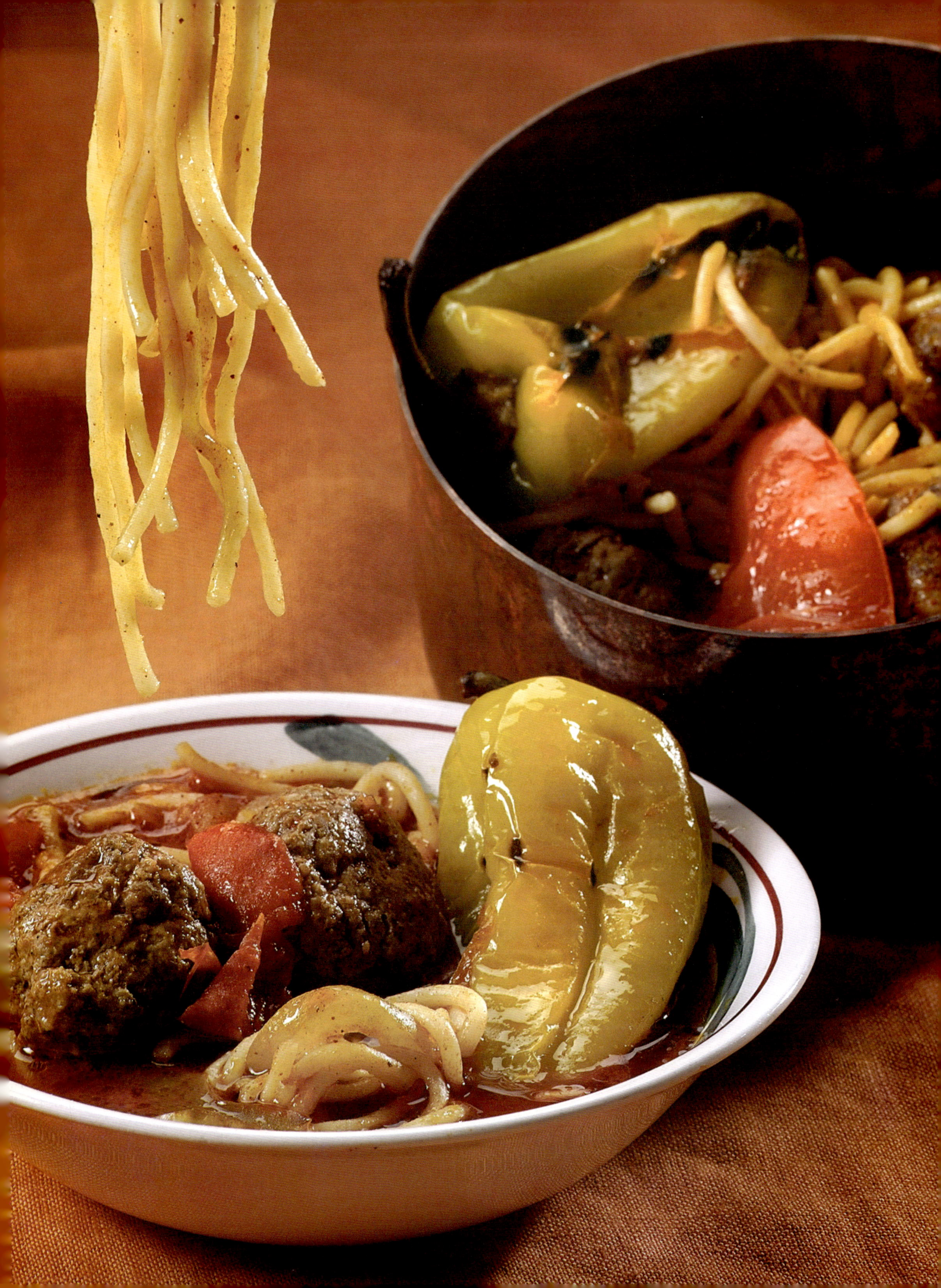

ALBÓNDIGAS CON FIDEOS
Meatballs and Pasta

Serves about 6

This is the Yucatán version of *sopa de albóndigas*. Here fresh mint is used in the broth rather than mixed in the ground meat. Other unique touches include the roasted *chile güerito* and the *recado rojo*. My wife makes the best *albóndigas con fideos*. I love going home and finding out that she's made it. This is the ultimate in comfort food.

1. Mix the ground pork and beef with 1 1/2 teaspoons salt and pepper. Form the *albóndigas* (meatballs) about 1 1/2 inches in diameter (golf-ball sized).

2. Heat vegetable oil in a hot frying pan and brown the *albóndigas*. Place in a large stockpot.

3. Reserve 1 tablespoon of the fat from the browned meatballs and heat in the same frying pan. Add the tomatoes, onion, garlic, and green and red bell peppers. Sauté until the onions become translucent.

4. Cover the meatballs in the stockpot with water until it reaches the level of about 1 inch above the meatballs. Add remaining 1 teaspoon salt, the sautéed vegetables, mint and *chiles güeritos*. Bring slowly to a boil.

5. Take about 1/2 cup water from the pot with the *albóndigas* and dissolve the *recado rojo*. Strain into the pot.

6. Cover and simmer until the *albóndigas* are cooked, about 20 minutes.

7. Add the *fideos* to the pot and bring to a boil again. Cover the pot, turn off the heat, and let the pasta cook about 15 minutes. Adjust salt.

To serve: Spoon 3–4 *albóndigas* per serving into a deep dish with *fideos* and broth. Serve with corn tortillas.

Ingredients

1 pound ground pork

1 pound ground beef

2 1/2 teaspoons salt (divided)

1 teaspoon ground black pepper

2–3 tablespoons vegetable oil

4 plum tomatoes, quartered lengthwise

1/2 medium white onion, sliced

4 cloves garlic, peeled

1/2 green bell pepper, sliced

1/2 red bell pepper, sliced

Water

2-4 sprigs fresh mint

2 *chiles güeritos*, roasted (with or without seeds)

1 1/2 teaspoons *recado rojo* (see recipe)

1 pound *fideos* (or vermicelli)

CARNE MOLIDA

Ground Beef with Sofrito

Serves about 6

INGREDIENTS

3–4 plum tomatoes, chopped

1/2 white onion, chopped

1/4 green bell pepper, chopped

1/4 red bell pepper, chopped

1/2 cup water

2 pounds lean ground beef

1 1/2 teaspoons salt

1 teaspoon ground black pepper

This is a simple dish that can be enjoyed any day of the week. It's a popular dish in the Yucatán because it's economical and easy to make. It's also really, really tasty and deserves some respect. It is similar to Cuban *picadillo*.

1. In a blender, purée the tomatoes, onion, green and red bell peppers and water.

2. Pour the purée into a large frying pan over high heat, and add the ground beef, salt and pepper. Bring to a boil.

3. Lower to medium heat, and break up any large lumps of ground beef. Cook uncovered until most of the moisture has evaporated, about 30 minutes. Adjust salt.

To serve: Serve with *frijoles de la olla* (see recipe) and corn tortillas.

Notes: A versatile dish, *carne molida* can used to top *salbutes* (see recipe) and to stuff empanadas (see recipe).

Buth negro de carne molida

Ground Beef with Recado Negro

Serves about 6

Buth negro de carne molida is great for tacos or *tortas* (sandwiches). In fact, you might find it served as a *botana* (a light snack) in cantinas (neighborhood bars) with cold beer. Or the tacos might be served at such family festivities as baptisms, birthday parties or other daytime gatherings. However, they wouldn't be served at anything as big and important as a wedding. The *recado negro* adds the distinct burnt and charred taste favored by the Maya to the meat.

1. Add 1/2 cup water and the meat to a large pan over high heat and bring to a boil. Lower to medium heat.

2. Dilute *recado negro* in the remaining 1/2 cup water and strain into the pan.

3. Add the tomatoes and epazote and cook uncovered for about 25 minutes.

3. Add the chopped egg whites, mix well and cook for about 5 more minutes. Adjust salt.

4. Remove to a serving bowl and top with whole egg yolks.

To serve: For individual servings, spoon meat into a deep dish topped with 1 egg yolk. Accompany with *frijoles de la olla* (see recipe) and corn tortillas.

Ingredients

1 cup water (divided)

2 pounds lean ground beef

3 tablespoons (2 ounces) *recado negro* (see recipe)

2 cups chopped plum tomatoes

10 fresh epazote leaves, chopped

Salt, if needed

6 hard-cooked eggs (separate the yolks and egg whites; chop the egg whites, but leave the yolks whole)

HÍGADO ENCEBOLLADO
LIVER SMOTHERED IN ONIONS

Serves about 6

INGREDIENTS

Juice from 3–4 *naranjas agrias* (or limes) (about 1/3 cup)

1 tablespoon *recado para bistec* (see recipe)

1 teaspoon salt

3 pounds liver, in 1/2-inch slices

2–3 tablespoons vegetable oil

4 medium red onions, sliced

GARNISHES

Green leaf lettuce leaves

Pico de gallo (see recipe)

One of the most classic ways of preparing liver is to smother it in caramelized onions, lots of them. The Yucatecan take on this is to add that extra layer of flavor by marinating the meat in *recado para bistec*. The onion of choice is, of course, the red onion.

1. Dilute the *recado para bistec* in *naranja agria* juice (or lime juice) and salt to make marinade in a nonreactive bowl.

2. Add the liver to the marinade and marinate for up to 30 minutes.

3. Heat vegetable oil in a hot frying pan. Fry the liver for about 30–45 seconds on each side or until no more blood runs out. Repeat until all of the liver is fried. Set aside, keeping covered and warm.

4. In the same pan in which you fried the liver, add the onions and any marinade that was left. Sauté until the onions become caramelized.

To serve: To serve family style, line a serving platter with green leaf lettuce leaves. Fan slices of meat on top and smother with onions. Garnish platter with *pico de gallo*. Serve with *arroz blanco* (see recipe), *frijoles de la olla* (see recipe) and corn tortillas.

Game Meats

BISTEC DE VENADO
TENDERLOIN OF VENISON

Serves about 6

This recipe is essentially the same as *bistec de vuelta y vuelta* (see recipe) except that venison is the star. Game meat has been a food staple in the Yucatán for centuries. In fact, Yucatán is called "*la tierra del faisán y del venado*" ("the land of the pheasant and the deer"). Since pre-Columbian times, the Maya were skilled hunters, and the eating of game meats continues as a tradition. Today, the meat is raised on farms and ranches and not caught in the wild since, for example, the diminished herds of wild deer in the Yucatán are protected. The venison I use in my restaurant comes from providers in Australia, New Zealand and the United States. If you aren't used to eating venison, you might find the taste of the meat strong, but you will also note that it is more tender than beef. (See more on game meat in Glossary.)

TO PREPARE THE MEAT

1. Dilute the *recado para bistec* in *naranja agria* juice (or lime juice) and salt in a nonreactive bowl to make a marinade.

2. Pound the venison medallions into thin cutlets. (See notes in *bistec de vuelta y vuelta* for tips on how to pound cutlets.) Add to the marinade and marinate for up to 30 minutes.

3. Heat the vegetable oil in a hot frying pan. Add the cutlets and quickly fry, about 30 seconds on each side. Set aside and repeat until all cutlets are fried. Set aside, keeping them warm and covered.

4. In the same pan in which you fried the meat, add the onions and any marinade that was left. Sauté until the onions are caramelized. Set aside, keeping warm and covered.

TO PREPARE POTATOES

1. Soak potato slices in water with salt for 1 hour.

2. Dry with paper towels.

3. Fry over a medium heat in vegetable oil until cooked through and golden brown on the outside.

To serve: Place a slice of meat on a leaf of green leaf lettuce and accompany with caramelized onions, potatoes, and slices of *plátanos fritos* along with *pico de gallo* and radish garnishes. *Arroz blanco*, *frijoles colados* (see recipes) and corn tortillas complete the meal.

BISTEC DE VENADO

Juice from 3–4 *naranjas agrias* (or limes) (about 1/3 cup)

1 tablespoon *recado para bistec* (see recipe)

1 teaspoon salt

2 pounds venison tenderloin, sliced into 1/8-inch medallions

2 tablespoons vegetable oil

2 medium red onions, thinly sliced

POTATOES

2 Russet potatoes, peeled and sliced into 1/8-inch rounds

Water

1 teaspoon salt

2 tablespoons vegetable oil

GARNISHES

Green leaf lettuce leaves

Plátanos fritos (see recipe)

Pico de gallo (see recipe)

Radishes to make decorative garnishes (optional)

PIPIÁN DE VENADO
Venison in Pumpkin Seed Sauce

Serves about 6–8

Ingredients

1 gallon water

1 tablespoon salt

1 pound venison neck bones

3–3 1/2 pounds venison tenderloin, cut into 1 1/2-inch cubes

6 plum tomatoes, quartered

3 cups *pepitas de calabaza tostadas sin cáscara* (see recipe)

1 sprig fresh epazote

1 *chile serrano*

1 cup *masa harina* (see Glossary)

1 cup warm water (or chicken, beef or pork stock)

Garnishes

Plum tomatoes, chopped

Whole pumpkin seeds, toasted

Fresh epazote sprigs

If you have tried and enjoyed *costillas en pipián* (see recipe), give this recipe a try. The venison gives it a much different taste, of course, but one that is just as delicious.

1. Bring the water and salt to a boil in a large pot. Add the neck bones and lower heat to medium low. Cook covered for 15 minutes, adding more water if the level drops. Skim the foam that rises to top with a slotted spoon and discard.

2. Add the venison. As it returns to a boil, again skim the foam that rises to the top with a slotted spoon and discard.

3. Add the tomatoes, ground pumpkin seeds, epazote and *serrano chile*. Cover and simmer over medium heat for 30 minutes or until the meat falls off the neck bones and the venison is tender.

4. Remove the meat from the pot and place in a covered bowl to keep warm. Remove any bones too.

5. To make the sauce, liquefy the contents of the pot in a blender or with a handheld emulsion blender.

6. In a separate bowl, mix the *masa harina* and warm water or stock until well blended. Add this slowly to the pot, stirring until the sauce thickens as desired. If the sauce is still a bit grainy, liquefy again until smooth; if too thick, add more water or stock.

7. Return the venison to the sauce and heat for 5 minutes. Adjust salt. Don't stir too much as to cause the meat to break apart. (Remember, don't discard the neck bones . . .)

To serve: Spoon the *venado en pipián* over *arroz blanco* (see recipe) and top with chopped tomatoes, pumpkin seeds and epazote sprigs. Serve with corn tortillas.

SAH KOL DE VENADO
Venison with White Sauce

Serves about 6

This is the more exotic version of *sah kol de pavo* (see recipe). Remember, *salsa blanca* is also called *sah kol*. I recommend that you make the *sah kol* while the venison cooks. That way it will be ready when it comes time to serve this dish.

Preparing the meat

1. Add the water, venison, garlic, oregano, salt, pepper and cilantro to a large pot and bring to a boil. Skim the foam that rises to the top with a slotted spoon and discard. Lower to simmer, cover and cook until the meat is tender and breaks apart easily, about 1–1 1/2 hours.

2. Remove the venison and let cool. Then break into chunks, removing the tendons.

Preparing the "sofrito" (sautéed vegetables)

1. Heat the vegetable oil in a skillet and add the tomatoes, onion, and green and red bell peppers, and sauté over a medium-high heat until the onion is translucent, about 5–7 minutes.

2. Add the chunks of venison to the *sofrito* and mix well.

Putting it all together and Serving

1. For each serving of *sah kol de venado*, place about 1/4–1/3 cup of the *sah kol* into a deep or wide soup bowl. Place about 1 cup of the venison-vegetable mix on top. Serve with corn tortillas.

The meat

1/2 gallon water

2 pounds venison flank steak

1 head garlic, roasted

1/2 teaspoon dried oregano

1 tablespoon salt

1/2 teaspoon ground black pepper

2 sprigs fresh cilantro

1 recipe *salpicón* (see recipe)

The sofrito

2 tablespoons vegetable oil

3 plum tomatoes, chopped

1/2 white onion, chopped

1/3 green bell pepper, chopped

1/3 red bell pepper, chopped

The sauce

2 cups *sah kol* (see recipe)

Salpicón de Venado
Shredded Venison Salad

Serves about 6

Ingredients

1/2 gallon water

2 pounds venison flank steak

1 head garlic, roasted

1/2 teaspoon dried oregano

1 tablespoon salt

1/2 teaspoon ground black pepper

2 sprigs fresh cilantro

1 recipe *salpicón* (see recipe)

Garnishes

Chiltomate (see recipe)

Chiles habaneros (optional)

The recipe is basically the same as *salpicón de res* (see recipe). And just like that dish, it is best served and eaten immediately after preparing. In fact, make the *salpicón* while the venison cooks or is cooling. Then you'll be ready for the big toss.

1. Add the venison, water, garlic, oregano, salt, pepper and cilantro to a large pot and bring to a boil. Skim the foam that rises to the top with a slotted spoon and discard. Lower to simmer, cover and cook until the meat is tender and breaks apart easily, about 1–1 1/2 hours.

2. Remove the venison and let cool. Then finely shred the meat, removing the tendons.

3. In a large bowl add the shredded meat and *salpicón*. Toss until well mixed. Adjust salt.

To serve: Serve family style in a large bowl with *chiltomate* (see recipe) and whole *chiles habanero* as garnishes. And, yes, *frijoles colados* (see recipe) and corn tortillas are called for.

On the Wild Side Game meats made up part of the ancient Mayan diet since the Maya did not practice animal husbandry on a wide scale. They took advantage of what nature offered, which included deer, peccary, armadillo, iguana, wild turkey (they did have a domesticated variety) and other fowl, agouti, paca, turtle, etc. In addition, the Maya ate eggs from various fowl and reptiles. And they ate dog (the Xoloitzcuintle), as did other neighboring peoples. For more on game meats, see Glossary.

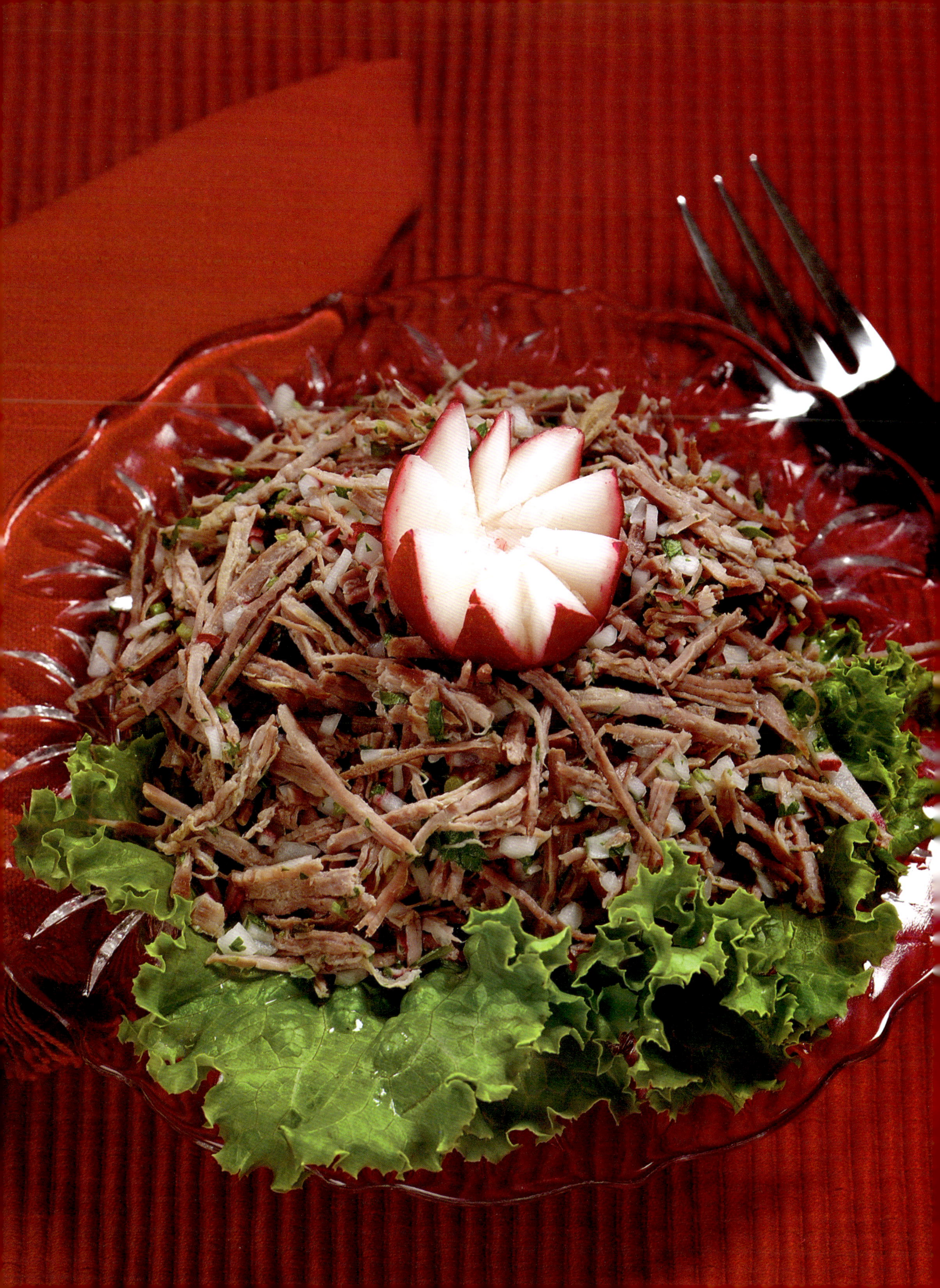

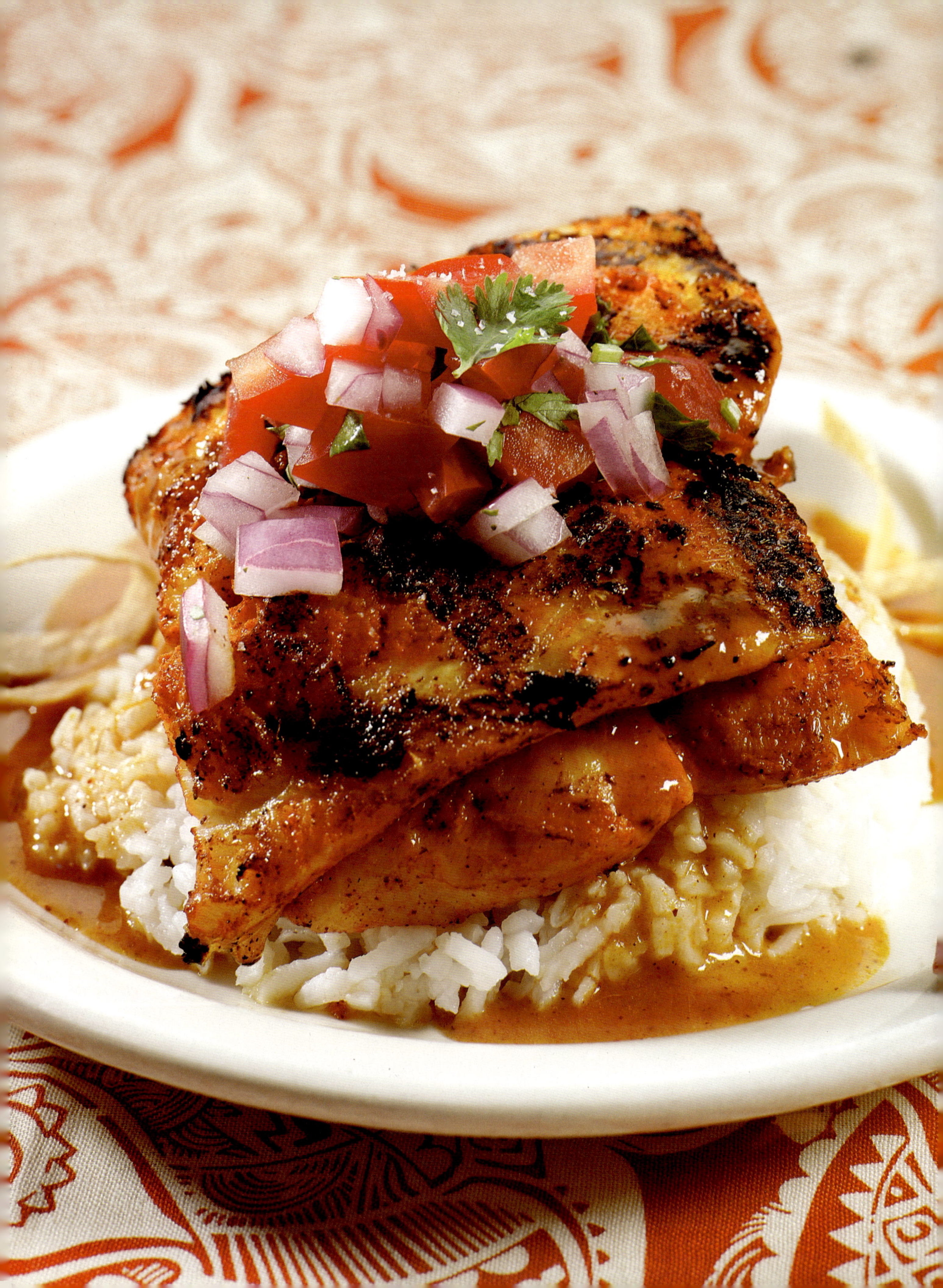

CHAPTER 8

SEAFOOD...
PESCADOS Y MARISCOS

No surprise that *yucatecos* take full advantage of the bounty that the sea offers. The Yucatán Peninsula's unique position places it where the Yucatán Channel connects the Gulf of Mexico and the Caribbean Sea. *Yucatecos* are definitely spoiled by regular access to fresh catches year-round.

In this collection of recipes you will find dishes that actually make great appetizers or starters but that can also be light meals. Other dishes are definitely main courses.

Always look for the freshest seafood available. The other option, of course, is frozen.

An interesting tidbit of information is that the cause of the mass extinction of dinosaurs is believed to have occurred off the coast of the Yucatán Peninsula. Scientists have found what is called the Chicxulub Crater and evidence that this is where an asteroid hit that eventually brought an end to the reign of the dinosaur.

Opposite page: Tikin xic *(page 125) swimming in* salsa de achiote para tikin xic *(page 16) and topped with* pico de gallo *(page 13).*

Above right, from top: The ever-present naranjas agrias *and* limas agrias; *mangroves of Laguna Nichupte in Cancún, Quintana Roo; and Chef Cetina with a fresh catch on a recent trip to the Yucatán.*

Ceviche de Pescado

Fish Ceviche

Serves about 6–8

Ingredients

2 pounds sole or red snapper (or other firm, mild white fish, such as grouper or halibut) cut into 1/4-inch pieces

1/3 cup lime juice (about 4–6 limes)

1 tablespoon salt

1 teaspoon ground black pepper

4 plum tomatoes, seeds and pulp removed, diced

1/2 red onion, diced

1/2 bunch fresh cilantro, finely chopped (without stems)

4 tablespoons olive oil

1 *chile habanero,* sliced (optional)

Lime wedges

The essence of the sea is yours every time you make ceviche. The trick is starting with the freshest fish possible and allowing it to marinate in its tangy, lime-juice preparation. Again, it's all about fresh, fresh, fresh. It's a great starter or light entrée.

1. Marinate the fish in a nonreactive bowl in the lime juice, salt and pepper. Cover and refrigerate for 3 hours or overnight.

2. Just before serving, add the tomatoes, onion, cilantro and olive oil. Toss. Add the *chile habanero,* if desired.

To serve: Serve with lime wedges and tortilla chips or saltine crackers. The ceviche also makes a good tostada.

Notes: The folks who eat the freshest ceviche are without a doubt the fishermen who ply the waters off the coast of the Yucatán Peninsula. Conveniently, they take all the necessary ingredients they need to make ceviche *in situ.* They have access to the most important ingredient—the freshest catch of the day.

Tip: Use a spoon to scrape the inside of the tomatoes to remove the seeds and pulp.

A Lime By Any Other Name It's confusing trying to get a handle on limes and what to call them. What's the difference between a Persian lime, a Mexican lime and a Key lime? For our purposes, we are going to make this simple. A Persian lime is the most common lime found in markets across the United States. Some may be imported from Mexico and, as a result, are sometimes labeled "Mexican limes." Key limes are also known as Mexican limes and are smaller, have more seeds, are more acidic and have a stronger perfume than their sister. They get yellow as they ripen. We will let others debate whether a Mexican lime is really a distinct kind of lime. There's also the *lima agria,* an entirely different fruit. For more information, see Glossary. And, remember, when *yucatecos* say "*limón,*" they are referring to lime, not lemon.

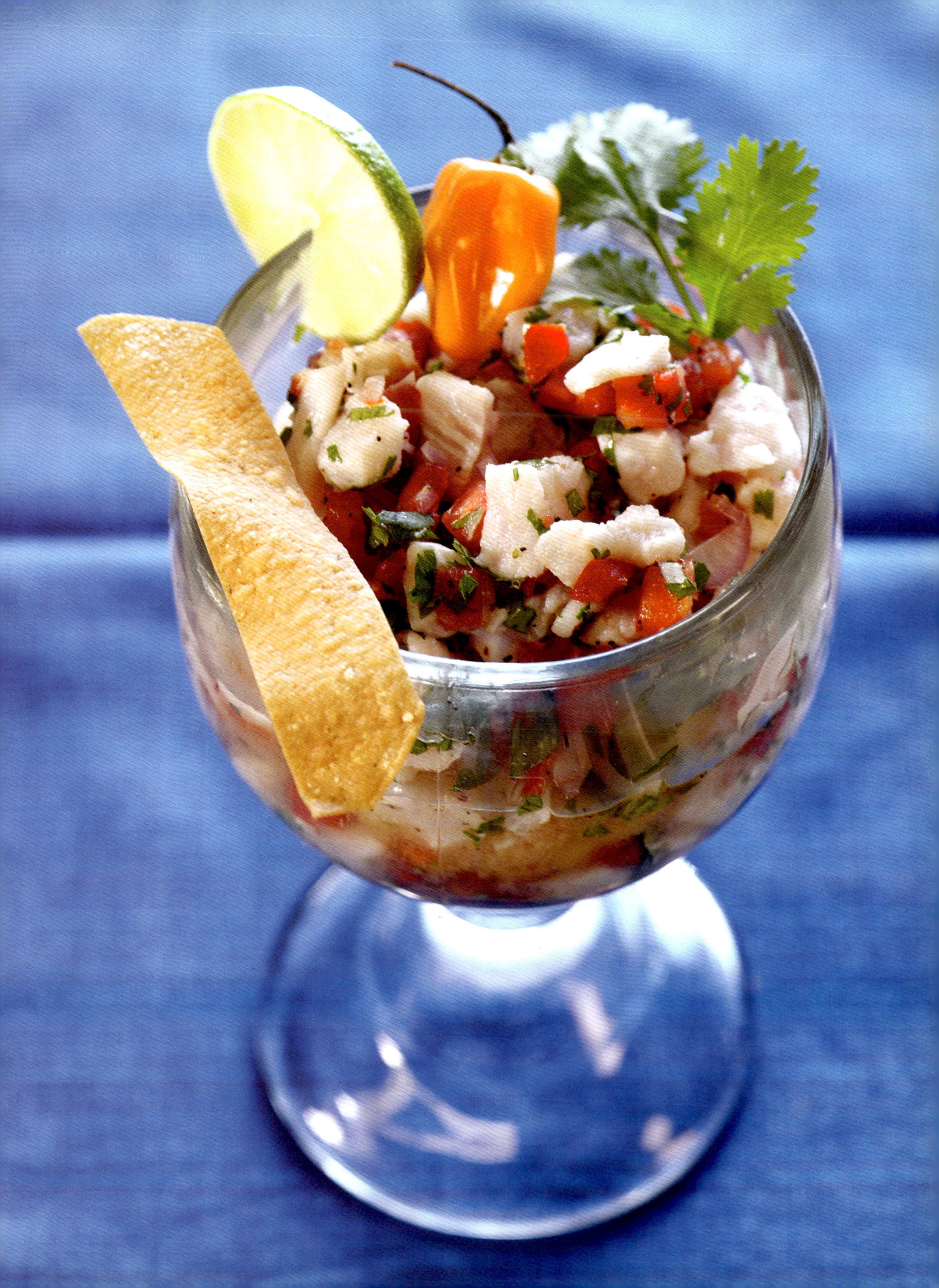

Ensalada mixta de mariscos

Mixed Seafood Salad

Serves about 6–8 (left in photo at right)

Ingredients

1 pound cooked shrimp, tails removed and sliced in half lengthwise (jumbo, about 23 per pound)

1 pound sliced cooked octopus

1 pound cooked squid, sliced into rings

1/3 cup lime juice (about 5–6 limes)

1 teaspoon salt

1 teaspoon ground black pepper

3 plum tomatoes, seeds and pulp removed, thinly sliced

1 medium red onion, thinly sliced

1/2 bunch fresh cilantro, finely chopped, no stems

4 tablespoons olive oil

1 *chile habanero,* thinly sliced (optional)

Lime wedges

This ceviche-like seafood salad is very simple to make. You'll notice that all the seafood is cooked because traditionally the only ceviche made with raw seafood in the Yucatán is *ceviche de pescado* (see recipe). You can chill this *ensalada mixta de mariscos* before serving it, or eat it right after you give it its final toss. It's good as a refreshing appetizer, a snack or a light meal. It's also great for parties.

1. Put the cooked and sliced shrimp, octopus and squid in large bowl. Add the lime juice, salt and pepper. Mix well.

2. Add the tomatoes, onion, cilantro and olive oil. Add the *chile habanero* if desired. Toss and adjust salt. Chill or serve right away.

To serve: Whether you serve it in a large bowl family style, or dish it up in individual servings, don't forget the tortilla chips or saltine crackers—and wedges of limes.

Note: Scallops are a nice addition to this mixed seafood salad. If you'd like to add them, then use 12 ounces each of cooked shrimp, octopus, squid and scallops. You can also use conch.

Tip: Use a spoon to scrape the inside of the tomatoes to remove the seeds and pulp.

Opposite page, from r. to l.: Ensalada mixta de mariscos *and* cóctel de camarones (*page 120*).

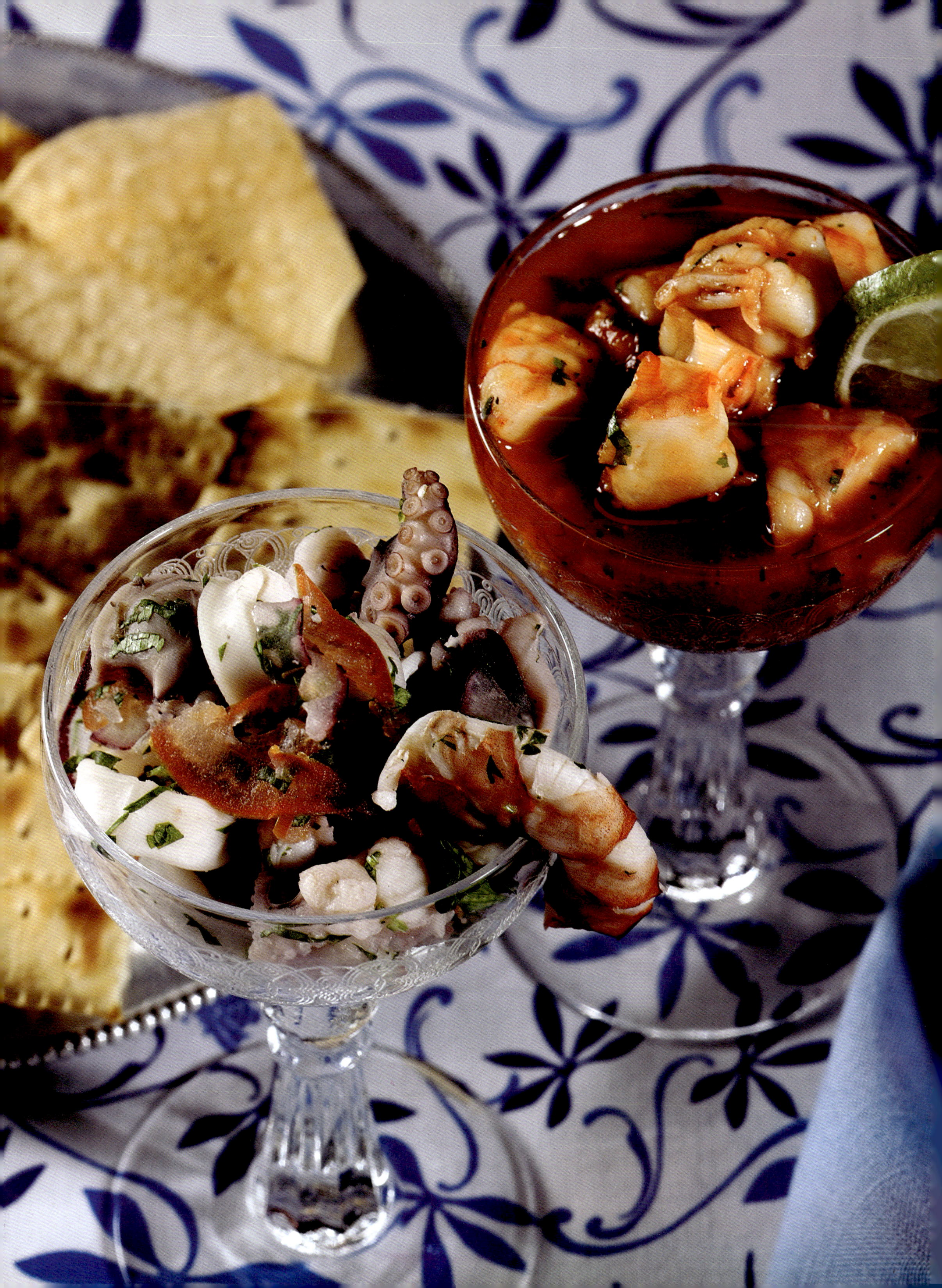

Pulpo en su tinta

Octopus in its Own Ink

Serves about 6–8

Ingredients

1/3 cup olive oil

2 cups chopped plum tomato

1 small white onion, chopped

4 cloves garlic, peeled and minced

1/2 green bell pepper, diced

1/2 red bell pepper, diced

1 teaspoon salt

2 pounds sliced cooked octopus

5 bay leaves

2 tablespoons octopus ink (thawed if frozen) (see notes)

1 cup dry white wine

Juice of 1 lime

A great appetizer and even better entrée, *pulpo en su tinta* is an extraordinary dish. And it's easier to prepare than it might seem. The glistening black sauce is singular as is the fresh scent of the sea. Start with fresh or frozen octopus, just make sure to cook it first if it is raw. But do not overcook, as the octopus will get tough.

1. Heat the olive oil in a frying pan. Add the tomatoes, onion, garlic, green and red bell peppers, bay leaves and salt. Sauté for 6–8 minutes until cooked.

2. Add the octopus and stir.

3. Dilute the octopus ink in the wine, add to the pan with octopus and vegetables. Lower heat and simmer uncovered for about 15 minutes.

4. Just before removing from heat, add lime juice. Adjust salt, if needed.

To serve: As an appetizer, serve with soda crackers or tortilla chips; as a light entrée, serve with *arroz blanco* (see recipe).

Notes: Finding octopus ink may be a bit challenging. Start by asking at your local grocer's seafood section or visit a seafood market. Sometimes specialty markets, such as Italian or Spanish, carry packets of octopus ink. You can also substitute with squid ink. By the way, a nice Sauvignon blanc is a good wine choice for this recipe.

CALAMARES EN ESCABECHE

PICKLED SQUID

Serves about 6–8

If you find yourself on the beach in the Yucatán, you might be offered *tacos de calamares en escabeche* or other seafood fixings *en escabeche*. Like *pulpo en su tinta, calamares en escabeche* is a good starter or light entrée. If you recall from *pollo en escabeche* (see recipe), this is a "pickled" dish.

PREPARING THE STOCK AND SQUID

1. Bring the water to a boil and add the squid and salt. Bring back to a hard boil for 10–15 minutes until the squid is tender.

2. Remove the squid and reserve the stock.

3. Slice the squid into 1/4-inch rings.

PREPARING THE ESCABECHE

1. Mix the *recado para escabeche* and vinegar. Add the onions, garlic, chiles, bay leaves and oil. Mix well.

2. Bring 1/2 gallon of the reserved stock to a boil and add the squid and the marinated onion mixture. Boil for 5 minutes. Adjust salt.

To serve: Serve in a deep dish with *arroz blanco* (see recipe) and corn tortillas.

Notes: For the variety, try this dish substituting the squid with octopus, scallops or fish.

THE STOCK AND SQUID

1 gallon water

5 pounds squid, bodies not tentacles,

1 tablespoon salt

THE ESCABECHE

1 tablespoon *recado para escabeche* (see recipe)

1/2 cup white vinegar

3 medium red onions, cut into eighths

1 head garlic, roasted

6 *chiles güeritos,* roasted

5 bay leaves

2 tablespoons olive oil

1/2 gallon reserved squid stock

Cóctel de Camarón
Shrimp Cocktail

Serves about 6–8 (right in photo on page 117)

Cocktail sauce

2 cups ketchup

Juice of 2 limes

Juice of 2 oranges

1 teaspoon ground black pepper

1 teaspoon salt

2 tablespoons olive oil

1/2 can (6–8 ounces) orange soda

Shrimp

6 cups cooked shrimp (about 3 pounds)

1/2 cup finely minced fresh cilantro

1/2 white or red onion, finely minced

1 *chile habanero,* minced (optional)

Lime wedges

A classic starter or appetizer, shrimp cocktails are also a popular snack or *botana* in the Yucatán. This recipe is very easy to prepare and is sure to be a hit any time you serve it. Your guests will not be able to stop eating it, nor will they ever guess the secret ingredient.

1. Mix all the ingredients listed for the cocktail sauce—ketchup, lime and orange juice, pepper, salt, olive oil, orange soda—in a large bowl.

2. Add the shrimp, cilantro, onion and the *chile habanero* (if desired) to the cocktail sauce and stir well.

3. Serve right away or chill in the refrigerator for a couple of hours or overnight.

To serve: Bring out your favorite cocktail glasses (12–16 ounces) and dish up the shrimp cocktail. Add lime wedges as a garnish. Serve with soda crackers and/or tortilla chips. This might not be very Yucatecan, but sliced celery goes well with this shrimp cocktail. By the way, the secret ingredient is the orange soda.

Creatures of the Sea: Shrimp

Use either fresh or frozen shrimp unless otherwise noted. If frozen, make sure the shrimp is whole and uncooked, and not peeled or deveined. Also, buy shrimp according to size. In the United States, shrimp is sold by count and this rating is by size and weight of fresh or frozen shrimp in the shell without the head on. The count represents the number of shrimp in a pound for the various size categories. Shrimp is generally labeled by name and count. For example, U15, referred to in *camarones empanizados* (see recipe), is a "colossal" with an average of 14 shrimp per pound. You can always buy a size that looks good to you, but keep in mind that larger shrimp are better for frying and grilling. Adjust recipes if needed.

Camarones Empanizados

Breaded Shrimp

Serves about 6

Breaded shrimp is a universally popular dish. However, marinating the shrimp before breading adds an extra tanginess to the dish, giving it that Yucatecan touch.

1. Make a marinade by mixing the lime juice, garlic, salt and pepper in a nonreactive bowl. Marinate the shrimp in this for 5–10 minutes. Drain and pat dry with paper towels. Discard marinade.

2. Dredge each shrimp lightly in the flour, then dip in the beaten eggs, and finally in the breadcrumbs, making sure it is well covered. Set aside on a dish.

3. Heat the oil in a hot frying pan over low to medium heat (not too hot). Fry the shrimp for about 2 minutes on each side until golden. Do not over cook.

To serve: Serve with *salsa tártara*, *pico de gallo* and *arroz blanco* (see recipes). Serve with corn tortillas, French rolls, *bolillos* or *pan de sandwich*, the white-crusted, Yucatecan, white bread (see Glossary).

Ingredients

Juice of 2–3 limes

1 teaspoon chopped garlic

1 teaspoon salt

1 teaspoon ground black pepper

2 pounds shrimp (colossal or #U15, see side bar), peeled, deveined and butterflied with tail left on

1 cup all-purpose flour

2 eggs, beaten lightly with 2 tablespoons water

2 cups bread crumbs or Panco

1/2 cup vegetable oil

Garnishes

Salsa tártara (see recipe)

Pico de gallo (see recipe)

Pan de Cazón
Fish Tortilla Stack

Serves 6

Ingredients

4 cups water

3 pounds filets of sole or red snapper (or other mild, firm, white fish)

1 head garlic, roasted

1 sprig fresh cilantro

1 sprig fresh mint

1 pinch dried oregano

1 tablespoon salt

1 teaspoon ground black pepper

4 tablespoons vegetable oil

20 fresh epazote leaves

3 cups *salsa de tomate* (divided) (see recipe)

1 cup *frijoles colados* (see recipe)

24 corn tortillas

3 tablespoons *sofrito de tomate* (see recipe)

6 *chiles habaneros,* roasted (optional)

If ever there was a seafood tortilla stack, this is it. Each serving is a four-tortilla tower. For an extra punch, use the prepared tortillas for *panuchos* (without the toppings, see recipe) instead of regular tortillas. In the Yucatán—or more specifically in Campeche, where this dish is from—this dish is made with dogfish (*cazón*). But since this fish is hard to get here, there are several good substitutes. However, like all other dishes that traditionally call for *cazón,* it is kept in the dish's name. See notes below and Glossary.

1. In a pan, bring the water to a boil. Add the fish, garlic, cilantro, mint, oregano, salt and pepper, and simmer for about 15 minutes or until the fish easily falls apart. Remove the fish, let cool and shred. (Discard the stock or save for other purposes.)

2. Heat the oil in a hot frying pan and sauté the epazote until the leaves release their fragrance.

3. Add the fish and sauté just until heated. Add 1 cup of the *salsa de tomate* and cook for about 15 minutes.

To construct the *pan de cazón*: Take a warmed tortilla and spread a smear of *frijoles colados* and top with about 2 tablespoons of the fish. Repeat two more times. Top with the fourth and final tortilla and smother with *salsa de tomate.* Top all of this with dollops of *sofrito de tomate* and a roasted *chile habanero.*

Notes: In some parts of the world *cazón*, a type of shark, is a fish that has been overfished and is considered a vulnerable or threatened species. There are, however, plenty of good substitutes. See side bar below and Glossary for more information.

Cazón: To Catch or Not to Catch *Cazón* or dogfish is a type of shark. In some parts of the world, it is considered a vulnerable or threatened species. Hard to find, use another white fish or even canned albacore. The term *cazón* is still used in a couple of recipes—*chile x'catic relleno de cazón, empanadas de cazón* and *pan de cazón* (see recipes)—because they are such traditional dishes and that's how they are best known. See Glossary for more information on *cazón*.

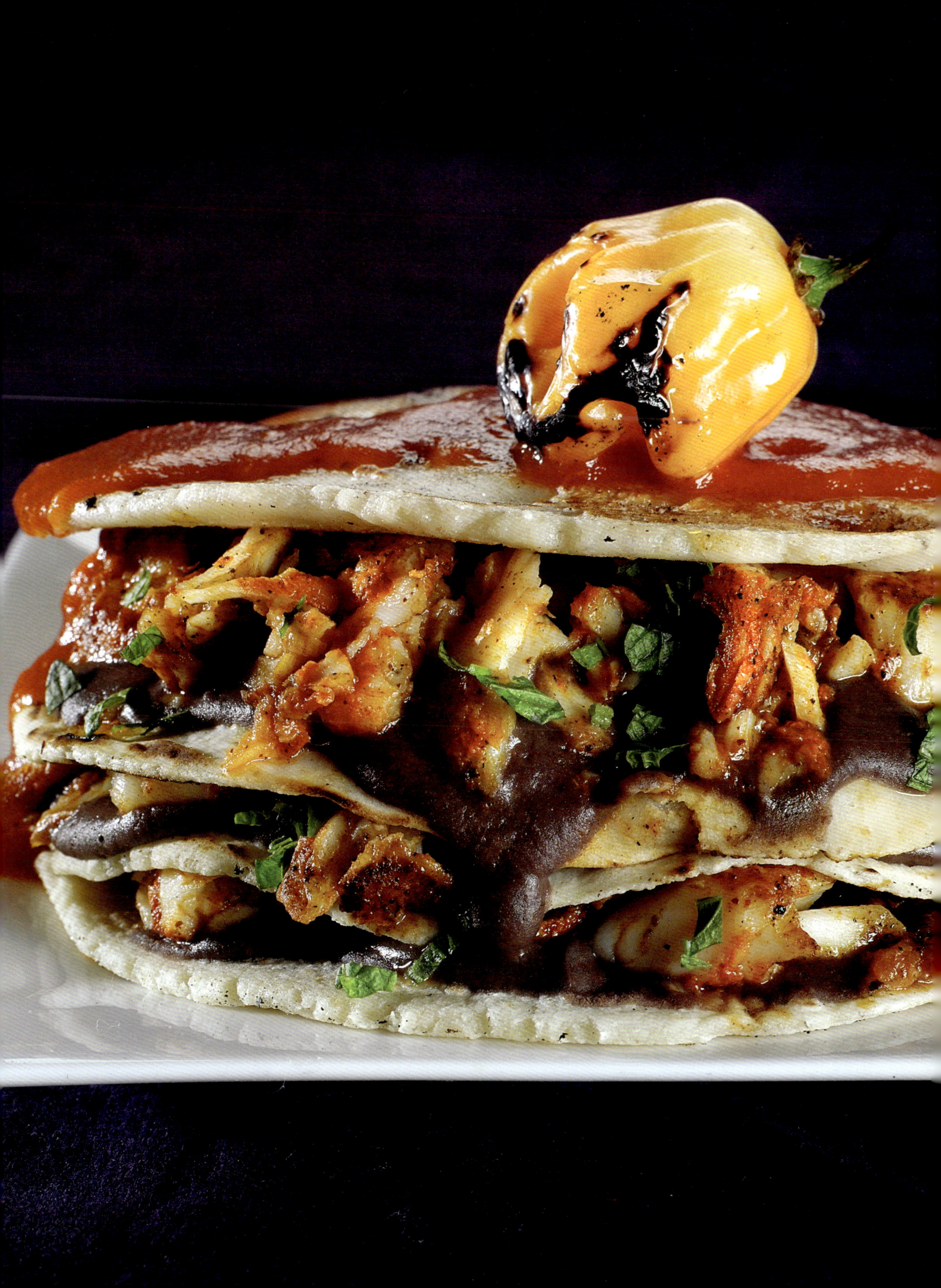

Pescado Empanizado

Breaded Fish

Serves about 6–8

Ingredients

Juice of 2–3 limes

1 teaspoon chopped garlic

1 teaspoon salt

1 teaspoon ground black pepper

6–8 filets of sole or red snapper, about 3 ounces each

1 cup all-purpose flour

2 eggs, beaten lightly with 2 tablespoons water

2 cups bread crumbs or Panco

1/2 cup vegetable oil

Garnishes

Salsa tártara (see recipe)

Pico de gallo (see recipe)

This is a another universally popular seafood dish. But like *camarones empanizado* (see recipe), the fish gets a boost of tanginess because it is first marinated in seasoned, lime juice. It's also flexible. Almost any firm white fish will work.

1. Make a marinade by mixing the lime juice, garlic, salt and pepper in a nonreactive bowl. Marinate the fish filets in this for 5–10 minutes. Drain and pat dry with paper towels. Discard unused marinade.

2. Dredge each fish filet lightly in the flour, then dip in the beaten eggs and finally in the breadcrumbs, making sure it is well covered. Set aside on a dish.

3. Heat oil in a hot frying pan over medium heat (not too hot). Fry the fish filets for about 2 minutes on each side until golden. Do not over cook.

To serve: Serve with *salsa tártara* and *pico de gallo* (see recipes). *Arroz blanco* (see recipe) goes well with this dish too. And as might be expected, so do corn tortillas, a French roll, *bolillo, pan de sandwich* (see Glossary) or regular white bread.

A dollop of salsa tártara *(page 17) is good on your* pescado empanizado, *but maybe another one is even better.*

TIKIN XIC

GRILLED FISH WITH ACHIOTE RUB

Serves about 6–8 (photo on page 112)

Much like ceviche, fishermen in the Yucatán were experts at making *tikin xic*. If they were unable to return home on fishing expeditions, they would camp on shore and prepare this dish for themselves. Much like making *cochinita pibil* (see recipe) the traditional way, they would dig pits in the sand and line them with stones covered by wood or charcoal. After getting this hot, they would cover with a crisscross of palm branches followed by palm leaves. They would then put the fish directly on the leaves or wrap it first in plantain leaves. The name means "*ala seca*" or "dried wing" because in times past, shark fins were used. I remember a time, unfortunately, when the fins were cut off and the rest of the shark's body was tossed aside. In this recipe, sharks fins are replaced with a mild, firm, white fish. This dish comes from Playa Lancheros, a tourist attraction in Isla Mujeres off the coast of the state of Quintana Roo where *tikin xic* is a much-served dish. After returning to the beach following fishing trips, visitors' catches are prepared—*tikin xic*, or course—and served to them.

1. Make a marinade by mixing the *recado rojo* in the lime juice and salt in a nonreactive bowl. Add the fish and marinate for no more than 30 minutes.

2. In a large frying pan, heat the vegetable oil over a medium-high heat. Add the filets and fry on each side for about 2 minutes, making sure to brown to ensure the *recado rojo* is "toasted" in order to bring out the flavor of the achiote.

To serve: To prepare a serving, smear a couple of tablespoons (or more) of *salsa de achiote para tikin xic* on a plate. Place a mound of *arroz blanco* (see recipe) in the center of a plate, and place a fish filet on top of the rice. Garnish with pico de gallo and serve with corn tortillas.

INGREDIENTS

1 1/2 tablespoons (1 ounce) *recado rojo* (see recipe)

Juice of 2–4 limes

1 tablespoon salt

6–8 filets of sole or red snapper (or other mild, firm, white fish), about 8 ounces each

4 tablespoons vegetable oil

GARNISHES

Salsa de achiote para tikin xic (see recipe)

Pico de gallo (see recipe)

SNACKS: LITE BITES Going out "snacking" (*botanear*) is a favorite pastime in the Yucatán. *Cóctel de camarón, calabacitas fritas, xec* and *papadzules* (see recipes) are popular *botanas*, great washed down with a cold beer or other refreshing drink. In Campeche, *cóctel de camarón* is made with *camarón de pacotilla* from the Laguna de Chompotón, which are these teeny, tiny shrimp. I always wonder how these tiny crustaceans get peeled and deveined. Or maybe they don't.

126   Sabores Yucatecos: A Culinary Tour of the Yucatán

Chapter 9

Tamales

Food wrapped in leaves and cooked is an age-old tradition around the world. In Mexico, cooks from ancient to modern times have reached culinary heights using this technique to make tamales. They are eaten throughout Mexico, and each region has its own version of delectable bundles of *masa* (corn dough) wrapped in corn husks, banana leaves, *hoja santa*, avocado leaves or even the inner layer of the maguey leaf (*pencas de maguey*). Most contain a filling or stuffing—savory or sweet—but not all do.

Yucatán boasts its own regional tamales. Here the preferred wrapper is banana leaves, and the *masa* preparation and fillings are a signature of the region.

If you are familiar with tamales or are an experienced tamal maker, the first thing you will notice is that the *masa* of choice is not *masa para tamales* (corn dough for tamales) but *masa de maíz para tortillas* (corn dough for tortillas). This choice delivers a light and moist dough.

The best place to get *masa* is at a *tortillería,* where they grind and prepare the *masa* for different uses. *Tortillerías* are springing up almost everywhere these days. Sometimes you can find *masa* in the deli section at supermarkets. Or you can buy a bag of *masa harina,* and follow the directions for making the *masa*. Just remember to ask for or make *masa para tortillas,* not *masa para tamales* nor *masa preparada para tamales*.

Among the collection of tamal recipes here are the unique *tamal colado* and *brazo de reina*. And there is the casserole-style tamal, *mucbi pollo,* made to celebrate *Hanal Pixan* or Day of the Dead. (*Hanal Pixan* means "*comida de las almas*" or "food for souls" or "food for the spirits.")

Opposite page, from l. to r.: Vaporcitos de pollo (129), *vegetarian* vaporcitos *and* vaporcitos de cochinita pibil.

Above right, from top: Piles of fresh banana leaves, a tortillería *doing a brisk business, and shelling* espelón *beans.*

STOP: READ ME FIRST!

NOTES

- Food scoops are a convenient kitchen tool to use to make uniform-sized tamales.

- I prefer to steam tamales in a rectangular steamer rather than in traditional, round, tamal steamers or *tamaleras* (see Tools). It's too easy to overcook tamales when packed into a traditional steamer. Steaming them single-layered in a rectangular streamer produces more tender tamales.

- If you layer the tamales in the steamer, more cooking time might be required.

- Notice how the banana leaf color changes from green to brownish green as it steams.

Before you make any of the tamales presented here, learn a bit about banana leaves and how to stuff and fold tamales prior to steaming.

GET TO KNOW YOUR BANANA LEAF

You can use frozen or fresh banana leaves to wrap your tamales. Frozen leaves only need to be thawed before using and are the easiest to find. Fresh leaves need to be prepared by either passing the leaves quickly over a flame (do not to burn or char) or by blanching in boiling water for a few seconds.

Notice how the veins run so that when you cut the leaves to the dimensions indicated, the veins run horizontally or lengthwise. Also note that one side of the leaf is smooth while on the other side you can feel vein ridges. Tamal fillings should be placed on the smooth side. So, smooth side up, ridge side down, veins horzontal. Finally, remove the thicker, center stem (that usually runs along the edge of a piece of a leaf) before using. You can use scissors or a sharp knife to cut the leaves.

TAMAL FOLDING 101

Follow these easy instructions to fold your tamales in their banana-leaf wrapper. The only things you need to note are the sizes of leaves required, how much *masa* is requested and if the tamal takes a filling or not. The *tamal horneado* is the only tamal that is baked, and the *brazo de reina* has its own special folding instructions.

a. Banana leaf: Cut out large rectangles of the banana leaves to the size indicated, the veins should run lengthwise.

b. *Masa*: Place a banana leaf rectangle, smooth side up, centered on a tortilla press. Place the requested amount of *masa* (suggested food scoops are noted to give you uniform-sized tamales) in the center of the banana leaf and place a piece of plastic wrap on top. Press down on the tortilla press to make a "tortilla" to the size indicated. Open and remove the plastic. (If you don't have a tortilla press, use a pie tin or frying pan.)

c. Filling: For tamales with fillings, place the requested amount of filling in the center of the "tortilla."

d. Folding: Lift one of the long ends of the banana leaf and ease 1/3 of dough over the filling and gently peel back the leaf. Then fold the other end over to enclose the filling and leave folded. (No part of the leaf should be folded into the tamal.) Lift the first end over again to complete the "bundle." Then lift by the two ends and fold under to form a rectangular "packet." (See photo insets ❸ and ❹ on page 137.)

MASA DE MAÍZ One kind of *masa de maíz* (corn dough) is used widely in Yucatecan cooking—*masa de maíz para tortillas* (corn dough for tortillas). It can be purchased at a *tortillería* (where *masa* and tortillas are freshly made). If you prefer, make your own *masa* from *masa harina* (a special, dry, corn flour), which you can find at most well-stocked grocery stores. Just follow the directions on the back of the package to make the dough. Two cups *masa harina* (to which you add salt and water added) will give you about a pound of dough. Then add any other ingredients called for in the recipe whether it's *salbutes* or tamales. (See *masa de maíz* and *masa harina* in Glossary; and tortilla press in Tools.)

VAPORCITO DE POLLO
CHICKEN TAMALES WRAPPED IN BANANA LEAVES

Makes about 15 tamales (photo on page 126)

These popular tamales are very common throughout the Yucatán. Remember to use *masa para tortillas* (corn dough for tortillas) rather than *masa para tamales* (corn dough for tamales). And as to lard, you just can't leave that out. Find good quality lard, not the hard, white blocks sold in supermarkets. That kind is partially hydrogenated to prolong shelf life and doesn't taste as good as the creamy, golden lard found in Latino markets or from your butcher. Please note that the stock that results from preparing the chicken is the stock you can use to make the *salsa de achiote para tamales* (see recipe).

MASA PARA VAPORCITO (CORN DOUGH FOR VAPORCITO TAMALES AND OTHER TAMALES)

- 2 pounds *masa de maíz para tortillas* (corn dough for tortillas)
- 10 ounces lard
- 1/2 teaspoon salt
- Water

1. Mix the corn dough, lard, salt and enough water to make a dough that is smooth, soft and pliable. You do not want a *masa* that is watery. Cover with plastic wrap or moist cloth so it does not get dry, and set aside.

THE MEAT FILLING (MAKE AHEAD IF POSSIBLE)

- 1 recipe *caldo de pollo* (see recipe)
- 1 recipe *salsa de achiote para tamales* (see recipe)

1. Make the *caldo de pollo* as instructed in the recipe.

2. Strain the stock, and reserve to make the *salsa de achiote para tamales*.

3. When cool enough to handle, shred the chicken by hand—not with a knife. The meat should not be too finely shredded.

4. Make the *salsa de achiote para tamales* as instructed using the reserved stock.

5. Mix the shredded chicken with the *salsa de achiote para tamales*.

TO ALSO HAVE READY

- Banana leaves, thawed if frozen or prepared if fresh (see Glossary and Techniques)
- 1 recipe of *masa para vaporcito* (as instructed above)
- Chicken filling (as instructed above)

You are now ready to assemble your tamales . . . (refer to column above right).

ASSEMBLING THE TAMALES

Follow the instructions in "Tamal Folding 101" for the (a.) banana leaf, (b.) *masa*, (c.) filling, and (d.) folding using the specifications indicated.

1./a. Banana leaf: Cut out 12" x 8" banana leaf rectangles.

2./b. *Masa*: Place about 2 1/2 ounces (or use a #20 food scoop) of the *masa* in the center of the banana leaf and press out a 6- to 8-inch "tortilla."

3./c. Filling: Place about 2 tablespoons (about 2 ounces) of the chicken with sauce in the center of the "tortilla." (Try other fillings, such as *cochinita pibil* (see recipe), as shown in photograph on page 126

4./d. Folding: Fold the tamal as explained.

5. Place the tamales in a single layer in a rectangular steamer. Cover with aluminum foil, place on stovetop burners and steam for about 30 minutes or until the banana leaf is easily separated from the dough. Let rest for 10 to 15 minutes before eating.

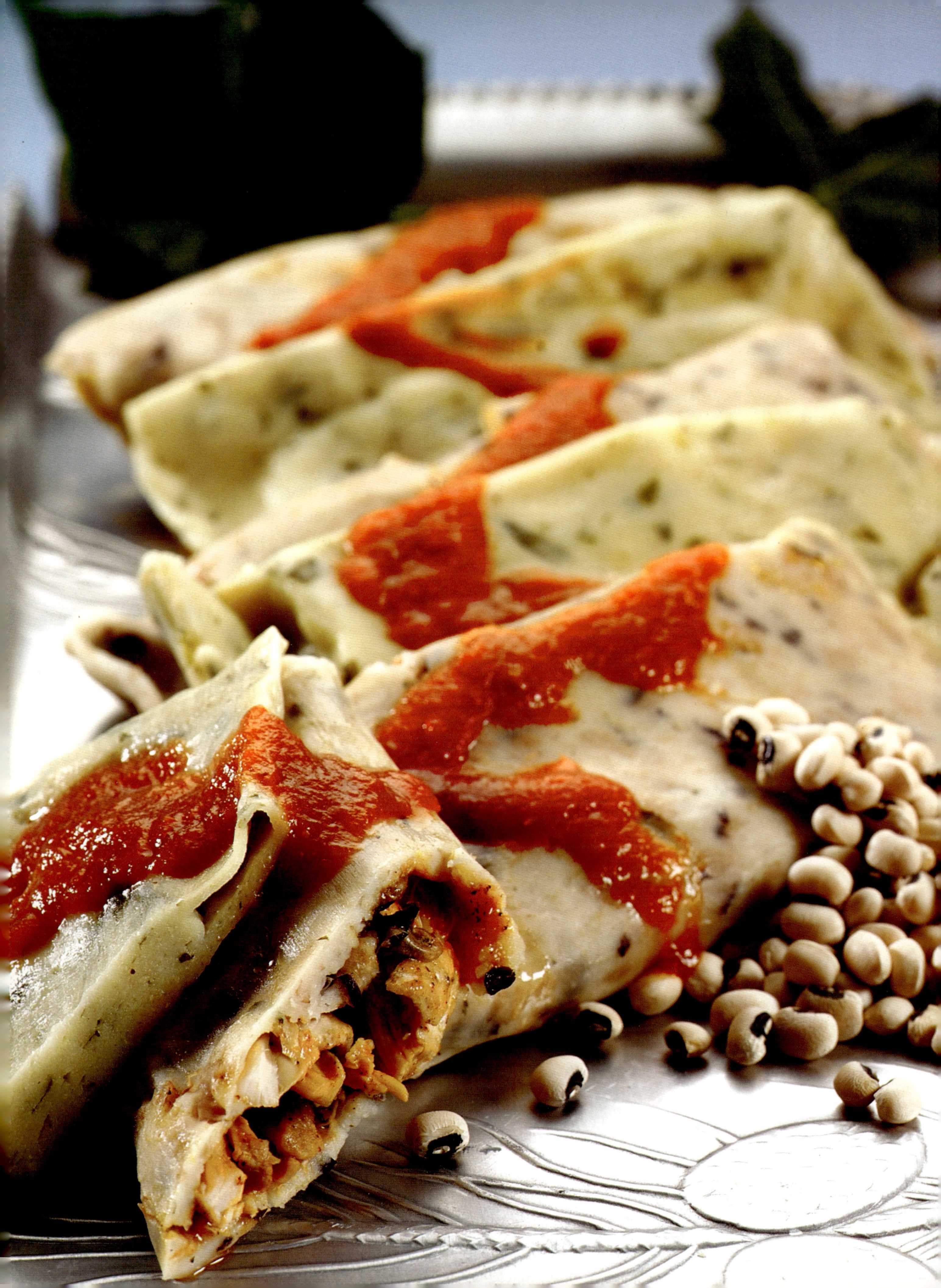

VAPORCITO DE ESPELÓN
BLACK-EYED PEAS TAMALES WRAPPED IN BANANA LEAVES

Makes about 15 tamales

Espelón is a fresh bean used widely in the Yucatán. Also known as *frijol tierno*, you can find vendors in markets in the Yucatán, shelling the pods, and packaging the beans for sale. While *espelones* are still hard to find this side of the border, black-eyed peas can be used.

THE MASA

1 recipe *masa para vaporcito* (see recipe) (with lard or corn oil, see notes)

1 pound *espelón* (or cooked black-eyed peas)

1. Make the *masa* as indicated for *vaporcito de pollo*.

2. Add the *espelones* and mix well.

TO ALSO HAVE READY

Banana leaves, thawed if frozen or prepared if fresh (see Glossary and Techniques)

1 recipe *sofrito de tomate* (see recipe)

You are now ready to assemble your tamales . . . (see column to right)

VAPORCITO DE CHAYA
CHAYA TAMALES WRAPPED IN BANANA LEAVES

Makes about 15 tamales

You should already be familiar with *chaya* as it has starred in *huevos con chaya* and *crema de chaya* (see recipes). (See Glossary for more information.) But as a refresher, *chaya* leaves are used much as spinach. Here it speckles the *masa* with dark green and gives the tamal a fresh taste.

THE MASA

1 recipe *masa para vaporcito* (see recipe) (with lard or corn oil, see notes)

2 cups chopped *chaya* leaves (or spinach), fresh or thawed and drained if frozen, chopped

1. Make the *masa* as indicated for *vaporcitos de pollo*.

2. Add the *chaya* (or spinach) and mix well.

TO ALSO HAVE READY

Banana leaves, thawed if frozen or prepared if fresh (see Glossary and Techniques)

1 recipe *sofrito de tomate* (see recipe)

You are now ready to assemble your tamales . . . (see column above right)

ASSEMBLING THE TAMALES
(VAPORCITO DE ESPELÓN AND VAPORCITO DE CHAYA)

Follow the instructions in "Tamal Folding 101" for the (a.) banana leaf, (b.) *masa*, (c.) filling, and (d.) folding using the specifications indicated.

1./a. Banana leaf: Cut out 12" x 8" rectangles of the banana leaves.

2./b. *Masa*: Place about 2 1/2 ounces (or use a #20 food scoop) of the *masa* in the center of the banana leaf and press out a 6- to 8-inch "tortilla."

(c. Filling: This tamal has no filling. However, as an option, you can use a meat filling for either tamal. The chicken filling used for *vaporcito de pollo* is an excellent choice.)

3./d. Folding: Fold the tamal as explained.

4. Place the tamales in a single layer in a rectangular steamer. Cover with aluminum foil, place on stovetop burners and steam for about 30 minutes or until the banana leaf is easily separated from the dough. Let rest for 10 to 15 minutes before eating.

Notes: To make either of these tamales vegetarian, use 10 ounces of corn oil instead of the lard called for in preparing the *masa para vaporcito* (see recipe).

More notes: However, if you do like meat fillings for your tamales, you can prepare the same filling used in *vaporcito de pollo* (see recipe) or even use *cochinita pibil* (see recipe) as a filling.

Opposite page: Vaporcitos de espelón *and* vaporcitos de chaya—*vegetarian and chicken-filled examples.)*

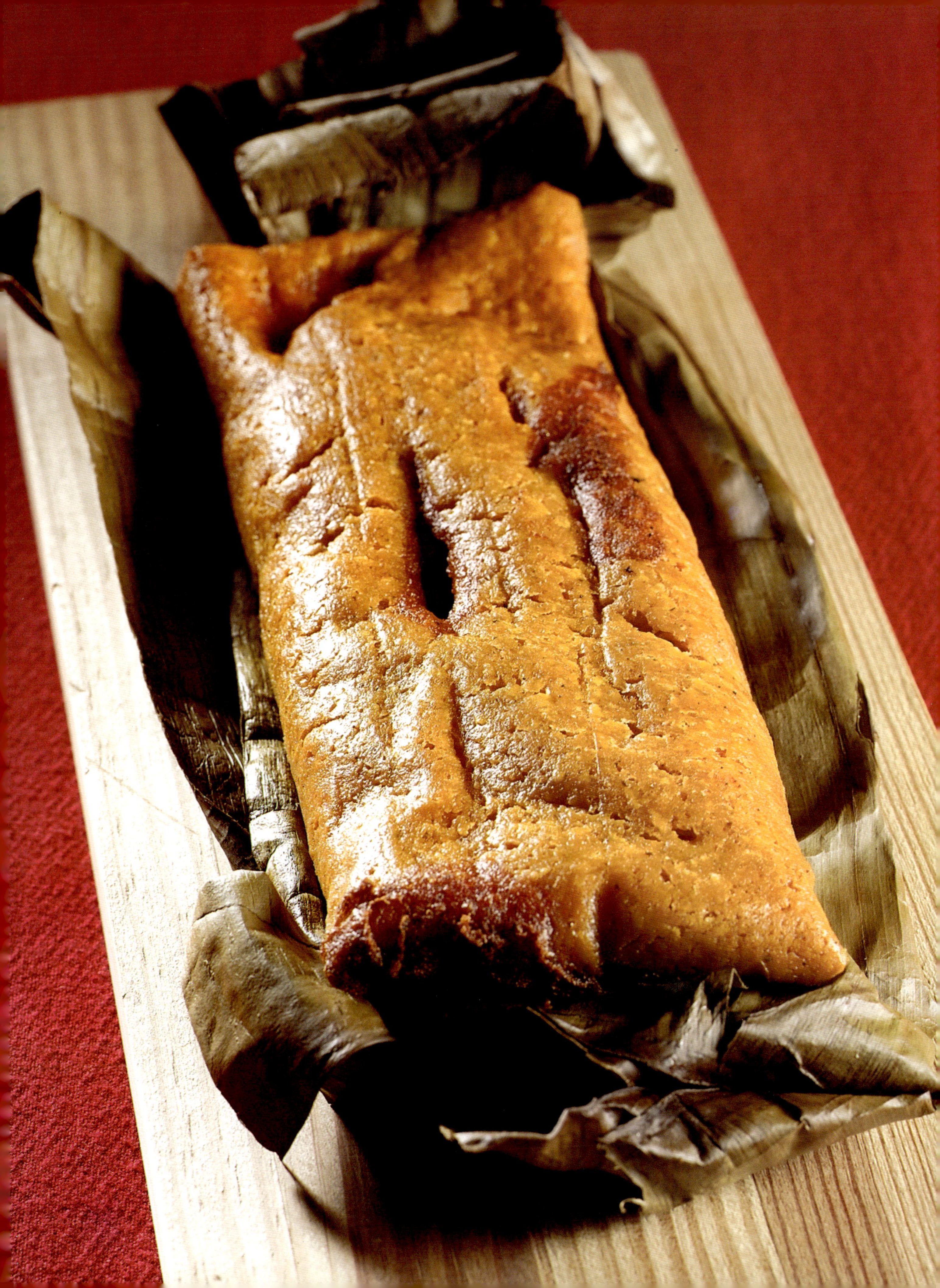

TAMAL HORNEADO
BAKED TAMAL

Makes about 12 tamales

These extra-large tamales make a hearty meal—all you need is one. They are extremely crunchy and crispy on the outside because of the baking, not like your average *tamal*. They used to be cooked *pibil* style, just like the Maya might have done it in pre-Columbian times. They lend themselves well to fillings of pork and venison.

To make them, you need to refer to other recipes in the book as indicated. If you have already made *vaporcitos de pollo* you will be familiar with them.

THE MEAT FILLING (MAKE AHEAD IF POSSIBLE)

   1 recipe *caldo de pollo* (chicken stock, see recipe)

   1 recipe *salsa de achiote para tamales* (see recipe)

1. Make the *caldo de pollo* as instructed in the recipe.

2. Strain the stock, and reserve to make the *salsa de achiote para tamales*.

3. When cool enough to handle, shred the chicken by hand—not with a knife. The meat should not be too finely shredded.

4. Make the *salsa de achiote para tamales* as instructed using the reserved stock.

5. Mix the shredded chicken with the *salsa de achiote para tamales*.

TO ALSO HAVE READY

   Banana leaves, thawed if frozen or prepared if fresh (see Glossary and Techniques)

   2 1/2 recipes *masa para vaporcito* (see recipe)

   Chicken filling (as instructed above)

   6–7 hard-cooked eggs sliced

   3–4 plum tomatoes, thinly slices

   24–30 fresh epazote leaves

You are now ready to assemble your tamales . . . see column on right).

ASSEMBLING THE TAMALES

Follow the instructions in "Tamal Folding 101" for the (a.) banana leaf, (b.) *masa,* (c.) filling, and (d.) folding using the specifications indicated.

1./a. Banana leaf: Cut out 12" x 10" rectangles of the banana leaves.

2./b. *Masa*: Place about 6 ounces (or use a #5 food scoop) of the *masa* in the center of the banana leaf and press out a 10-inch "tortilla."

3./c. Filling: Place about 3 tablespoons (about 3 ounces) of the chicken filling, 2–3 slices of hard-cooked egg, 2–3 slices of tomatoes and 2–3 epazote leaves in the center of the "tortilla."

4./d. Folding: Fold the tamal as explained.

5. Place the tamales on a sheet pan (cookie sheet) and place in a pre-heated 500°F oven for about 1 1/2 hours. The *tamal* should be well cooked—toasty and crispy. The banana leaves will be crinkly like paper.

Tamal colado de pollo

Strained Chicken Tamal

Makes 30–35 tamales

These are very special tamales. You will be taken by their airiness. The challenge is in nailing the technique required to make the translucent *masa*. Even mine don't turn out as light, airy and gelatinous as my mother's *tamales colados*. Note that you need the same filling as used in the *vaporcito de pollo* recipe. Pork and venison work well as alternative fillings.

The meat filling (make ahead if possible)

- 2 recipes *caldo de pollo* (chicken stock, see recipe)
- 1 recipe *salsa de achiote para tamales* (see recipe)

1. Make the *caldo de pollo* as instructed in the recipe, making sure to increase the ingredients.

2. Strain the stock, and reserve to make the *salsa de achiote para tamales*.

3. When cool enough to handle, shred the chicken by hand—not with a knife. The meat should not be too finely shredded.

4. Make the *salsa de achiote para tamales* as instructed using the reserved stock.

5. Mix the shredded chicken with the *salsa de achiote para tamales*.

Preparing the masa

- 1 gallon chicken stock (reserved from preparation of *caldo de pollo,* see above)
- 4 pounds *masa para tortillas*
- 1/2 cup lard
- Salt, if needed

1. In a blender, mix 1 gallon of the reserved chicken stock and the *masa*. Do in batches of about 4 cups of stock to 2 full handfuls of *masa*.

2. Strain each batch through cheesecloth or a very fine sieve—the finer the better—into a large pot. You will get a mixture that is very watery—like an *horchata* or watery gruel.

3. Stir in the lard until well incorporated.

4. Over a medium heat, stir the liquefied and strained *masa* with a wooden spoon. Once it starts to thicken, lower heat and, like making polenta, continue stirring so that the mixture does not stick to the bottom of the pan or burn. Cook for 15–20 minutes or until the spoon stays upright when inserted into the *masa*.

5. Adjust salt.

6. Set aside, but keep the *masa* warm.

Assembling the Tamales

Follow the instructions in "Tamal Folding 101" for the (a.) banana leaf, (b.) *masa,* (c.) filling, and (d.) folding using the specifications indicated.

1./a. Banana leaf: Cut out 12" x 10" rectangles of the banana leaves.

2./b. *Masa*: Place about 5 ounces (or use a #8 food scoop) of the *masa* in the center of the banana leaf and press out a 6- to 8-inch "tortilla." The *masa* may start to spread, so quickly move on to the filling;

3./c. Filling: Place about 2 tablespoons (2 ounces) of the chicken filling in the center of the "tortilla."

4./d. Folding: Fold the tamal as explained.

5. Place the tamales in a single layer in a rectangular steamer on stovetop burners and steam covered with aluminum foil for 25–30 minutes or until the banana leaf is easily separated from the dough. Let rest for 10 to 15 minutes before eating.

To serve: A tender *tamal colado* goes great with hot chocolate or *atole.*

Notes: If you don't make *vaporcitos de pollo* first, make sure to read that recipe carefully because many steps are the same.

TO ALSO HAVE READY

Banana leaves, thawed if frozen or prepared if fresh (see Glossary and Techniques)

Prepared *masa* (as instructed above)

Chicken filling (as instructed above)

You are now ready to assemble your tamales . . . (refer to column on opposite page at far left).

BRAZO DE REINA

Queen's Arm Tamal

Makes about 12 tamales

Ingredients

2 recipes *masa para vaporcito* (about 4 pounds *masa*) (see recipe)

2 cups chopped *chaya* leaves (or spinach), fresh or thawed and drained if frozen (see Glossary)

20 hard-cooked eggs, chopped

2 cups *pepitas de calabaza tostadass sin cáscara* (ground, toasted, pumpkin seeds, see recipe)

Banana leaves, thawed if frozen or prepared if fresh (see Glossary and Techniques)

Garnishes

Salsa de tomate (see recipe)

Toasted pumpkin seeds, hulled or unhulled (see recipe)

These curiously named tamales are unique to the Yucatán and hearken back to pre-Columbian times. Mayan murals hint at tamales that were stuffed, rolled and sliced. And as corn and pumpkin seeds figured in the Mayan diet, who is to say they weren't the first to make these pinwheel tamales way back when. Vegetarians love these tamales, and on the catering side of our business, customers frequently pick these tamales as appetizers. Its name possibly refers to the shape of the tamal, but who was the queen?

1. Mix the *masa* with the *chaya* (or spinach) until well blended.

2. Cut out large 12" x 10" rectangles of the banana leaves, the veins should run lengthwise.

3. Place about 6 ounces (or use a #5 food scoop) of the corn dough in the center of the banana leaf, smooth side up. With your fingertips, press out an 8-inch tortilla. ❶

4. Sprinkle about 2 tablespoons of the pumpkin seeds on the tortilla. Follow that with about 2 tablespoons of the hard-cooked eggs on the lower third of the tortilla. ❷

5. To make your tamal roll, start at one end and lift up and fold over a third of the tamal and carefully peel the banana leaf from the *masa*. Then, fold over the other third and roll the tamal. ❸ Basically you are creating a spiral. Be careful to not roll the banana leaf into the roll.

6. Then lift by the two ends and fold the ends under. ❹

7. Place the tamales in a single layer in a rectangular steamer on stovetop burners and steam covered with aluminum foil for about 25–30 minutes or until the banana leaf is easily separated from the dough. Let rest for 10 to 15 minutes. (If you layer the tamales in the steamer, more cooking time might be required.)

8. Remove the banana leaf and slice each tamal into 8 slices crosswise to reveal the spiral of fillings.

To serve: Arrange the slices of one *tamal* on a plate and top with *salsa de tomate* and a sprinkling of pumpkin seeds.

CHAYA: LEAFY GREEN Also known as tree spinach, *chaya* (*Cnidoscolus aconitifolius*) is a perennial shrub, native to the Yucatán Peninsula. The shrub can grow quickly into a tree and produces leaves that exude a milky sap when cut. It is popular in Mexican and Central American cuisines. The leaves must be cooked before eaten, however, as the raw leaves are toxic. *Chaya* is a good source of protein, vitamins, iron, calcium and antioxidants. In recipes calling for *chaya*, spinach—fresh or frozen—can be substituted. (See Glossary.)

Opposite page—
Brazo de reina
inset photographs:
❶
❷
❸
❹

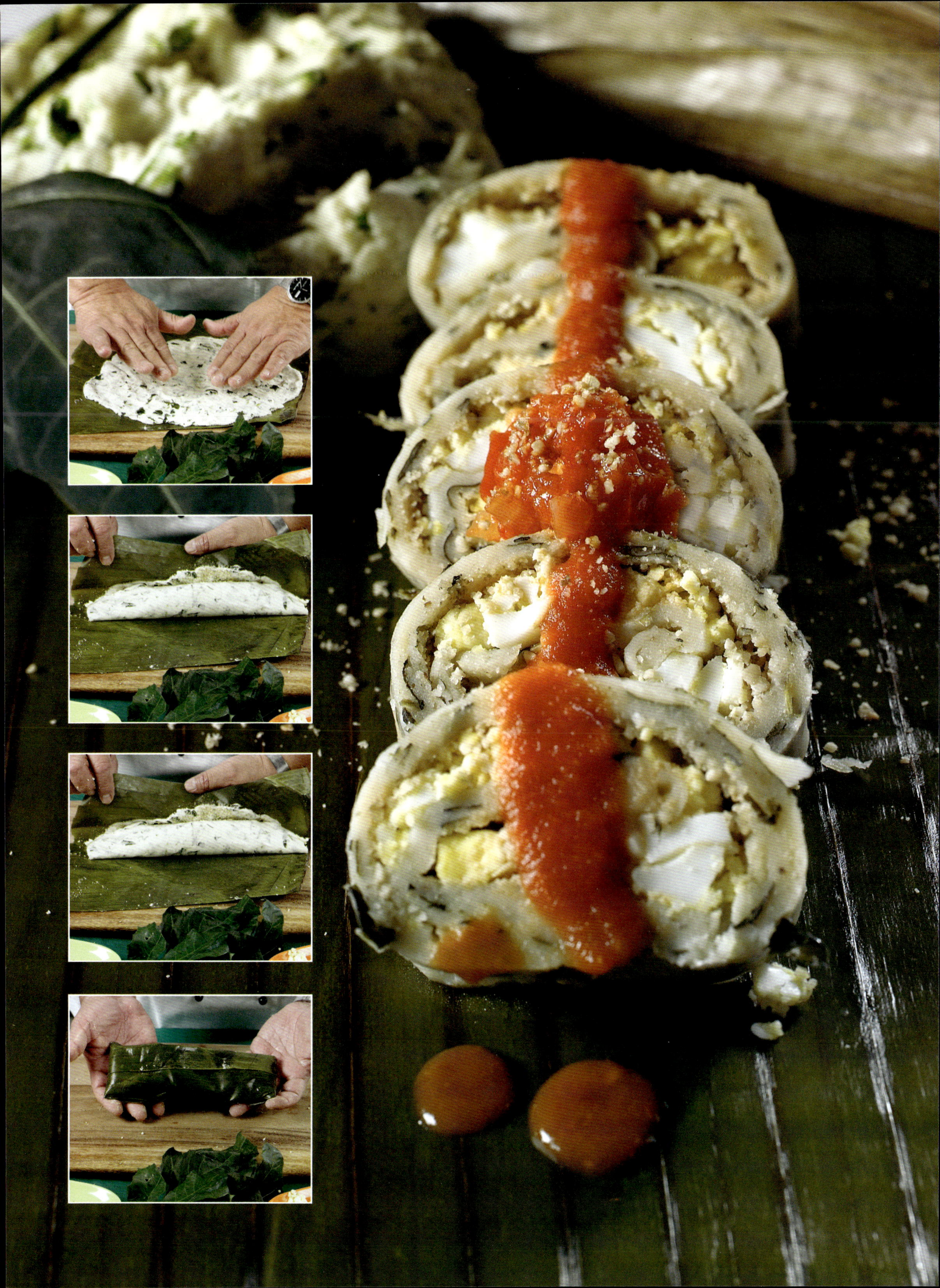

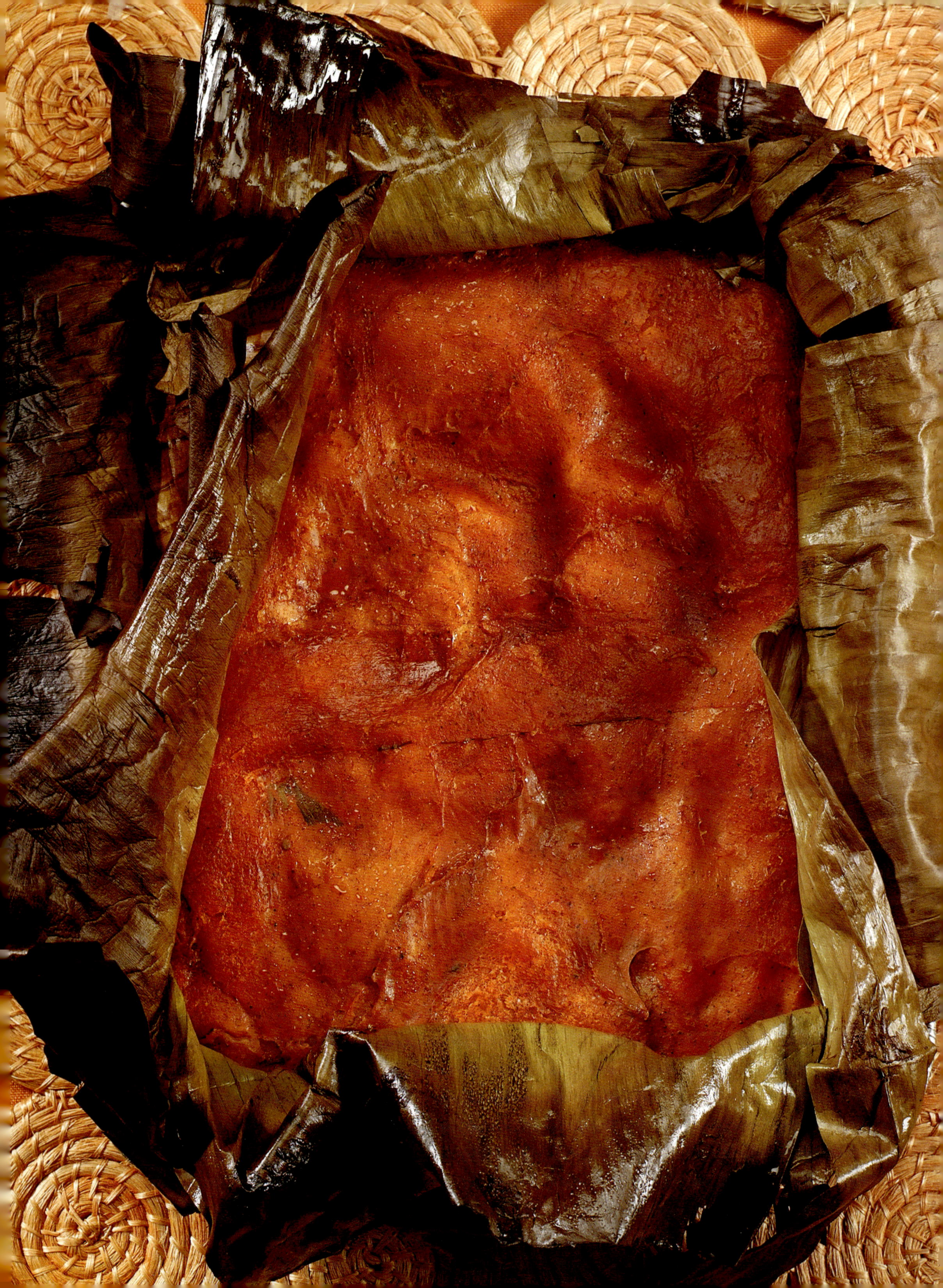

MUCBI POLLO
CHICKEN TAMAL PIE

Serves about 6–8

In the Yucatán, this casserole-like dish is traditionally served for Hanal Pixan or Día de los Muertos (Day of the Dead) celebrations. These honor dead family members and friends on November 2, a time when it is believed the dead return in spirit. *Mucbi pollo* is prepared as an offering to them. How did this tradition begin? In pre-Columbian times the Maya believed that when a person died, his or her soul or spirit did not leave the body for seven days. To help the dead on their journey, the Maya would put a *mazorca* or corncob in the dead person's mouth for sustenance. Over time the *mazorca* became a ball of *masa*.

TO MAKE THE MEAT FILLING (MAKE AHEAD IF POSSIBLE)

1. Make the *caldo de pollo* as instructed in the recipe.

2. Strain the stock, and reserve to make the *salsa de achiote para tamales*.

3. When cool enough to handle, shred the chicken by hand—not with a knife. The meat should not be too finely shredded.

4. Make the *salsa de achiote para tamales* as instructed using the reserved stock.

5. Mix the shredded chicken with the *salsa de achiote para tamales*.

ASSEMBLING THE MUCBIL POLLO

1. Preheat the oven to 500°F.

2. Line a 12" x 10" baking dish with banana leaves with enough extra to fold over and cover the *mucbi pollo* once the dish is filled.

3. Take 1 1/2 pounds of the *masa* and press onto the bottom and up the sides of the banana-leaf-lined baking dish.

4. Spread the filling (shredded chicken mixed with the salsa) on top of the *masa* in the baking dish.

5. Follow with a layer of the sliced tomatoes, a layer of sliced hard-cooked eggs, and a layer of the epazote leaves. Add the *chile habanero*, if desired.

6. Take the remaining 1/2 pound of *masa*, place between 2 pieces of plastic wrap, and spread or roll out the *masa* to a 12" x 10" rectangle. Peel off the top piece of plastic wrap and flip the *masa* carefully on top of the "casserole." Remove the remaining plastic wrap, and seal the edges of the *masa* completely.

7. Top with a large piece of banana leaf and fold over the ends of the leaves that you had left hanging over when you originally lined the baking dish. The leaves should cover the "tamal" completely.

8. Bake the *mucbi pollo* at 500°F for 2 hours, or until it comes out crispy and toasty on top and along the edges.

MEAT FILLING

1 recipe *caldo de pollo* (see recipe)

1 recipe *salsa de achiote para tamales* (using reserved broth from *pollo asado*) (see recipe)

FOR ASSEMBLING THE MUCBI POLLO

Banana leaves, thawed if frozen or prepared if fresh (see Glossary and Techniques)

1 recipe *masa para vaporcito* (divided) (see recipe)

Filling as instructed above and to left

1–2 plum tomatoe, sliced

2–3 hard-cooked eggs, sliced

10–15 fresh epazote leaves

1 *chile habanero,* sliced (optional)

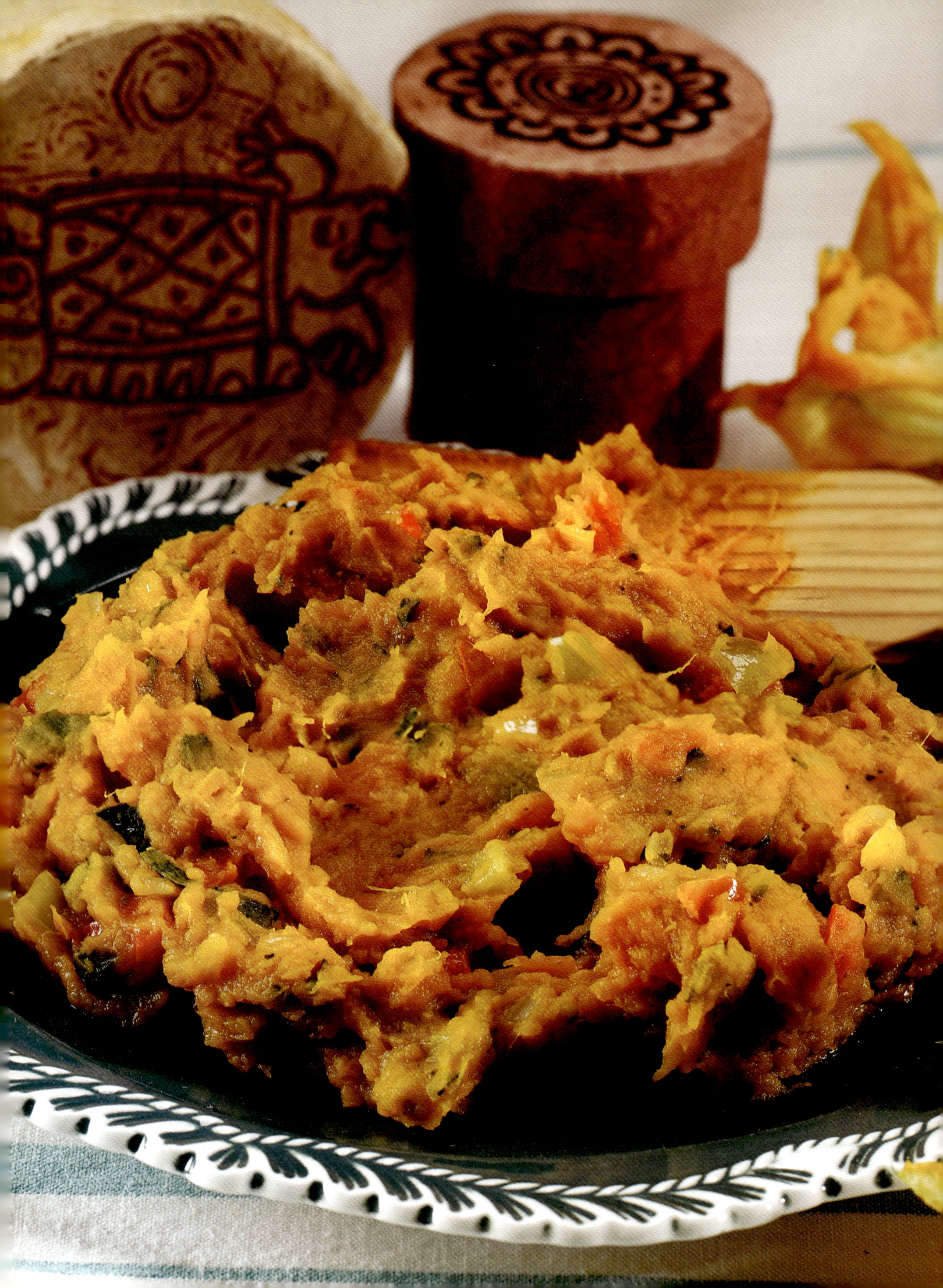

CHAPTER 10

SIDES . . .
PARA ACOMPAÑAR

In this chapter you will find recipes for many of the toppings, accompaniments and side dishes that pair with the recipes provided in other chapters. Much like the *recados* and salsas in Chapter 1, master them and you can put together an authentic and complete Yucatecan meal.

As you have discovered, *yucatecos* really love their red onions, and you will find the three most popular recipes here. Notice the subtle differences between the three. Are the onions sliced or diced, roasted or not? It makes a difference.

Then you will find recipes for black beans (see side bar on page 149 and Glossary), which are eaten throughout the region. Get comfortable making the first recipe—*frijoles de la olla*—and you will have a head start on the other black bean recipes.

The next selection of recipes are for rice dishes, ranging from the simple *arroz blanco* to the made-for-a-party *suflé de arroz*. While *arroz blanco* is often noted as a side dish to many dishes in this book, you can use almost any other rice dish if you prefer.

Finally, you will find vegetable sides as well as the ever-popular *plátanos fritos* (fried plantains).

Opposite page: Calabacitas fritas (page 151).

Right, from top: Calabacitas *found in the Yucatán; water delivered house to house back in the day, Campeche, Campeche; and seasoned ibes that are used to make* polkanes, *another popular* antojito *in the Yucatán.*

CHAPTER 10: SIDES/PARA ACOMPAÑAR   141

Cebolla para Cochinita Pibil

Chopped Pickled Red Onions

Makes about 6 servings (pictured on page 82)

Ingredients

1 medium red onion, chopped

1/4 cup white vinegar

1/4 cup water

3/4 teaspoon salt

Yes, this is what complements a succulent *cochinita pibil* (see recipe). It takes only minutes to throw this together. It also goes well with *akat de codillos* and savory empanadas (see recipes).

1. Place the chopped onion in a large bowl.

2. Add the vinegar, water and salt. The onions should be completely covered.

3. Cover with plastic wrap and let stand for 15 minutes—in or out of the refrigerator—or serve immediately.

Cebolla para Panuchos

Sliced Pickled Red Onions

Makes about 6 servings (pictured on page 22)

Ingredients

1 medium red onion, thinly sliced

1/4 cup white vinegar

1/4 cup water

3/4 teaspoon salt

Panuchos and *salbutes* are always topped with this version of pickled red onions. Note that the onion is sliced, not chopped or diced. And the thinner you slice the onion, the better. Is the slice transparent?

1. Cut the onion in half lengthwise and slice across very thinly. Place the sliced onions in a large bowl.

2. Add the vinegar, water and salt. The onions should be completely covered.

3. Cover with plastic wrap and let stand for 15 minutes—in or out of the refrigerator—or serve immediately.

Cebolla para Poc Chuc

Diced Roasted Pickled Red Onion

Makes about 6–8 servings (pictured on page 88)

Ingredients

3 small red onions, roasted

1/3 cup white vinegar

1/2 teaspoon salt

3 sprigs fresh cilantro, chopped

By its name, you can tell this is the preferred accompaniment to *poc chuc* (see recipe). Please note that the onions are slow roasted before they are diced.

1. Roast the onions on direct heat or on a *comal* (griddle or skillet) over low to medium heat until they give to the touch, like a rubber ball. If the heat is too high, the onions will burn and not cook through. Let rest and cool.

2. Take off the charred skin and dice the onion.

3. Add the vinegar, salt and cilantro to the diced onions. Mix well.

4. Cover with plastic wrap and let stand for 15 minutes—in or out of the refrigerator—or serve immediately.

FRIJOLES DE LA OLLA (OR FRIJOL KABAX)

BLACK BEANS IN A POT

Serves about 6–8 (pictured on page 82)

Black beans are the beans of choice in the Yucatán. This preparation is basic and simple, and provides that basic steps for other black bean recipes that follow. All are common side dishes.

1. Bring the water to a boil and add the beans. Skim the foam from top if needed and bring back to a boil. Lower heat slightly.

2. Cook another 1 1/2–2 hours until the beans are tender. About 15 minutes before reaching that point, add the *epazote* and salt. Adjust salt.

To serve: Always serve the beans in a bowl with plenty of bean broth.

Notes: Your beans are cooked if you can easily mash a bean in your finger. I do not soak my beans in water before cooking. Covering the pot is optional, however, either way don't let the level of water drop below the beans.

INGREDIENTS

1 pound dried black beans, sorted and rinsed

1 gallon water

3 sprigs fresh epazote

1 tablespoon salt

FRIJOLES NEGROS GUISADOS

STEWED BLACK BEANS

Serves about 6–8

Here is another take on black beans. Basically, it's the same as the *frijoles de la olla* recipe (above) with the addition of a couple of ingredients that make a big difference. On top of that, you cook the liquid down and give these beans a bit of a mash before serving.

1. Follow the directions for *frijoles de la olla*—steps 1 and 2 (above).

3. Once cooked, drain the beans in a colander. Discard water or reserve to make *moros y cristianos* (see recipe).

4. In a large pot, heat the oil over a medium-high heat, and add the chopped onion and fry until translucent.

5. Add the beans to the sautéed onion and cook for 30 minutes or until much of the moisture is reduced, but not completely.

Notes: You can also mash the beans a bit with a potato masher if you like that added texture.

INGREDIENTS

1 pound dried black beans, sorted and rinsed

1 gallon water

3 sprigs fresh epazote

1 tablespoon salt

4 tablespoons olive oil (or vegetable oil, bacon fat or lard)

1/2 white onion, chopped

ONIONS, RED THAT IS In the Yucatán, many dishes just wouldn't be complete without a red onion garnish or topping. And there are three popular ways to prepare them. Count them: 1. *Cebolla para cochinita pibil*; 2. *Cebolla para panuchos*; 3. *Cebolla para poc chuc*. You'll note that these "relishes" bear the name of the dish they accompany. But they are great with other dishes too. Pay particular attention to how they are sliced or diced or roasted.

Frijoles colados
Puréed Black Beans

Serves about 8–10

Ingredients

1 pound dried black beans, sorted and rinsed

1 gallon water

3 sprigs fresh epazote

1 tablespoon salt

4 tablespoons oil (vegetable oil, bacon fat or lard)

1/2 white onion, chopped

These creamy beans are what make *panuchos* (see recipe) extra special. That smear between layers of *masa* with tasty toppings is heavenly.

1. Follow directions for *frijoles de la olla*—steps 1 and 2 (on page 143).

3. Purée the beans in a blender with enough broth to be able to purée. You may have to do in batches.

4. In a large pot, heat oil over a medium-high heat, and the sauté chopped onion and fry until translucent.

5. Add the bean purée to the sautéed onion and continue cooking over low heat until reduced by half. The consistency should be like a thick sauce. Adjust salt.

Plátanos fritos
Fried Plantains

Serves about 6–8

Ingredients

4 large ripe plantains (see Glossary)

1/2 cup vegetable oil

Fried plantains are popular throughout the Caribbean, of which the Yucatán claims a corner. They are most often served as a side dish or are used to top mounds of white rice in *arroz blanco con plátanos fritos* (see recipe). You will also need them for *arroz con plátanos*, *huevos motuleños* and *pollo ticuleño* (see recipes). Served with *media crema* they also make a simple dessert (see notes).

1. Peel the plantains (see Techniques). Slice each plantain crosswise at an angle into about 1/4-inch slices (about 8–10 slices per plantain).

2. Heat oil in a frying pan and add slices. Fry about 2–3 minutes on each side or until golden. They should be slightly crunchy on the outside and tender on the inside.

Notes: For dessert, you can simply slice the peeled plantain in half lengthwise and fry. Serve with generous spoonfuls of *media crema* (see photo on page 159).

More notes: Pick plantains that are yellow with black spots and that give slightly to the touch. Avoid those that are unripe and hard and green or those that are overripe and too soft and mostly black. About 4–6 slices make a single serving.

Ensalada de verduras

Vegetable Salad

Serves about 6–8

This lightly dressed, tri-color, vegetable salad can be enjoyed any time and is often partnered with *pollo asado* (see recipe). However, it is also typically served at the Christmas Eve dinner alongside the *pavo asado* (see recipe).

1. Peel the carrots and potatoes and slice crosswise into 1/8-inch slices. (Slice carrots at an angle.)

2. Bring the water to a boil in a pot. Add potatoes and boil for about 3 minutes or until al dente. Place in an ice bath to stop cooking.

3. Bring the water back to a boil and add the carrots to the water and boil for about 5 minutes or until al dente. Place in an ice bath to stop cooking.

4. Bring the water back to a boil and add the unpeeled beets to the water and boil for about 20–25 minutes or until tender. Place in an ice bath to stop cooking and then peel and slice into 1/8-inch slices.

5. Drain the vegetables and arrange on a platter alternating each vegetable and squeeze the juice of the *naranja agria* (or lime) on top and sprinkle with salt and pepper to taste.

To serve: Serve family style on a platter at room temperature or chilled. Alternate the sliced vegetables for an attractive presentation.

Notes: Do not peel or slice the beets before boiling because the slices will lose their vibrant color in the process. And make sure to boil the beets after the carrots and potatoes so as to not stain those vegetables red.

Ingredients

1/2 gallon water

2 large carrots

2 medium Russet potatoes

2 beets (or canned sliced beets)

Juice of 1–2 *naranjas agrias* (or limes)

Salt, to taste

Ground black pepper, to taste

Arroz Blanco

White Rice

Serves about 6–8 (pictured on page 82)

Ingredients

3 tablespoons vegetable oil

3–4 tablespoons finely diced white onion

2 cloves garlic, peeled and crushed

2 cups long grain rice

4 cups water or chicken stock

1 1/2–2 teaspoons salt (if not using salted chicken stock), or to taste

This may be the most-called-for rice dish. One of the tricks to making good rice is to not burn the rice when frying, not to use too much water and to lower the heat after bringing the water to a boil.

1. Heat the oil in a large frying pan and add the onion and garlic. Sauté over a medium-high heat until the onions are translucent.

2. Add the rice and fry until it turns golden and opaque. Do not burn the rice.

3. Add the water and the salt to the rice (it will sizzle). Cover and bring the water to a boil. Reduce the heat to a very low simmer for about 20 minutes or until the moisture is gone and the rice is plump and tender. Turn off the heat and let the rice rest for 5–10 minutes.

Notes: If using salted chicken stock instead of water, adjust salt later if needed.

Arroz con cebolla y tomate

Rice with Onions and Tomatoes

Serves about 6–8 (pictured at right)

Ingredients

3 tablespoons vegetable oil

2 plum tomatoes, finely diced

1/2 cup finely diced white onion

2 cloves garlic, peeled and minced

2 cups long grain rice

4 cups water or chicken stock

1 1/2–2 teaspoons salt (if not using salted chicken stock), or to taste

Rice dishes accompany many dishes in the Yucatán, and this one goes with just about any main course. Basically, it's an enhanced *arroz blanco* and can take its place with any meal.

1. Heat the oil in a large frying pan and add the tomatoes, onions and garlic. Sauté for about 6–8 minutes until the vegetable are tender.

2. Add the rice and fry until the rice turns golden and opaque. Be careful not to burn the rice.

3. Add the water and salt to the rice (it will sizzle). Cover and bring the water to a boil and reduce the heat to a very low simmer for about 20 minutes or until the moisture is gone and the rice is plump and tender. Turn off the heat and let the rice rest for 5–10 minutes.

Opposite page, clockwise from top left:
Arroz con cebolla y tomate (this page),
moros y cristianos, arroz con azafrán, and
arroz con cilantro (see recipes).

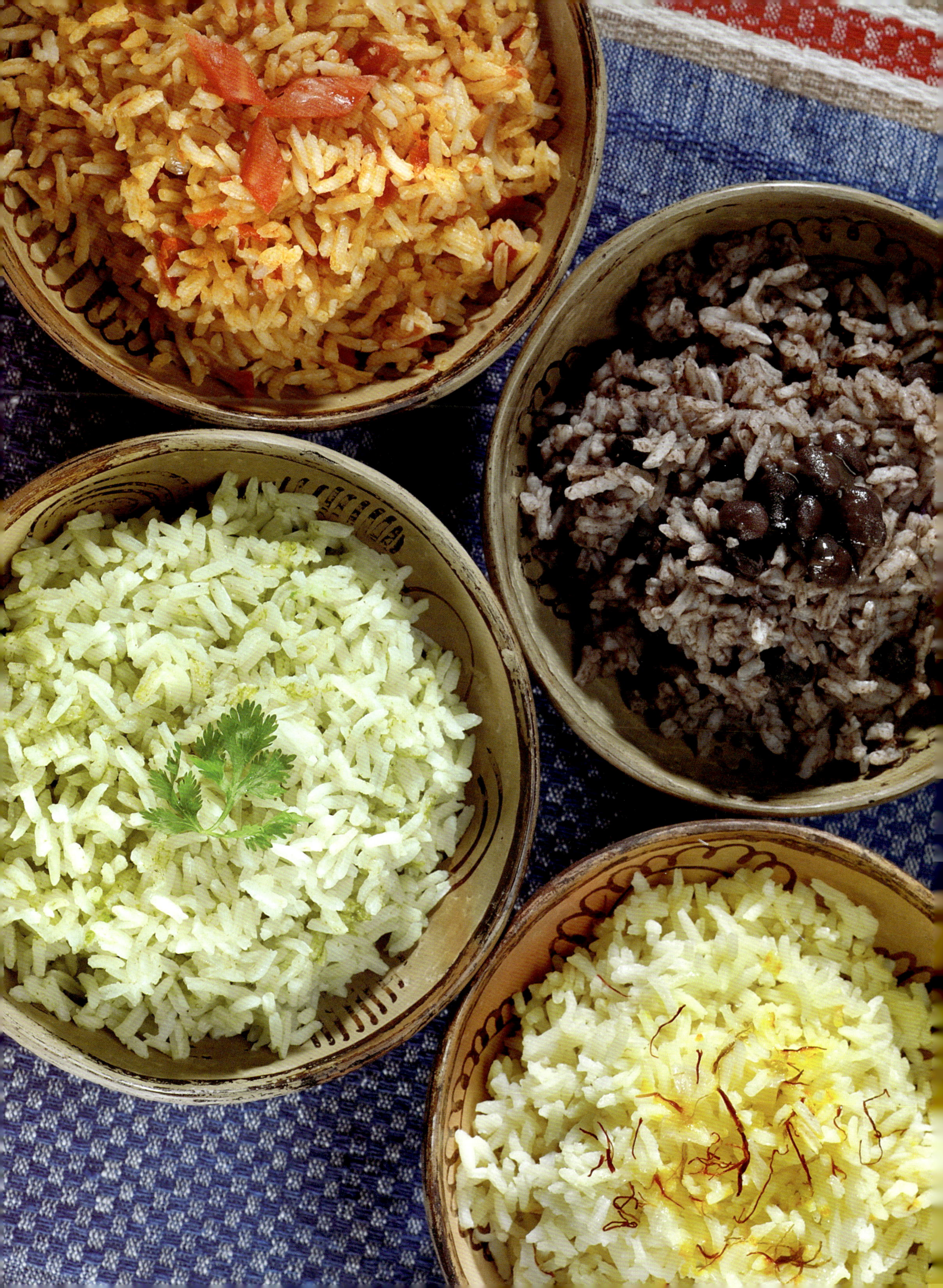

Arroz con Cilantro

Cilantro Rice

Serves about 6–8 (photo on page 147)

Ingredients

3 tablespoons vegetable oil

1/2 cup roughly chopped white onion

2 cloves garlic, peeled and diced

2 cups long grain rice

4 cups water (or chicken stock)

1/3 bunch fresh cilantro, rinsed and without end of stems

1 1/2–2 teaspoons salt (if not using salted chicken stock), or to taste

This rice dish gets a little extra something, not to mention color, from the cilantro. It goes great with any number of dishes.

1. Heat the oil in a large frying pan and add the onion and garlic. Sauté until the onions are translucent, about 6–7 minutes.

2. Add the rice and fry until the rice turns golden and opaque. Be careful not to burn the rice.

3. In a blender add the water and cilantro and purée. Pour into the rice and add salt (it will sizzle). Bring to a boil, cover and reduce the heat to a very low simmer for about 20 minutes or until the moisture is gone and the rice is plump and tender. Turn off the heat and let rice rest for 5–10 minutes.

Arroz con Azafrán

Saffron Rice

Serves about 6–8 (photo on page 147)

Ingredients

3 tablespoons vegetable oil

2 plum tomatoes, finely diced

1/2 cup finely diced white onion

2 gloves cloves, peeled and minced

2 cups long grain rice

4 cups chicken stock

Salt, to taste (see notes)

1 pinch saffron

In the Yucatán, this is the favored rice dish to accompany *puerco empanizado* (see recipe), not to mention Yucatecan fried chicken. You will notice that the recipe is the same as that for *arroz con cebolla y tomate* except that it calls for chicken stock and saffron. It also can serve as a base for paella.

1. Heat the oil in a large skillet and add the tomatoes, onion and garlic. Sauté over medium-high heat until the onions are translucent.

2. Add the rice and fry until it turns opaque and golden. Do not burn rice.

3. Bring the chicken stock to a boil and add the saffron. Turn off the heat and seep the saffron until it releases its color and flavor, about 5–6 minutes.

4. Add the saffron-infused chicken stock to the rice (it may sizzle). Bring to a boil, cover and reduce the heat to a very low simmer for about 20 minutes or until the moisture is gone and the rice is plump and tender. Turn off the heat and let the rice rest for 5–10 minutes.

Notes: If the chicken stock you used has salt or is low in sodium, you may not need to add salt to the rice. If the stock has no salt, add up to 2 teaspoons of salt.

Moros y Cristianos
Black Beans and Rice

Serves 6–8 (photo on page 147)

If you are fond of Cuban food, you've no doubt run across this quaintly named bean-and-rice dish. The literal translation of the dish is "Moors and Christians," perhaps a politically incorrect reference to skin color, but acknowledgement of the time when the Moors occupied the Iberian Peninsula from 711 A.D. to about the time of the "discovery" of the New World. Regardless, it is a filling side dish and is even better with fried plantains.

1. Heat the oil in a large frying pan and add the tomatoes, onions and garlic. Sauté over high heat until the onions are translucent, about 6–7 minutes.

2. Add the rice and fry until turns opaque and golden. Be careful not to burn the rice.

3. Add the bean broth and beans (from *frijoles de la olla*) to the rice (it will sizzle). Bring the water to a boil, cover and reduce heat to a very low simmer for about 20 minutes or until the moisture is gone and the rice is plump and tender. Turn off the heat and let *moros y cristianos* rest for 5–10 minutes. Adjust salt.

Ingredients

3 tablespoons vegetable oil

2 plum tomatoes, finely diced

1/2 cup finely diced white onion

2 garlic cloves, peeled and minced

2 cups long grain rice

4 cups black bean broth (from *frijoles de la olla,* see recipe)

1 cup cooked beans (from *frijoles de la olla,* see recipe)

Salt, to taste

Black Beans: Protein Powerhouse Beans, a diverse group of legumes that come in many sizes and colors, are an important food stuff that originated in the New World. The common bean has been cultivated in the Americas for thousands of years. It may have originated in Peru, spreading to all parts of the Americas and becoming an important source of protein. The bean of choice in the Yucatán is the black bean (*frijol negro* or black turtle bean). Black beans—and beans, in general—are very easy to cook. I do not soak mine before cooking.

Suflé de Arroz

Rice Soufflé

Serves about 6–8

Rice

3 tablespoons vegetable oil

2 cups long grain rice

4 cups water

1 teaspoon salt

Suflé fixings

1 can (7.6 ounces) *media crema* (or heavy cream) (see Glossary)

1 cup diced ham steak

1 cup diced cheddar cheese

1 cup corn kernels (drained if canned, thawed if frozen)

1 large red bell pepper, roasted and chopped

This rice dish is a party food, especially in demand at children's parties alongside a variety of tasty canapés. That doesn't mean you can't enjoy it with an everyday meal if you want to.

1. Heat oil in a large frying pan. Add the rice and fry until it turns opaque and golden. Be careful not to burn the rice.

3. Add the water and salt to the rice (it will sizzle). Bring the water to a boil, cover and reduce heat to a very low simmer for about 20 minutes or until the moisture is gone and the rice is plump and tender. Turn off the heat and let the rice rest for 5–10 minutes.

4. Chill rice.

5. Add the cream, ham, cheese, corn and red bell pepper to the chilled rice and mix well. Adjust salt.

CALABACITAS FRITAS

FRIED SQUASH

Serves about 6–8 (photo on page 140)

Although this dish sounds like a side dish, in the Yucatán it is also served as a *botana* or *aperitivo*—a snack. In the Yucatán, a squash that resembles a small, dark green and squat kabocha would be used. This recipe calls for kabocha squash, which is a close match. It has a lovely yellow-orange color, creamy texture and sweet taste.

1. Wash the squash well. Slice in half, remove the stem, and scoop out the seeds. Then cut into 1-inch-thick slices.

2. Bring the water to a boil, add the squash and cook for 5 minutes or until it is tender but not overcooked. Drain and set aside.

2. Heat the oil in a large frying pan and add the tomatoes, onion, red and green bell peppers, and salt. Fry until the onion is translucent.

3. Mash the squash and add to the sautéed vegetables. Mix well and add the *salsa de tomate* and cook over low heat for about 6–7 minutes.

4. When ready to serve, top with cheese.

To serve: Serve family style in a large bowl or platter, topping with the grated cheese when ready to serve.

INGREDIENTS

1 kabocha squash (about 3 pounds)

1/2 gallon water

3 tablespoons vegetable oil

3 plum tomatoes, diced

1/2 medium white or yellow onion, diced

1/2 cup diced green bell pepper

1/2 cup diced red bell pepper

1 teaspoon salt

1/2 cup *salsa de tomate* (see recipe)

1/2 cup baby Edam cheese, grated (or Gouda cheese)

CURTIDO DE REPOLLO

CABBAGE RELISH

Serves about 6–8 (pictured on page 30)

If you are fond of *pupusas*, a popular Salvadoran treat, you may be familiar with a version of this tangy, cabbage relish. In the Yucatán, it often accompanies *kibis* (see photo on page 30) or is served on the side with *tortas* (sandwiches). It can even be used to make vegetarian *tortas* and *panuchos*.

1. Toss all of the ingredients in a large mixing bowl. Adjust the vinegar and salt.

Notes: Go ahead and make this dish in advance and refrigerate, as the longer it marinates, the better it tastes.

INGREDIENTS

1/4 head green cabbage, julienned (finely sliced)

1/4 large red bell pepper, julienned

1/4 large green bell pepper, julienned

1 carrot, shredded

4–6 sprigs fresh cilantro, finely chopped

2–4 tablespoons white vinegar

1–1 1/2 teaspoons salt

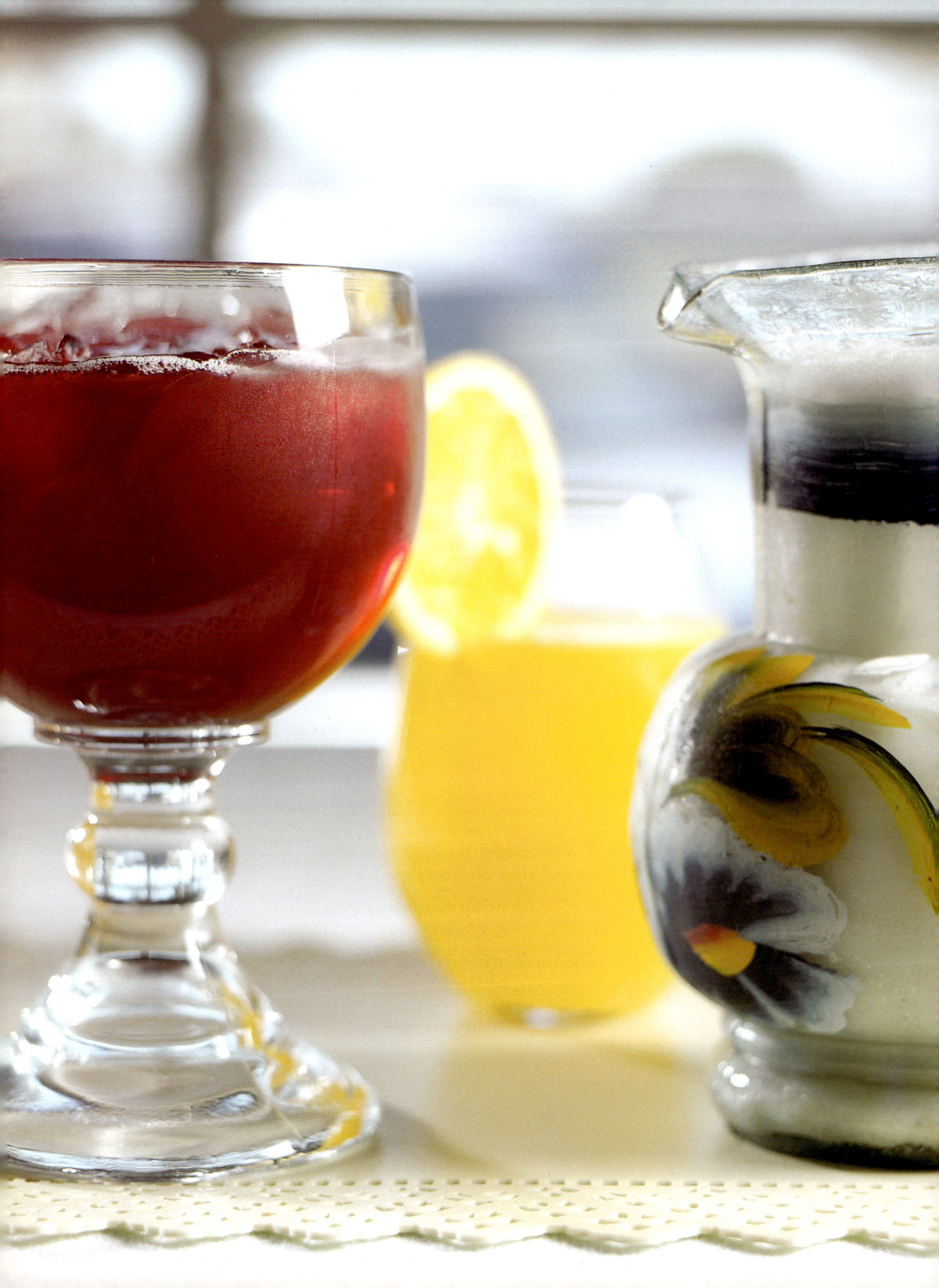

CHAPTER 11

BEVERAGES...
REFRESCOS

Fruit beverages run the course in the Yucatán from fresh juices to shakes. Most of them are really easy to make. As to some of the tropical fruits called for, some are easy to find, while others are easier to find in the form of frozen pulp in Latino or Asian supermarkets. For the more exotic fruits, you might just have to wait until they show up in a specialty or farmer's market near you.

The fruit beverages that call for milk, such as *plátano con leche* or *papaya con leche* (see recipes), you may have heard called *licuados* in other parts of Latin America.

Non-fruit drinks included in this chapter include *horchata*, a traditional rice-based drink found throughout Mexico; and *agua de jamaica,* made from an infusion of the sepals and calyces of a hibiscus flower.

There are lots of variables when it comes to making these drinks, so use the recipes as a guide. You may need more of the fruit than noted in the recipe, for example, if they aren't very juicy. Or if you like drinks more concentrated or less sweet, simply use less water or sugar.

If you are in the Yucatán and want a brew to quell your thirst, a chilly Carta Clara (lager), Negra León (amber) or Montejo (pilsner), might hit the spot.

As an aperitif or after-dinner drink, you can't get more typical than Xtabentún, a liqueur made with anise seed, fermented honey and rum. True Xtabentún is made with honey that bees extract from the flowers of the Xtabentún vine (related to morning glory). You can drink it straight, on the rocks, add it to coffee, or in unique mixed drinks. You can buy this liqueur on-line, but wouldn't it be more fun to bring back a bottle after a trip to the Yucatán?

Opposite page, fom l. to r.: Agua de jamaica *(page 157),* naranjada *(page 154) and* horchata *(page 154).*

Right, from top: Exotic *pitayas*; dancers wearing traditional dress perform in the town square in Mérida, Yucatán; and ripe papayas.

CHAPTER 11: DRINKS/REFRESCOS 153

Horchata

Rice Drink

Makes about 30 large servings (photo on page 152)

Té de canela (Cinnamon Tea) and Syrup

1/2 gallon water

4 cinnamon sticks

1 pound rice flour

2 pounds sugar

1 teaspoon almond extract

1 tablespoon vanilla extract

Horchata

1/4 gallon prepared syrup

4 quarts water

Making *horchata* is a two-step process. First, you make a tea of cinnamon, then a rice-flour syrup. These are then added together to make a refreshing drink that is great with *cochinita pibil* (see recipe). Don't be put off by the large quantities of ingredients called for. You'll be glad you made enough.

To make the té and Prepared Syrup

1. Bring the water to a boil with the cinnamon sticks and boil for 10 minutes.

2. In a large bowl, add 1/4 gallon of the cinnamon tea (from step 1) with the rice flour, sugar, almond extract, and vanilla extract. With a handheld emulsion blender, mix well.

To make the horchata

1. Blend the prepared syrup and the water

2. Serve the *horchata* in tall glasses on ice

Notes: You can keep syrup refrigerated for up to 2 to 3 months. However, once you mix the syrup with water, it is best served the very same day.

Naranjada

Orange Drink

Makes about 6 servings (photo on page 152)

Ingredients

Juice of 12–14 oranges (navel, Valencia or Texas)

3 quarts water

1/2 cup sugar

This simple drink is found in the Yucatán wherever fresh drinks or *aguas frescas* are made. Unlike orange juice, this has a hearty dose of water putting it in the "drink" category. If you prefer your drink "juicier," add more orange juice or less water. Something else that is common in the Yucatán is the *chineros* who entice you to buy fresh oranges to enjoy on the spot. They have hand-powered machines that peel the oranges that they then serve with salt and chile. In the Yucatán oranges are called "*chinas*."

1. Juice the oranges and add the water and sugar. Make sure to dissolve the sugar thoroughly. Chill and/or serve on ice.

Notes: I am very sensitive to the nuances between the different oranges. Once you cut the oranges, they start to get *amargo* or bitter, and how fast that happens depends on the orange. If you use navel oranges it is best to serve the *naranjada* right away. If you select Valencia oranges the drink will keep a day; with Texas oranges it keeps for up to 2 days.

REFRESCO DE DE NARANJA AGRIA

SEVILLE ORANGE DRINK

Makes about 6 servings

You've been introduced to the Seville orange or *naranja agria* already (see Glossary). As you might imagine, its pungent and extra-strength flavor makes for a wonderfully refreshing beverage. The recipe is the same as for *naranjada* except for the quantity of sugar. This tart fruit needs more sweetness. Do not use bottled *naranja agria* juice to make this drink.

1. Juice the *naranjas agrias* and add the water and sugar. Make sure to dissolve the sugar thoroughly. Chill and/or serve on ice.

INGREDIENTS

Juice of 12–14 *naranjas agrias* *(Seville oranges (Jan/Feb))*

3 quarts water

1 cup sugar

LIMONADA

LIMEADE

Makes about 6 servings

Here's yet another 1-2-3 fruit drink recipe. If you use the smaller Key limes, also known as Mexican limes (see side bar on page 114), you may need to adjust the recipe slightly. You might need more fruit and/or more sugar. Interestingly enough, lemons are not that commonly found or used in the Yucatán—hence "limeade" instead of "lemonade." But if all else fails, you can use regular or Meyer lemons too.

1. Juice the limes and add the water and sugar. Make sure to dissolve the sugar thoroughly. Chill and/or serve on ice.

INGREDIENTS

Juice of 6–8 limes, Persian or Key

3 quarts water

1 cup sugar

REFRESCO DE GUANÁBANA

GUANÁBANA DRINK

Makes about 4–5 servings

Guanábana—a tropical fruit with a delicate fragrance, color and taste (see Glossary)—lends itself to a delicious beverage and a cooling sorbet (see recipe). Other common names for the fruit include *graviola* and Brazilian pawpaw. Because the fresh fruit might be hard to find, look for the frozen pulp. You can find it in Latino or Asian markets.

1. Let the pulp partially defrost until soft and pliable.

2. In a blender add the pulp, sugar and water and blend until well mixed. Chill and/or serve on ice.

Notes: If you want to make *refresco de mamey* or mango, just substitute the frozen pulp of those fruits in this recipe.

INGREDIENTS

1 package (12 ounces) frozen pulp of *guanábana*

3/4 cup sugar

2 quarts water

CHAPTER 11: DRINKS/REFRESCOS 155

Refresco de Sandía

Watermelon Drink

Makes about 4–5 servings

Ingredients

2 cups chopped watermelon

3/4 cup sugar

2 quarts water

Nothing makes you think of summer like a nice, cold watermelon. Here's another way to enjoy it. A seedless water melon is best.

1. In a blender add the watermelon, sugar and water and blend until well mixed. Chill and/or serve on ice.

Refresco de Pitaya

Dragon Fruit Drink

Makes about 4–5 servings (the fruit is pictured on page 153)

Ingredients

2 cups peeled and chopped *pitaya*

3/4 cup sugar

2 quarts water

Pitaya is the fruit of a cactus (see Glossary). It is very common in the Yucatán, where it is cultivated. Its exotic look is sure to impress as is its kiwi-like taste. Try it freshly sliced or make ice cream.

1. Mash the *pitaya* and mix well with sugar and water. Chill and/or serve on ice. Garnish with a slice of lime.

Plátano con Leche

Banana Shake

Makes about 3 servings

Ingredients

3 cups milk

2 bananas, sliced (or 3–4 *guineos*)

3 tablespoons sugar

4 drops of vanilla extract

If you've got milk and bananas, give them a whirl in a blender for a simple, yet yummy drink. If you can find the petite bananas I call *guineos*, then the drink will be even tastier.

1. Put the milk, bananas, sugar and vanilla extract in a blender and blend.

2. Serve right away in tall glasses, but do not serve on ice. Finish it with a sprinkling of cinnamon.

Mamey con Leche

Mamey Shake

Makes about 3 servings (fruit is pictured on page 159 and 181)

Ingredients

1 package (12 ounces) frozen *mamey* pulp

3 cups milk

3 tablespoons sugar

Mamey (see Glossary), with its sandpaper skin, hides a delicious interior. Cut one open and you get a burst of vivid, burnt orange and a pulp that can be scooped out with a spoon like custard. Hard to get stateside, look for the frozen pulp. Try this with frozen *guanábana* pulp too.

1. Partially defrost *mamey* pulp until pliable.

2. Put the pulp, milk and sugar in a blender and blend. Serve right away.

Papaya con Leche

Papaya Shake

Makes about 3 servings (the fruit is pictured on page 153)

Papayas (see Glossary) are relatively easy to find year-round and are delicious served sliced with a spritz of lime. Put in a blender with some milk and sugar and you've got *papaya con leche*.

1. Put the papaya, milk and sugar in a blender and blend.

2. Serve right away.

Notes: Make sure to serve this refreshing drink right away. Let it sit for a bit and it gets bitter and off tasting.

Ingredients

2 cups roughly chopped papaya, peeled and seeded

3 cups milk

3 tablespoons sugar

Agua de Jamaica

Hibiscus-flower Drink

Makes about 10 servings (photo on page 152)

Slightly astringent and colored a lovely, deep burgundy, this drink is particularly refreshing. Dried hibiscus flowers, or actually the dried sepals and calyces of *Hibiscus sabdariffa* flowers (see "jamaica" in Glossary), are infused in water to make a concentrate that is then mixed with water and sugar to make the drink. It's easy to stain clothes and countertops when making this beverage, so be careful. Use glass or stainless steel pots and bowls.

Making the concentrate

1. Put the hibiscus flowers in large pot and cover with 1/2 gallon of water. Bring to a boil, then lower to high simmer for 20 minutes.

2. Strain the flowers, returning them to the pot. Reserve the infused water on the side.

3. Pour the remaining 1/2 gallon of water over flowers. Bring to a boil, then lower to high simmer for another 20 minutes.

4. Strain flowers and discard.

5. Combine the two batches of infused waters. Because the flowers will have absorbed a lot of water, you will end up with about 2 1/2 quarts (or 10 cups) of *jamaica* concentrate.

Making the agua de jamaica

1. Mix the concentrate, water and sugar. Blend well and chill and/or serve on ice.

Notes: The extra concentrate will keep refrigerated for several months if you can resist using it all. As for the straining, you can use a regular strainer, but I prefer to use paper filters because it results in a very crystalline *agua*. In fact, I prefers to use paper filters when straining stocks and other liquids because it keeps out more impurities and results in cleaner, clearer liquids.

Jamaica concentrate (makes 1 gallon)

1/2 pound dried hibiscus flowers

1 gallon water (divided)

Agua de jamaica

1 quart *jamaica* concentrate (above)

2 quarts water

1 cup sugar

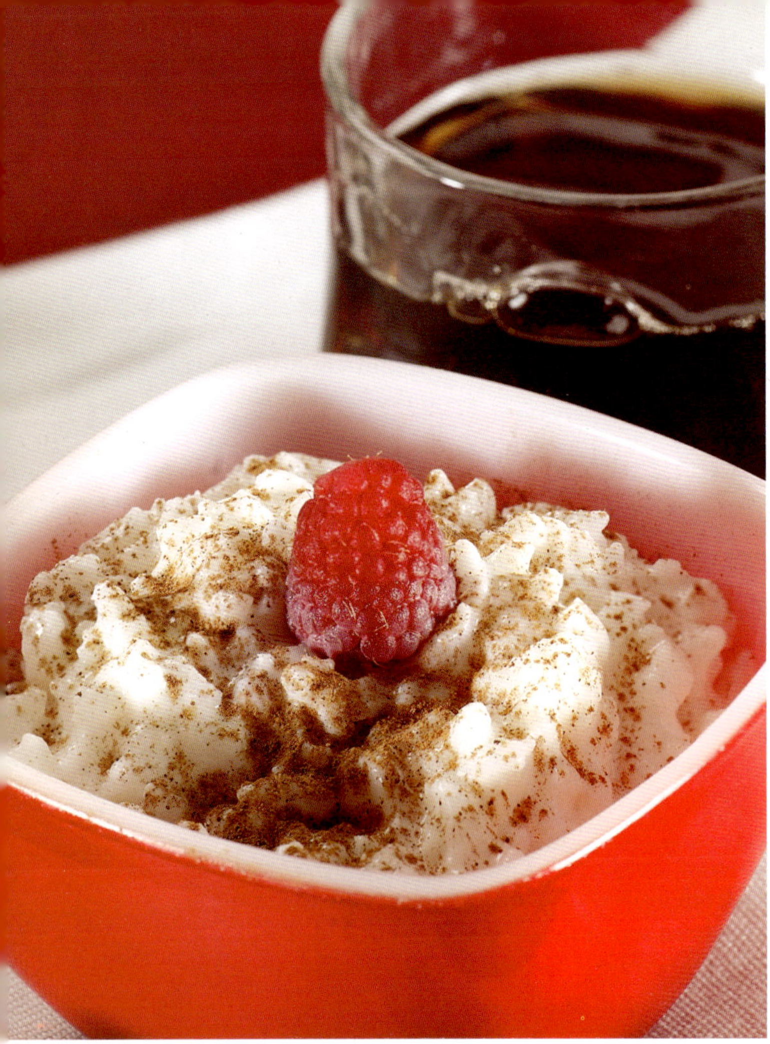

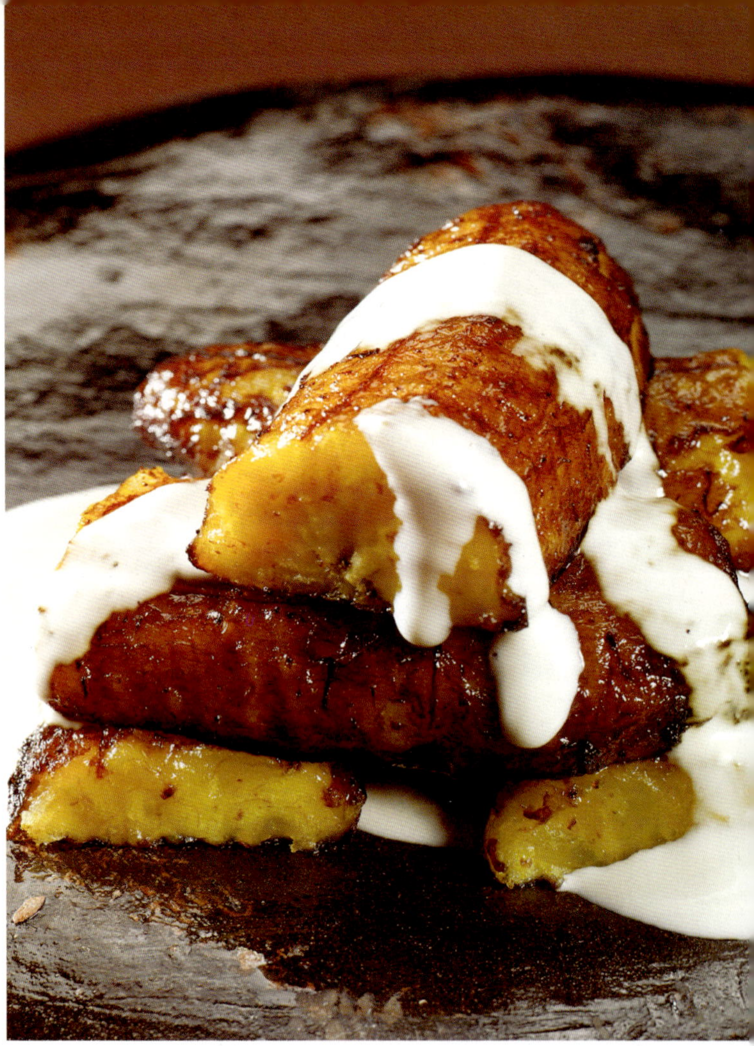

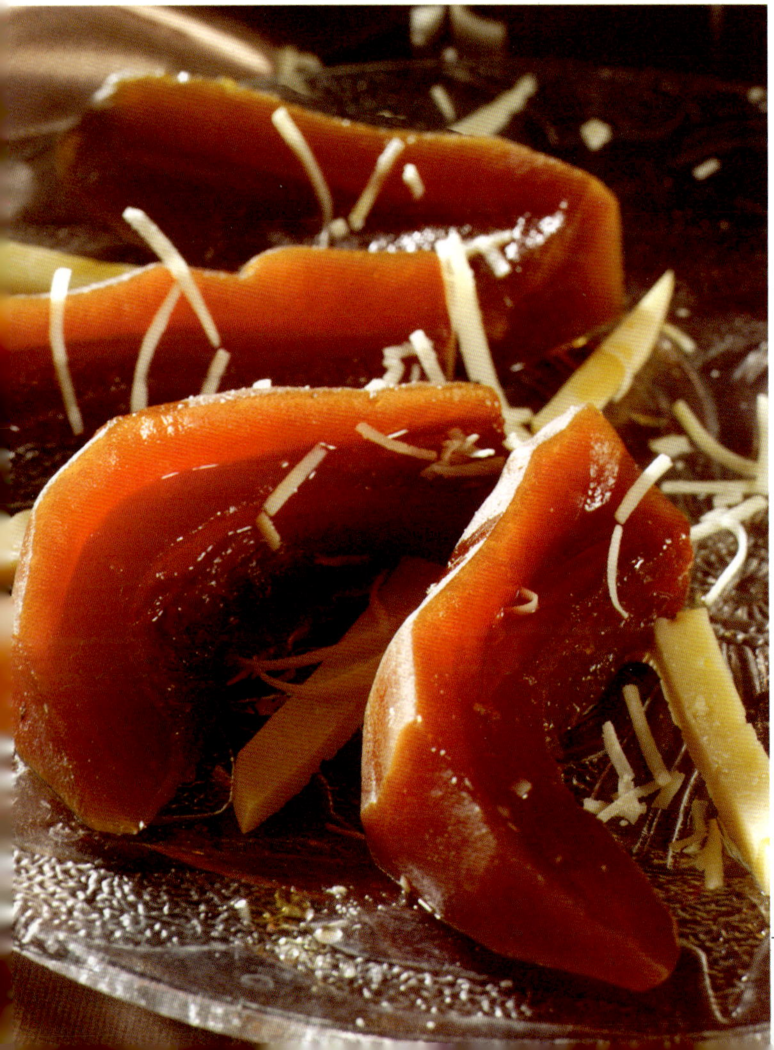

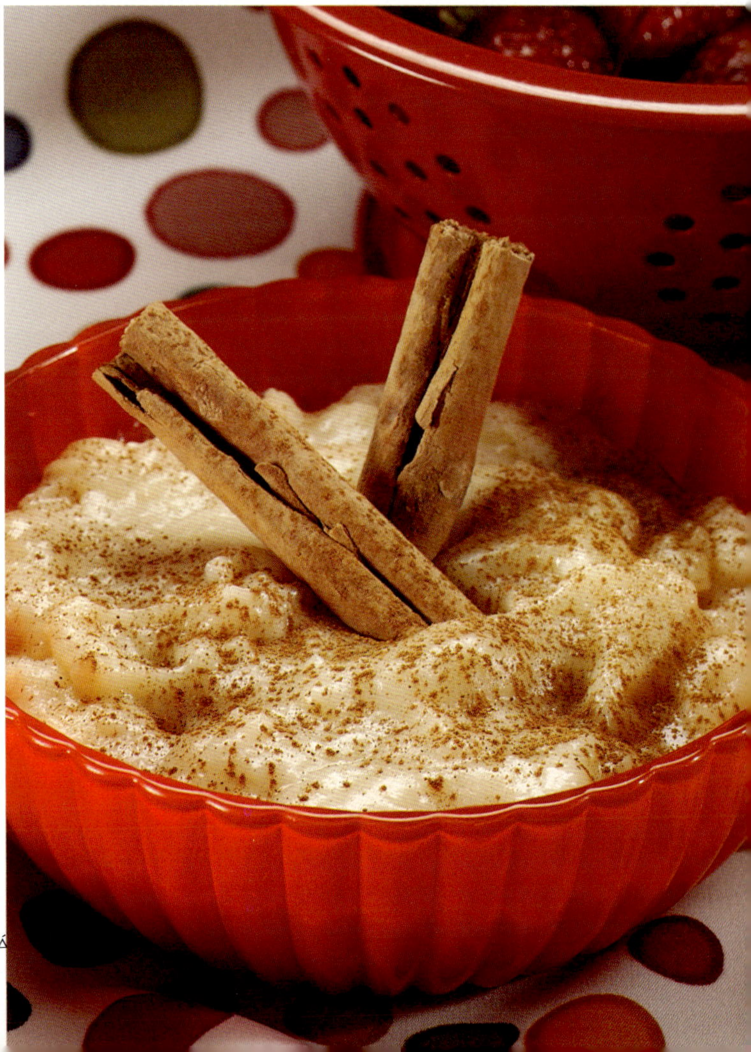

CHAPTER 12

DESSERTS...
POSTRES

Enough with the savory stuff already! What's for dessert?

While the Maya may have sweetened their foods and beverages with the honey produced by their highly prized honey bees (see Glossary) and put vanilla beans (see Glossary) to good use, surely the arrival of sugar cane and dairy products along with recipes from the Old World opened up a whole new world of sweet treats.

Among the recipes here are classics that came with the Spaniards and others. You will find a selection of custard-type desserts, such as flan, *crema española*, *crema de coco* and *arroz con leche*.

Other desserts reflect the peninsula's Caribbean connection and take advantage of such tropical fruits as papaya, *guanábana*, *maracuyá* and coconut. (See tropical fruits listed in Glossary.)

Finally, other sweet endings are particular to the Yucatán. *Caballeros pobres* or *pastelitos de atropellados* anyone?

Opposite page, clockwise from top left: Arroz con leche, *(page 164),* plátanos con crema *(page 144),* crema española *(page 164), and* papaya en almíbar *(page 165).*

Right, from top: Mazapán *sweets, in all shapes and colors, are made with pumpkin seeds versus almonds as in Spain; buying palm-woven hats in Becal, Campeche; and sliced* mameyes *reveal their lush interiors.*

FLAN
CARAMEL CUSTARD

Serves about 8

INGREDIENTS

1 1/2–2 cups sugar (divided) (see serving and cooking options below)

2 tablespoons water, if needed

6 eggs

2 cups whole milk

1 teaspoon vanilla extract

Flan is a very common dessert throughout Latin America. This recipe starts with a sugar caramel that coats the top of the flan, giving it its typical look and taste. Just be careful not to burn the sugar because you'll have to start all over again.

1. Melt 1 cup sugar in a pan over low heat, stirring constantly with a wooden spoon, until it reaches a golden, caramel-like color. Pour this caramel in equal amounts into the bottom of eight 4-ounce serving dishes or molds and tilt each one until the caramel coats the bottom and sides. (If needed, add a bit of water to make it easier to handle, but only after the caramelizing process.)

2. Beat the remaining 1 cup sugar, eggs, milk and vanilla extract until well blended, but do not over mix. Pour into the prepared dishes or molds.

3. Cover each dish or mold with plastic wrap and place in a baking dish. Fill the baking dish with water to at least halfway up the sides of the molds. Cover all with foil and cook on the stove over medium heat until firm, about 15–20 minutes or until a knife inserted in the center comes out clean.

To serve: Cool slightly and un-mold each flan on a small plate making sure the caramel isn't left behind. Should the flan stick, dip the dish or mold in warm water for just a few seconds.

SERVING AND COOKING OPTIONS
FLAN AND QUESO NAPOLITANO

You can also prepare the *flan* and *queso napolitano* in 9-inch cake pans. Caramelize the sugar right in the pan if using an aluminum cake pan, and tilt to coat the bottom and sides. Use 1/2 cup sugar for this. Pour the egg-milk mixture into the cake pan. Cover with foil, place in a baking dish filled with water at least halfway up the sides of the pan, and bake at 350°F for 45 minutes to 1 hour or until a knife inserted into the center comes out clean. Cool and unmold onto a platter. Should the *flan* or *queso napolitano* stick, dip the cake pan in warm water for just a few seconds. You can also refrigerate either and unmold later.

Queso Napolitano

Neapolitan Custard

Serves about 8

This is a variation of flan but with a punch of extra richness from the condensed milk. This version is particularly popular in the Yucatán, especially for the Christmas Eve meal. The instructions are the same as for the flan.

1. Melt the sugar in a pan over low heat, stirring constantly with a wooden spoon, until it reaches a golden, caramel-like color. Pour this caramel in equal amounts into the bottom of eight, 4-ounce, serving dishes or molds and tilt each one until the caramel coats the bottom and sides. (If needed, add a bit of water to make it easier to handle, but only after the caramelizing process.)

2. Beat the eggs, condensed milk, whole milk and vanilla extract until well blended, but do not over mix. Pour into the prepared dishes or molds.

3. Cover each dish or mold with plastic wrap and place in a baking dish. Fill the baking dish with water to at least half way up the sides of the dishes or molds. Cover all with foil and cook on the stove over medium heat until firm, about 15–20 minutes.

To serve: Cool slightly and unmold each *queso napolitano* on a small plate making sure the caramel isn't left behind. Should the custard stick, dip the dish or mold in warm water for just a few seconds.

Ingredients

1/2–1 cup sugar (see serving and cooking options on opposite page)

2 tablespoons water, if needed

5 eggs

1 can (14 ounces) condensed milk

1 1/2 cups whole milk

1 teaspoon vanilla extract

Crema de Coco

Coconut Custard

Serves about 6

Ingredients

2 cans (13.5 ounces each) coconut cream

3/4 cup sugar

3 eggs

3 tablespoons cornstarch

1/2 teaspoon vanilla extract

Ground cinnamon

This dessert is essentially *crema española* (see recipe) but uses coconut cream instead of whole milk. Who knows, you might even prefer this to *crema española* or *manjar blanco* (see recipe)! You'll just have to try them all.

1. In a blender add the coconut cream, sugar, eggs, cornstarch and vanilla extract. Blend until well mixed, but do not over mix.

2. Pour into a pot and heat over medium heat for 8–10 minutes, mixing constantly until it thickens but can still be poured.

3. Pour into individual serving dishes (or one large bowl to serve family style) and chill.

4. When ready to serve, sprinkle lightly with ground cinnamon.

Notes: The solids may have separated from the liquids in a can of coconut cream. So give the can a good shake before opening or a good mixing after opening it.

Manjar Blanco

Milk Custard

Serves about 6

Unlike *crema española* or *crema de coco* (see recipes), *manjar blanco* is gelatinous (like Jello), and if chilled in a square baking dish can be cut into squares to serve. Cinnamon lovers will love the very generous covering of ground cinnamon that should blanket this dessert.

1. Place the coconut cream, water, rice flour and sugar in a pot and heat over medium heat, mixing constantly until it thickens to the point where you can see the bottom of the pan as you stir or if you drop a dollop on a plate and tilt it, it does not run.

2. Pour into individual serving dishes (or in a 9-inch square baking dish) and chill.

3. When ready to serve, sprinkle extremely generously with ground cinnamon.

Ingredients

1 can (13.5 ounces) coconut cream

2 1/2 cups water

4 ounces rice flour (about 2/3 cup)

1/2 cup sugar

Ground cinnamon

Crema Española

Spanish Custard

Serves about 6 (photo on page 158)

Ingredients

3 cups whole milk

3/4 cup sugar

3 eggs

3 tablespoons cornstarch

1/2 teaspoon vanilla extract

Ground cinnamon

This silky, pudding-like dessert is easy to make and is a crowd pleaser. For a pretty presentation, pour into individual serving dishes and then chill. At least that way portions are controlled . . . unless folks go back for seconds or thirds. You had better make enough!

1. Beat the milk, sugar, eggs, cornstarch and vanilla extract until well blended, but do not over mix.

2. Pour into a pot and heat over medium heat for 8–10 minutes, mixing constantly until it thickens but can still be poured.

3. Pour into individual serving dishes or one large bowl to serve family style and chill.

4. When ready to serve, sprinkle lightly with ground cinnamon.

Arroz con Leche

Rice Pudding

Serves about 8–10 (photo on page 158)

Ingredients

2 cups water

1 cup short-grain white rice

2–3 cups whole milk (depending on preferred consistency)

1 can (14 ounces) condensed milk

1 cinnamon stick

2 teaspoons vanilla extract

Ground cinnamon

This classic dessert is particularly popular during the Christmas holidays. I likes my *arroz con leche* watery like an *atole*. In fact, there's something very satisfying about drinking *arroz con leche* with a warm *panucho* (see recipe).

1. In a pan, bring the water to a boil and add the rice. Reduce the heat to simmer, cover and let the rice cook for 15–20 minutes until the rice is fluffy and tender.

2. To the cooked rice add 2 cups milk, condensed milk, cinnamon stick, vanilla extract and pinch of salt. Stir over medium heat for another 10–15 minutes or until it thickens but can still be poured. If you like your *arroz con leche* less thick, add more milk.

3. Pour into individual serving dishes (or one large bowl to serve family style). Chill or serve at room temperature. Sprinkle lightly with cinnamon upon serving.

Notes: If you like, add shredded coconut, raisins and/or nuts to your *arroz con leche* toward the end of the cooking process.

Papaya en Almíbar
Papaya in Syrup

Serves 8–12 (photo on page 158)

This dessert is light, refreshing and not too sweet. Soaking the papaya slices in quicklime hardens the outside of the papaya but allows the syrup to seep in to sweeten the fruit. Be careful, however, because if you soak in the quicklime too long the fruit hardens. Other kinds of fruits work well too. Try the recipe with guava, apricot, peach, honeydew melon, cantaloupe, squash (kabocha or banana), as well as harder to find *tejocote* or *nance*.

1. Peel the papaya and cut in half, crosswise. Remove the seeds. Then slice each half into 12 wedges (about 1-inch wide).

2. In a large pot, dissolve the quicklime completely in 1 gallon water and add the papaya wedges. Soak for 1 1/2 hours.

3. Remove the papaya wedges and rinse in cold water several times until you have thoroughly removed the quicklime and the water runs clear.

4. In a large stockpot, add 2 cups sugar. Over a low heat, stir the sugar with a wooden spoon until the sugar melts and caramelizes, taking on a deep, brown color (like *piloncillo*). Be careful not to burn the sugar or you will have to start all over again.

5. Pour the remaining 1 gallon water into the caramelized sugar, mix well and raise heat. Let the sugar dissolve again if it seizes up with the addition of the water. Add the remaining 2 cups sugar, cinnamon sticks and papaya slices, and bring to a boil. Then reduce the heat to a simmer and leave covered for 3–3 1/2 hours or until the syrup is reduced by a quarter to one half.

6. Chill.

To serve: Serve 2–3 slices of papaya per person accompanied by a slice of baby Edam or Gouda cheese, and drizzle with a tablespoon or two of syrup.

Ingredients

1 papaya (about 3 pounds), not overly ripe

2 gallons water (divided)

1 tablespoon quicklime (see Glossary)

4 cups sugar (divided)

2–3 cinnamon sticks

Slices of baby Edam cheese (or Gouda cheese as a second choice)

HONEY: THE BUZZ

The ancient Maya domesticated stingless bees and practiced beekeeping. They harvested the honey and wax for personal use and as trade goods. The honey was used as a sweetener and antibiotic and as the main ingredient in an alcoholic beverage called "*balché*," which survives the Conquest. Hives were collected from the wild and placed in hollow logs close to home. The hives were often handed down from one generation to another. The bee was considered a link to the spirit world and a gift from Ah Muzen Cab, the bee god. Following the Conquest, the Maya paid tribute to their conquerors in honey and beeswax.

CABALLEROS POBRES
Poor Boys

Serves about 6

INGREDIENTS

2 French rolls (8-inch long each), sliced into 1-inch slices (about 6 slices per roll)

4 eggs

Vegetable oil

3/4 gallon water

2 cups sugar

2 cinnamon sticks

1/2 cup raisins

2 tablespoons sliced, blanched almonds

This humble dessert is the poor man's answer to *torrijas* (and even *torrejas*), a rich dessert that features *pan de leche* (a sweet milk bread) soaked in rich milk. These poorer relations are made with day-old bread and are soaked in a syrupy water. They are just as good.

1. Toast the bread slices in a 375°-400°F oven for about 7 to 8 minutes, making sure they are toasted on each side.

2. Separate the egg yolks from the egg whites. Beat the egg whites until they form soft peaks; gently fold in the egg yolks.

3. In a frying pan, heat the oil about 1-inch deep over medium heat.

4. Dip each slice of bread into the egg mixture, covering both sides. Place in the frying pan and fry until golden on both sides. Remove and drain on paper towels.

5. Bring the water to a boil in a large, wide stockpot (2–3 gallon). Add the sugar, cinnamon sticks, raisins and almonds. Boil for 5 to 6 minutes until flavors blend together and the syrup slightly thickens (but not as thick as maple syrup). Lower the heat to simmer. This is the syrup.

6. Add the battered and fried bread slices to the syrup. The slices will float, so use a large spoon to push them down until they absorb enough liquid to stay submerged. Simmer for 5 to 6 minutes.

7. Turn off heat, cover and let the bread slices rest for about an hour in the syrup. They will puff up.

To serve: Best served at room temperature, although some people like them warm like French toast. Two slices drenched in syrup, with raisins and almonds, make a single serving.

Note: It seems counter intuitive to submerge the fried and battered bread slices in the watery syrup, but that's what makes *caballeros pobres* juicy. However, it is important to get the balance of water and sugar right or the bread will get soggy. And when the slices are resting in the syrup it is important to cover the stockpot so they puff up.

BUÑUELOS DE YUCA

Cassava Fritters

Makes about 15 fritters

These are not exactly the same as New Orleans' famed beignets, but you get the same high when you eat one of them freshly made. Crunchy on the outside, soft on the inside and drenched in honey, you won't be able to eat just one—or three as recommended for a serving.

Preparing the yuca

1. Bring the water to a boil and add the *yuca*, lime juice and salt. Cook for about 20–25 minutes or until the *yuca* is tender.

2. Drain the *yuca* and mash. Take out the thick fibers that run through the pieces of yuca. Set aside.

Preparing the fritters

1. Combine the mashed *yuca*, salt, eggs and flour and mix well.

2. Pour oil into a hot skillet about 1-1 1/2 inches deep (or use a deep fryer at 375°F).

3. Using a teaspoon (dinnerware, not measuring teaspoon), drop a heaping spoonful of the batter into the hot oil and fry on both sides until golden. Remove and drain on paper towels.

4. While still warm serve drizzled with honey. Three fritters make a serving.

For the yuca (cassava)

1/2 gallon water.

1 pound frozen and peeled *yuca* (cassava)

Juice of 1 lime

1 tablespoon salt

For the batter

Mashed *yuca*

1 teaspoon salt

2 eggs

1/3 cup all-purpose flour

Vegetable oil

Honey

PASTELITOS DE ATROPELLADO
Sweet Potato and Coconut Turnovers

Makes about 20 turnovers

Ingredients

2 1/2 cups all-purpose flour

1 1/2 teaspoons salt

3/4 cup warm water

3/4 cup unsalted butter or margarine

2 pound yams or sweet potatoes, peeled and diced into 1-inch pieces

Water

1 cup unsweetened coconut, shredded

1 cup sugar

1 tablespoon vanilla extract

Powdered sugar

These turnovers are popular during the *fiestas decembrinas* (Christmas holidays). You can't eat just one of them, so don't think for a minute that you can make too many. To ante up the delight factor, serve with vanilla ice cream and fresh strawberries (as pictured on page 6).

1. Mix the flour, salt and warm water.

2. Melt the butter and while warm (not hot) add to the flour mixture. Mix well until it forms a pliable dough. Knead right in the mixing bowl for 1–2 minutes until smooth.

3. Divide the dough into balls about 1 1/2 inch in diameter (golf-ball size). Cover with plastic wrap or a moist towel to keep dough moist, and let rest at room temperature for an hour. Do not over handle.

4. In a pot, cover the yams or sweet potatoes in water. Cook until they are tender, about 15–20 minutes. Drain well.

5. Mash the yams or sweet potatoes and add the coconut, sugar and vanilla extract. Mix until well blended. Set aside.

6. Preheat oven to 350°F.

7. Roll out the balls of dough into 4 1/2- to 5-inch discs. Or use a tortilla press by placing a ball of dough between 2 sheets of plastic wrap and pressing down on tortilla press until desired the disc is achieved. (Remove top sheet of plastic wrap before filling.)

8. Place about 1 1/2 to 2 teaspoons of the yam or sweet potato and coconut filling in the center of each disc and fold the disc over. Using tines of a fork, seal the edges of the turnover.

9. Sprinkle a cookie sheet with flour and place the turnovers on the sheet. Bake for 25–30 minutes or until golden on the bottom. Cool on a rack.

10. When cool, toss in lots of powdered sugar and serve.

Notes: No surprise that you can make turnovers with different fillings. Try pineapple, *guayaba* (guava paste), or *guayaba* and cheese. Savory fillings include cheese (I like cheddar) and meat (like *carne molida,* see recipe). But don't leave off the powdered sugar—the sweet and salty tastes are wonderful.

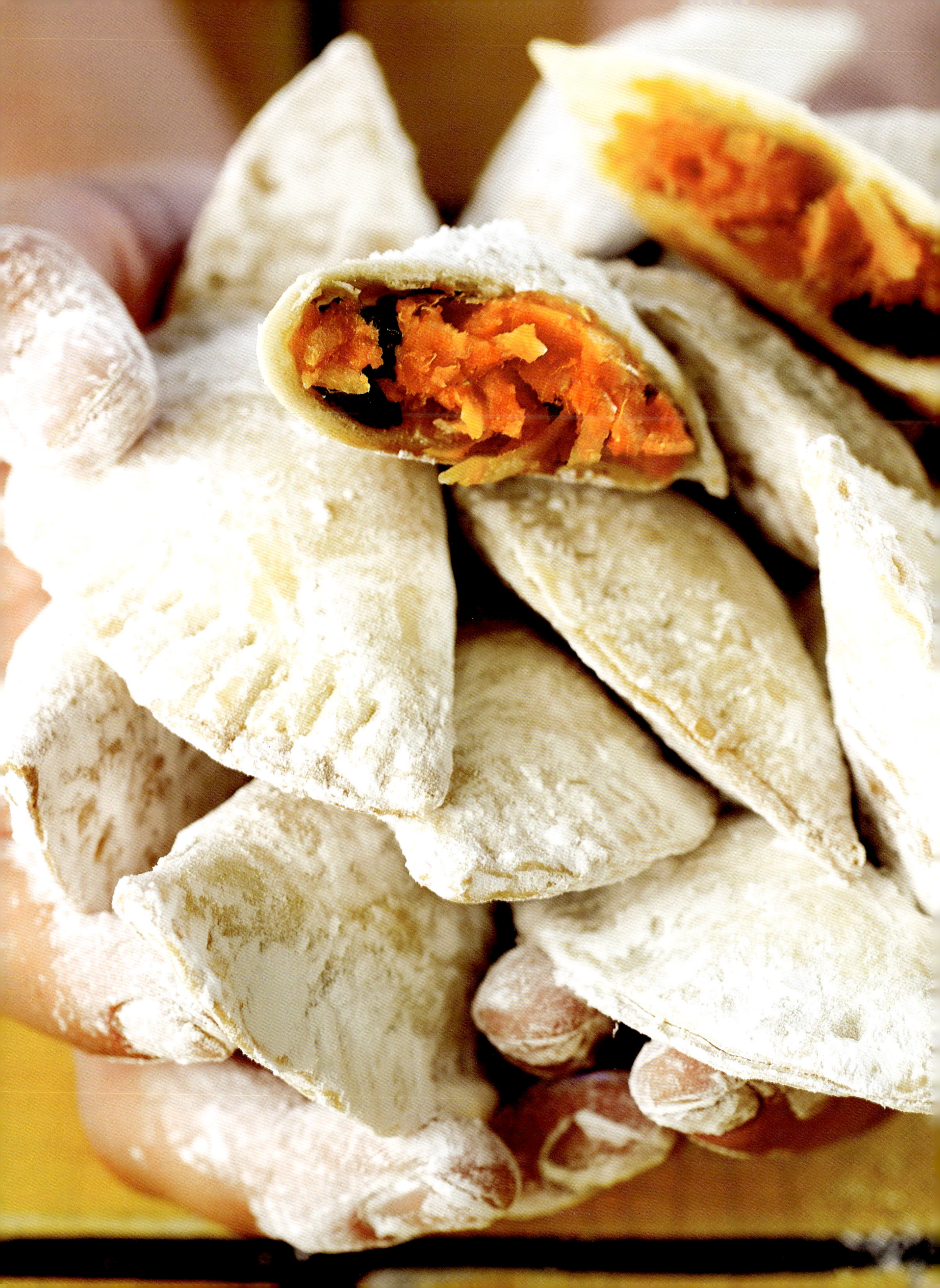

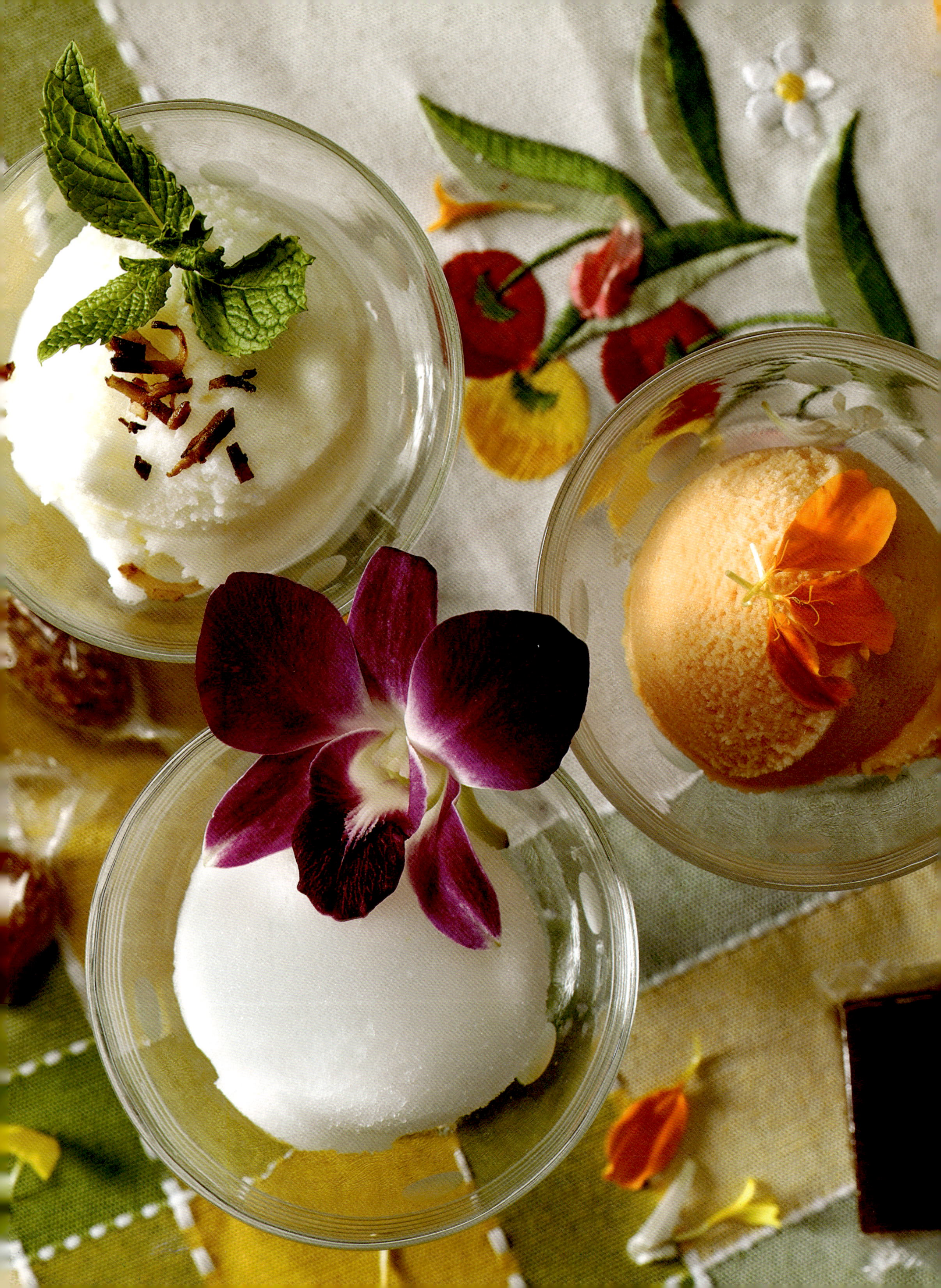

Sorbets and Ice Creams

Throughout the Yucatán, it is easy to find sorbets and ice creams made out of a wide variety of tropical fruits. Look for such flavors as mango, *nance, saramullo, anona, pitaya* and *zapote*. Street vendors on tricycles tempt with their wooden boxes harboring several flavors in containers surrounded by crushed ice and salt to keep the frozen treats cool for an entire day. They announce their approach with their telltale bell.

Sorbete de Guanábana
Guanábana Sorbet

Makes about 1/2 gallon (bottom in photo to left)

If you liked the *refresco de guanábana* (see recipe), you'll love this fragrant sorbet. Again, it's easy to make using frozen pulp.

1. Heat the water in a stockpot just to the point of boiling and add the sugar. Stir constantly with a wooden spoon or whisk until it losses its opaqueness and becomes clear. Do not boil.

2. Let the syrup cool.

3. Once the syrup is cooled, add the *guanábana* pulp and mix well. Pour into a glass bowl, cover and chill overnight or for 24 hours.

4. Place the chilled syrup and pulp mixture in an ice cream maker and process following the manufacturer's instructions.

Ingredients

1 3/4 cups water

1 1/2 cups sugar

2 packages (14 ounces each) frozen *guanábana* pulp, thawed

Sorbete de Maracuyá
Passion Fruit Sorbet

Makes about 1/2 gallon

Maracuyá (passion fruit, see Glossary) is not much to look at. Its smooth to wrinkly papery skin—whether yellow or purple—does not hint at the jeweled beads of flavor clustered inside. But once you get a taste of its heavenly tanginess, you'll be hooked. But because the fresh fruit can be hard to find and is generally costly, it's good to know that the frozen pulp works just fine in this sorbet recipe.

1. Heat the water in a stockpot just to the point of boiling and add the sugar. Stir constantly with a wooden spoon until it losses its opaqueness and becomes clear. Do not boil.

2. Let the syrup cool.

3. Once the syrup is cooled, add the *maracuyá* pulp and mix well. Pour into a glass bowl, cover and chill overnight or for 24 hours.

4. Place the chilled syrup and pulp mixture in an ice cream maker and process following the manufacturer's instructions.

Ingredients

1 3/4 cups water

1 1/2 cups sugar

2 packages (14 ounces each) frozen *maracuyá* pulp, thawed

Opposite page, clockwise from top left: helado de coco *(page 173),* helado de mamey *(page 173), and* sorbete de guanábana *(this page).*

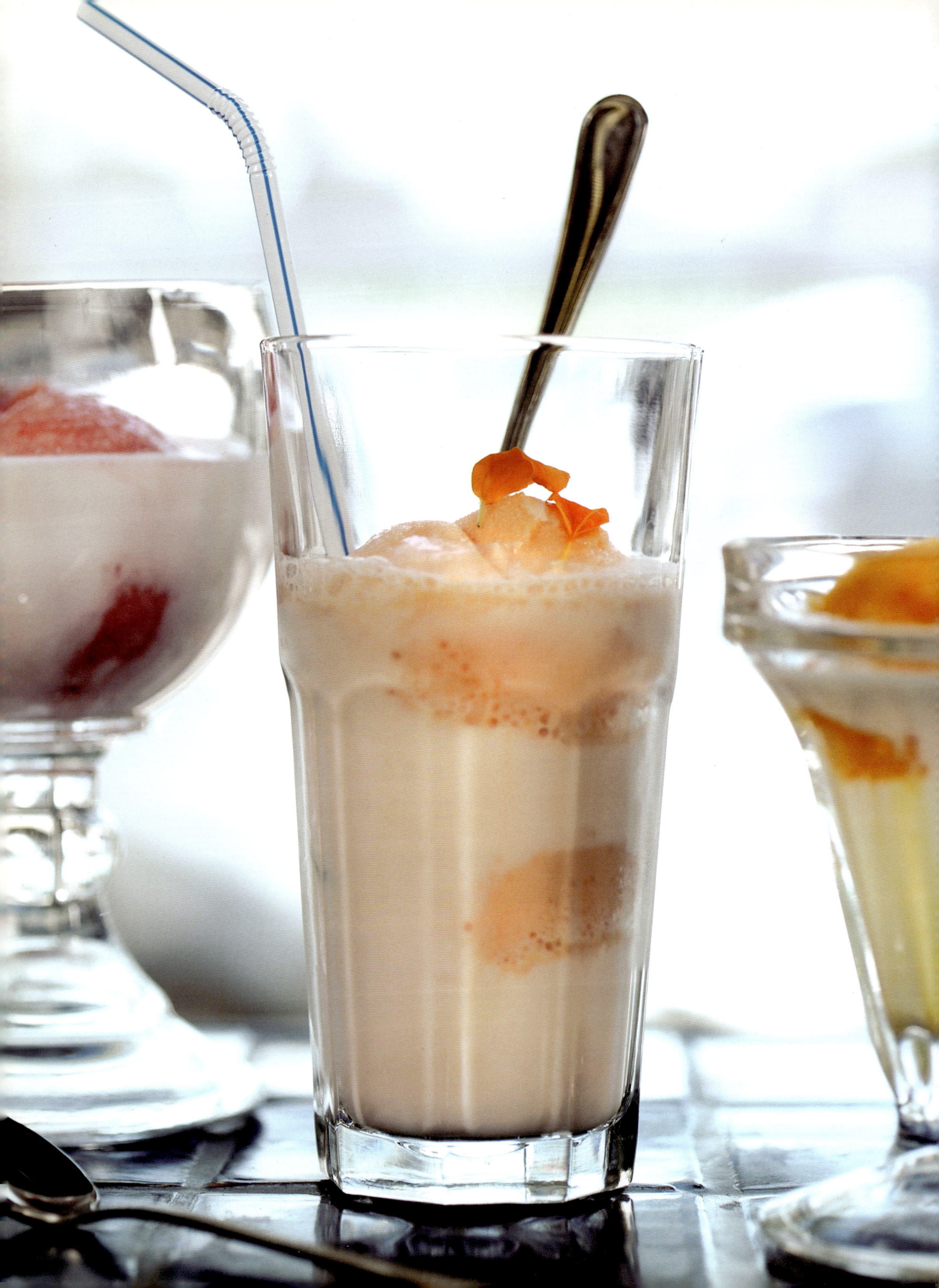

Helado de Mamey

Mamey Ice Cream

Makes about 1/2 gallon (right in photo on page 170)

Fresh *mamey* is hard to find so use the frozen pulp to make this ice cream that captures the beauty of the fruit's color and taste.

1. Heat the condensed milk and Half and Half in a stockpot just to the point of boiling. Stir constantly with a wooden spoon until it thickens slightly. Do not boil.

2. Let this mixture cool.

3. Once cooled, add the thawed *mamey* pulp and mix well. Pour into a glass bowl, cover and chill overnight or for 24 hours.

4. Place the chilled syrup-and-pulp mixture in an ice cream maker and process following the manufacturer's instructions.

Ingredients

1 can (14 ounces) condensed milk

2 cups Half and Half

2 packages (14 ounces each) frozen *mamey* pulp, thawed

Helado de Coco

Coconut Ice Cream

Makes about 3/4 to 1 gallon (left in photo on page 170)

Coconut ice cream was never easier to make. Toast some extra coconut flakes to sprinkle on top just before serving.

1. Toast the coconut in a non-stick frying pan over medium heat until fragrant and golden. Do not burn. Set aside.

2. Put the coconut cream, heavy whipping cream, sugar, vanilla and cinnamon stick in a saucepan. Simmer over a medium heat for 10–15 minutes until it slightly thickens, stirring constantly with a wooden spoon.

3. Add the toasted coconut flakes, mix well, and remove from the heat.

4. Chill the mixture in a covered glass bowl in the refrigerator overnight.

5. Strain the mixture and process in an ice cream maker following the manufacturer's instructions.

Ingredients

1 cup unsweetened coconut flakes, toasted

2 cans (13.4 ounces each) coconut cream

3 cups heavy whipping cream

1 1/4 cup sugar

1/2 teaspoon vanilla extract

1/2 cinnamon stick

Champola

Tropical Ice Cream Float

Makes 1 serving (various flavors of *champolas* in photo to left)

You can use any fruit-flavored ice cream in this float, but to make it extra special use an exotic one—such as *mamey, guanábana* or coconut. After all, that's the whole point of making it "tropical."

1. Put scoops of ice cream in a tall glass and pour milk over ice cream. Serve immediately.

Ingredients

2 scoops ice cream, your choice of flavors

Milk

TECHNIQUES

The following techniques will be helpful to you if you are not too familiar with some of the those required to prepare some of the dishes in this cookbook.

GRINDING OR CRUSHING HERBS, SPICES AND CHILES

Grinding or crushing herbs, spices and chiles before using releases their aromatic flavors and therefore better enhances their flavors in dishes. The best way to do this is by using a *molcajete* and *tejolote* (see Tools) or pestle and mortar. The texture achieved using this traditional method is distinct. But for convenience sake—and for large quantities—food processors and even blenders can be used. For hard seeds, spice or coffee grinders are best.

HANDLING CHILES HABANEROS

Because *chiles habaneros* are so hot, it's a good idea to use caution when handling them. Here are some tips that are good for handling hot chiles, like *habaneros*:
- Use plastic gloves when handling the chiles.
- Warn your guests if you have added *chile habanero* to your dishes.
- Offer *chile habanero* and hot salsas on the side, allowing everyone to add to their food at their own risk!
- If you didn't use a glove when handling, don't rub your eyes, and take care in the bathroom (men, especially).

PEELING A PLANTAIN

Plantains are harder to peel than your regular banana. To peel, cut off both ends. Then, with the tip of a knife, make a few slits lengthwise through the peel, being careful not to cut through to the fruit. Remove the peel in sections. The riper the plantain, the easier it is to peel.

PEELING CHILES

To prepare chiles to be stuffed for *chile x'catic relleno de atún* (see recipe), you are asked to remove the skin from the chiles. To do this, roast the chiles over an open flame, on a hot griddle or skillet until charred all around. Place chiles in a plastic bag and allow them to steam for 10–15 minutes. When you remove the chiles, you will find it easy to peel off the skin. Use your fingers (you might want to wear plastic gloves), a small pairing knife or rub the chiles with a clean cloth under cold water.

PIBIL

Pibil refers to a traditional way of cooking by the Maya that survives to modern times. Essentially it is the pit roasting of meats that allowed hunters to cook game meat to eat and to preserve until they were able to return home. Today, it is more common that pits are dug close to home and domestically raised pigs or cuts of pork meat are used. Home cooks will be happy to know that easier techniques have been developed to capture the essence of pibil-style cooking on a stovetop or in an oven. The Mayan word "*pibil*" means "buried." "*Pib*" means "pits." For more on *pibil*, see side bar on page 83.

PREPARING FRESH BANANA LEAVES

Banana leaves are used to wrap tamales or meats for cooking. Fresh banana leaves must first be softened. The easiest way to do this is by passing the leaves quickly over a flame of a gas burner. Be careful not to burn or char the leaves. You can also blanch in boiling water for a few seconds. Either method will make the leaves more pliable for handling and folding. For convenience sake, consider using frozen leaves that only need to be thawed. Frozen leaves, thawed, can be used right out of the bag. Also see "Get to Know Your Banana Leaf" on page 128 for more tips.

ROASTING CHILES, GARLIC, TOMATOES, ETC.

It is common in the Yucatán to roast chiles, tomatoes, onions, etc., to add depth of flavor to dishes. To do so, roast chiles, onion, garlic, etc., on direct heat on a gas burner or on a hot *comal* or in a skillet. (It will take a bit longer to roast in a skillet.) Do not remove the skin beforehand. Tomatoes are messier, so a *comal* or skillet is preferred. Make sure the heat is not too high. You want the chiles, etc., to cook while at the same time char on the outside. If the heat is too high you risk burning the outside while leaving the chiles, etc., raw on the inside. Caution: Make sure to work in a well-ventilated area when roasting hot chiles (like *habaneros*) as the fumes are choking. And wear plastic gloves when handling.

TORTILLA MAKING

Using *masa harina para tortillas* (see Glossary), make balls the size of a golf ball. Open a tortilla press and place a piece of plastic wrap. Place a ball of *masa* on top of the plastic wrap and lay another piece of plastic wrap on top. Close the press and press down firmly until you get a tortilla of the desired thickness and size. If you don't have a tortilla press, use a pie tin or frying pan. Make sure to press the corn dough between two layers of plastic wrap (or banana leaves). If you forget to do that you will be scraping dough off the press or other surface. For making *panuchos*, *salbutes* and *pastelitos de atropellados* (see recipes) note what size of ball of *masa* is requested. And note that for some tamales, banana leaves will take the place of the bottom piece of plastic wrap.

Tortilla strips
Crisp and crunchy tortilla strips are great soup toppers, and they are easy to make. Just stack a few corn tortillas and slice into thin strips. Separate and fry until crispy in hot oil. Drain on paper towels and sprinkle lightly with salt.

Tortilla test
The tortilla test is my alternative method to check to see if meats are cooked until tender. I take a corn tortilla and pinch off a piece of meat. If it comes off easily into the tortilla, it's done.

Tostadas
Tostadas are flat, crispy, fried, corn tortillas. They can be topped with beans, meats, lettuce, avocados, etc., for a crunchy treat. Here they are used for what could be called "layered" tostadas (*huevos motuleños* and *pollo ticuleño*, see recipes). They are best if made at home. Simply fry corn tortillas in vegetable oil until golden and drain on paper towels. If purchased, avoid those boxed, uniform, yellow-colored things called that claim to be "tostadas."

TOOLS

While it's fun to have specialized cooking tools, you don't always need then. Here we discuss some, but tell you how to improvise using what you already have in your kitchen.

Comal
A cooking tool long used in Mexico to cook tortillas, toast chiles, spices and vegetables, a *comal* is a smooth, flat griddle. The word comes from "*comalli*" in the Nahuatl language of the Aztecs. If you are in the market for a *comal*, look for one of cast iron, cast aluminum or carbon steel. Purchase one that is seasoned or season it yourself before using. Look on-line for tips on seasoning cookware. A griddle or skillet can be used too.

Molcajete
The Mexican version of the mortar and pestle, this rounded "bowl" on three legs was used throughout Mesoamerica to grind chiles and spices and mix salsas. While early *molcajetes* were more commonly made of ceramic, today we are more familiar with those made of heavy volcanic rock. Technically, "*molcajete*" is the mortar, while "*tejolote*" is the handheld pestle. Blenders and food processors can be used in place of *molcajetes*, but Mexican food *aficionados* (fans) prefer the texture of salsas made in a *molcajete*.

Nonreactive bowls and containers
As you will be making lots of marinades with such acidic ingredients as vinegar and citrus juices, it's best to use nonreactive bowls such as glass or stainless steel. Other types of containers that will work too are those made of food-grade plastic, ceramic, stoneware or anodized aluminum (not regular aluminum).

Plastic gloves
Disposable, plastic gloves are good to have handy for a variety of purposes. Use them to handle chiles to avoid the transfer of heat to your fingers and hands. Use them to hand mix ingredients in order to keep your hands clean. You might also want to use them when working with *recado rojo* so that you don't stain your fingers or hands. I recommend plastic or latex gloves that come in sizes from small to extra large because you can find a size that fits. The cheaper, clear, plastic gloves are fine, but may slip from your hand too easily.

Tamalera
A *tamalera* is a steamer especially designed for steaming tamales. You can find them in Latino markets or on-line. In many Mexican homes, steamers are often improvised from pots and pans and pie tins poked with holes. A *tamalera* is perfect to steam *arrolladitos de repollo* (see recipe). However, it is best to use rectangular steamers in which tamales lay flat in single layers. They are more conducive to Yucatán-style tamales.

Tortilla press
A tortilla press is a great tool to have around the kitchen. It will come in handy not only for making tortillas, but for making *panuchos, salbutes,* tamales and *pastelitos de atropellado* (see recipes). Basically, it flattens out a ball of dough into a perfectly round shape. They come in cast iron, cast aluminum, and wood. They even make electric tortilla presses that not only press out the dough but cook the tortilla at the same time. A cast iron press is good because the weight takes some of the effort out of the job. Regardless, they are not expensive and can be found in Latino markets and on-line at reasonable prices, with the exception of the much more expensive (and over-the-top) electric press. But, you don't need a press. A pie tin or frying pan will work just as well. See "Tortilla making" in Techniques.

Glossary

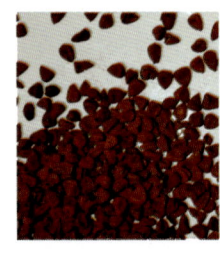

Achiote
Achiote is a bush-sized tree that produces the fruit pods that contain achiote or annatto seeds. These tiny, hard seeds are a rich chestnut color and are used in cooking for color and flavor. In the Yucatán, the ground seeds are mixed with spices and vinegar or citrus juices to make a paste, which is a signature ingredient in the region's cuisine. Its Latin designation comes from the Spanish *conquistador* Francisco de Orellana who explored the Amazon River. See side bar, page 84.

Al-sikbaj - See "escabeche."

Alcaparrado
"*Alcaparrado*" generally refers to a Mediterranean-influenced dish that contains olives, capers, garlic and raisins.

Allspice
Allspice is native to southern Mexico, Central America and the Greater Antilles. It comes from the dried, unripe fruit or berry of an evergreen tree. The green berries are dried in the sun. When brown they resemble large peppercorns, hence the Spanish name of "*pimienta*" or "*pimienta de Jamaica.*" The English name for this spice refers to the aroma it delivers of several spices, such as cinnamon, cloves, juniper, nutmeg and pepper. It is also called Jamaica pepper, *kurundu*, myrtle pepper and newspice. In ancient times, it was used to flavor chocolate and as an embalming agent. See side bar, page 17.

Avocado
The avocado tree is native to Latin America and produces the fruit that is used to make guacamole or is simply sliced or diced to use as a garnish. It is believed that it originated in southern Mexico. Technically, the fruit is a large berry with a large pit or seed. The word "avocado" comes from the Nahuatl word "*ahuacatl*" meaning "testicle." For the Aztecs, it was the "fertility fruit," hence its name. Avocados are very hard if unripe, but ripen quickly (place in a brown paper bag to speed up the ripening). If ripe, look for fruit that gives slightly when pressed. Common varieties include Hass and Fuerte. Avoid the football-sized avocados that are popular in Latin America for desserts and smoothies.

Baby Edam cheese
Edam is a Dutch cheese that comes in balls covered in two layers, the outer one of red, paraffin wax. The balls weigh between 3 and 4 pounds. As it ages, it takes on a strong flavor and is dryer and saltier than Gouda cheese. Baby Edam is less aged than regular Edam cheese, and is the cheese of choice in the Yucatán. See *queso relleno* to learn about this cheese's history in the Yucatán.

Banana leaves
Banana leaves are used in the Yucatán to wrap tamales and to cook or bake meats. It is much easier to use frozen leaves; all you need to do is thaw them out before using. They are readily available in Latino and Asian markets. To use fresh banana leaves, you must first soften them. See "Preparing fresh banana leaves" in Techniques. For more on banana leaves, see page 128.

Barra de Francés or Pan Francés
The roll of preference in the Yucatán, and a nod to European influences in that peninsula's culinary traditions, is the French roll. In fact, it's called *barra de francés* or *pan francés*. What distinguishes these rolls is the use of stems from the guano palm that are placed on top of each roll lengthwise that makes slicing the tops of the rolls unnecessary. *Barras* are leaner than your average *bolillos* (see entry), which make good substitutes.

Bell peppers/Chile dulce
Sometimes referred to as "sweet peppers," bell peppers come in an array of colors from bright yellow to deep burgundy. Unlike other fruits in the Capsicum famil, bell peppers are not hot. They are native to Latin America. Technically, in the Yucatán, a chile called "*chile dulce*" is used. But because it is hard to find stateside, green and red bell peppers can be used.

Black beans
Beans, a New World food, are a diverse group of legumes. The bean of choice in the Yucatán is the black bean (*frijol negro* or black turtle bean). The common bean, of which the black bean is one, has been cultivated in the Americas for thousands of years and may have originated in Peru. They are packed with protein and are very easy to cook. See side bar, page 149.

Bolillo
A *bolillo* is a typical bread roll in Mexico. Plump and oval in shape, it is crunchy on the outside and soft and

dense on the inside. They are probably the easiest rolls to find at *panaderías* or Mexican bakeries. But, remember, French bread is a closer match to what they enjoy in the Yucatán. Regardless, *bolillos* are good for *tortas* (sandwiches) or to serve warm with a dish.

Bulgar wheat
A whole grain, bulgar wheat is most often made from durum wheat. It is used widely in Middle Eastern cuisine. The Christian Lebanese who migrated to the Yucatán are credited with introducing bulgar wheat into the Yucatecan diet and *kibis* (see recipe). It is sold by size of grain from fine (#1) to course (#3). The name "bulgar" comes from the Persian word "*barghul*". See "*kibis*."

Cal/Cal Viva - See "quicklime."

Cazón
Cazón or dogfish is a type of shark. Unfortunately, in some parts of the world, it has been overfished and is considered a vulnerable or threatened species. Regardless, it is not an easy fish to find in markets. I recommend using another white fish, such as sole, red snapper, grouper, sea bass or halibut. Canned albacore is good too. The term *cazón* is still used in recipes because they are such traditional dishes. By the way, they are called dogfish because they travel and hunt in packs.

Chaya
Chaya is a shrub native to the Yucatán Peninsula. Its leaves are commonly used in cooking. However, the leaves are toxic if raw, so it is very important to cook them before eating. See side bar, page 136. Spinach, fresh or frozen, can be substituted for *chaya* in the recipes in this book.

Chayote
Chayote, also known as christophene, vegetable pear (due to its shape) and mirliton, is used much like potatoes in cooking. Native to Mesoamerica, it played an important role in the Mayan diet. Look for smooth, pastel green chayotes rather than the "spiny" ones. Peeling is optional and the seed is tasty. The root, stem and leaves are edible too.

Chile de Árbol - See "chiles."

Chile Dulce - See "bell pepper."

Chile Guajillo - See "chiles."

Chile Güerito - See "*chile x'catic*" in "chiles"

Chile Habanero - See "chiles."

Chile Serrano - See "chiles."

Chile X'catic - See "chiles."

Chiles
Chile peppers (or chili peppers) originated in the Americas, perhaps domesticated as early as 6,000 years ago according to archaeological evidence found in Ecuador. Christopher Columbus and his sailors were probably among the first Europeans to sample them. They called them "peppers" because their hot taste reminded them of the black and white peppercorns (from a completely different genus) they knew at home. Introduced to Europe, chiles eventually made their way around the world where they are cultivated and are integral ingredients in many cuisines. The chiles noted here are most used in the Yucatán and in this cookbook. Also see "Scoville scale."

Chile de Árbol
When ripe, this bright, red, petite chile is hotter than a *serrano chile*—15,000–30,000 on the Scoville scale. It is used fresh, dried or powdered, and is widely available in markets. Its name is a reference to its woody stem, hence the "tree chile." Attractive "ristras," popular in New Mexico, and wreaths are often made with dried *chile de árbol*.

Chile Dulce - See "bell pepper."

Chile Guajillo
Dark, red-brown *chiles guajillos* are dried Marisol chiles. They are about as hot as jalapeños and are commonly used in soups and stews. It is generally toasted and or soaked in warm water prior to use. Because of its thicker skin, it may require more soaking time than other dried chiles.

Chile Habanero
This chile (*Capsicum chinense*) is thought to have originated in the Yucatán Peninsula, which explains why it is so loved there. But, it is a very hot chile, rated 150,000–325,000 on the Scoville scale. Compare this with the jalapeño pepper that only rates 2,500–8,000 on the same scale. Green when unripe, look for orange or red, lantern-shaped chiles with smooth skin. Use plastic gloves when handling, and proceed with caution in

cooking unless you or those for whom you are cooking can really handle the heat. You can always offer the chile on the side. Although the chile probably did not originate in Havana, Cuba (as claimed by some), there was a great deal of trade between the peninsula and the island, which may have influenced its name. It got its Latin name after it was so widely disseminated around the world that some considered China as its place or origin.

Chile Serrano
Chile serrano originated in the mountains—or *serranías*—around the Mexican states of Hidalgo and Puebla in central Mexico, hence its name. Green at first, this petite chile ripens to red, yellow, orange or brown. It is hotter than a jalapeño; rated between 8,000–22,000 on the Scoville scale. As a result, handle and serve with care.

Chile x'catic (chile güerito or blond chile)
"*Chile güero*" is a generic name for yellow or light-green chiles, sometimes referred to as "blond chiles." In the Yucatán, a regional variety is called "*chile x'catic*" or "*chile güerito*." Sometimes they are hot, sometimes they are mild. A good substitute is the Hungarian wax chile.

Chorizo - See "*longaniza*."

Cilantro
Cilantro is the leaves and stems of coriander, an herb used widely throughout Mexico. Also known as Chinese parsley, it is native to southern Europe, North Africa and southwestern Asia and has been used in cooking since at least 5,000 B.C. It is mentioned in a Sanskrit text and the Bible. Buy as fresh as possible, avoiding limp stems and brown leaves. Sizes of bunches do vary, so adjust recipes as needed.

Coconut cream
Coconut cream is the milky, slightly sweet cream processed from the meat of a coconut. It comes in 14-ounce cans. Sometimes the cream can separate and rise to the top. Just shake the can vigorously before opening. Canned coconut milk can also be used.

Coconut milk - See "*coconut cream*."

Corn dough - See "*masa de maíz*" and "*masa harina*."

Dogfish - See "*cazón*."

Dragon fruit - See "*pitaya*."

Epazote
Epazote is an herb that was familiar to the Aztecs who called it "*epazotl*," giving us the name we know it by today. In addition to cooking, it was used as a medicine. Its fragrance is hard to describe, but citrus, savory, gasoline, mint and camphor come to mind. Europeans often found the herb "vile" or an acquired taste. It is used often in bean dishes as it may combat gassiness (if you know what I mean). Here it is used to flavor various dishes and as a garnish. It is also known as wormseed, Jesuit's tea, Mexican tea, pigweed, skunkweed, goosefoot or Herba Sancti Mariæ. Epazote can be found in Latino markets, however, you can also find suppliers of dried epazote on-line. One teaspoon of dried leaves is equivalent to about one branch or seven leaves of fresh epazote. Of course, fresh is best.

Escabeche
Escabeche refers to foods that are marinated in an acidic marinade. The acidity can come from vinegar or citrus juice, such as *naranja agria* or *lima agria* as used in the Yucatán. See side bar, page 66.

Fideos
In many parts of South America, *fideos* are thin pasta similar to vermicelli that comes coiled. Spaghetti is an adequate substitute. It is often toasted or sautéed in oil before using.

Galletas Globitos
A take on mini-fish-shaped crackers popular in the United States, Galletas Globitos are their counterpart in the Yucatán. They are hollow ovals about 1/2-inch long. They add a pleasant crunch and taste to any soup, especially *crema de chaya* (see recipe). Use fish-shaped crackers or crushed saltine crackers as substitutes.

Galletas Maria
Galletas María are simple, flat, round cookies that have their name and intricate decorations stamped into them. Inexpensive, they are great for dunking in milk and are used in or to accompany various desserts. Kids love them. As a style or kind of cookie, you will find them with different ladies' and brand names in grocery stores. In the Yucatán, Galletas María are also used crushed for breading meats like Panco crumbs, which can be substituted even if not delivering quite the same taste.

178 Sabores Yucatecos: A culinary Tour of the Yucatán

History records that the cookie was created in England in the late 19th century to commemorate the wedding of a duke of Edinburgh to a grand duchess of Russia. The cookies, also known as "Marie biscuits," became popular throughout Europe, especially Spain. Now they are enjoyed worldwide.

GAME MEATS

Game meats (meats from land animals hunted for food and not typically domesticated) figured prominently in the ancient Mayan diet since the Maya did not practice animal husbandry on a wide scale. As a result, they took advantage of nature's bounty that offered white-tailed and brocket deer, peccary, armadillo, iguana, wild turkey (they also had a domesticated variety) and other fowl, agouti, paca, coati (coatimundi) and turtle. In addition, the Maya ate the eggs from various fowl and reptiles. Also on the wilder side, the Maya ate dog (the Xoloitzcuintle, a native, hairless breed) and insects that neighboring cultures also ate. Recipes featuring venison link us to what the ancient Maya ate and are included in Chapter 7.

GARBANZO BEANS

The garbanzo bean, also known as chickpea, is an edible legume high in protein. For thousands of years, people have taken full advantage of its butter-like texture and nutty flavor. If you've had hummus, you've enjoyed those qualities. The beans are available either dried or canned.

GREEN LEAF LETTUCE

Green leaf lettuce is the preferred lettuce of the Yucatán. Whole leaves are used in plating and in *tortas* (sandwiches) or chopped for toppings. Look for fresh heads with loose, crumpled-looking leaves.

GUANÁBANA

Guanábana, or soursop, is a flowering evergreen tree native to Mexico, Central America, the Caribbean and parts of South America. The light, creamy pulp of the fruit has a flavor that some describe as a blend of pineapple, strawberry and citrus. The fruit resembles *chirimoya*. They are both in the same genus. For your convenience, buy frozen pulp in Latino or Asian markets. Look for it by other common names, such as *graviola*, Brazilian *pawpaw* or *durian benggala*.

GUANO PALM

The guano palm refers to several species of palm trees, many indigenous to the Caribbean and Mexico. The palm leaves were used by the Maya to build "pibs" (underground pits). Slivers of the leaves are also used to create the center slit or slash in *barras de francés* (French rolls, see entry) instead of slitting with a knife or razor.

HABANERO CHILE - See "chiles."

HERBS AND SPICES

Certain herbs and spices are used frequently in Yucatecan cooking. Herbs include: cilantro, epazote, mint and oregano. Of these, epazote is native to Latin America. (See "cilantro" and "epazote.")
Spices include: allspice, cinnamon, cloves, cumin, pepper, saffron and vanilla. Of these, allspice is native to southern Mexico, Central America and the Greater Antillles. Vanilla is native to Mexico and was cultivated in Mesoamerica. (See "allspice" and "vanilla.")
Fresh herbs are best, however, dried herbs can be used. Since dried herbs are more potent than fresh herbs, the general rule of thumb is to use a 1-to-3 ratio, i.e. 1 teaspoon of dried herbs for every 3 teaspoons (or 1 tablespoon) of fresh herbs.

HIBISCUS FLOWER - See "*jamaica*."

HONEY

The ancient Maya practiced beekeeping and domesticated stingless bees. They harvested the honey and wax for personal use and as trade goods. The honey was used as a sweetener and antibiotic and as the main ingredient in an alcoholic beverage called "*balché*," which survives the Conquest. Hives were collected from the wild and placed in hollow logs close to home. The hives were often handed down from one generation to another. The bee was considered a link to the spirit world and a gift from Ah Muzen Cab, the bee god. Following the Conquest, the Maya paid tribute to their new rulers in honey and beeswax.

HONEYCOMB TRIPE

Its definition is anything but appetizing: the lining of the reticulum (or second stomach) of a ruminant used as food. But honeycomb tripe when cleaned and cooked properly can make for delicious eating. You can purchase it fresh or in frozen blocks.

JAMAICA

Jamaica or roselle is a species of hibiscus native to the Americas. In Mexico, the dried flower, or more accurately the sepal and calyce, is used to make beverages. Refreshing *agua de jamaica* (see recipe) is slightly astringent, like cranberry juice, and is a beautiful burgundy color. In Latino markets you can find *jamaica* sold by the pound or in pre-wrapped packages. Avoid powdered mixes.

Jícama
Jícama is a vine native to Mexico. Most people know its edible root, which is most often eaten raw. After being introduced to the rest of the world, it has become particularly popular in Asia. Jícama has a slightly sweet pear or apple taste. It looks similar to a large turnip. Look for tubers that are firm, with dry roots and skin that is not bruised. Peel before eating.

Kibis
Kibis are the Yucatecan version of what are called *kibbeh* or *kibbe* in other parts of the world. A legacy of the Lebanese community that calls Yucatán home, *kibis* are fried meat-and-grain (in this case beef and bulgar wheat) patties that are great as appetizers or a light entrée (see recipe). Also see "bulgur wheat."

Lima
A common citrus fruit, *limas* or limes are used a lot in Yucatecan food. The juice and rind are used as ingredients, and wedges or slices garnish many dishes. While the limes found in most grocery stores will do, those marked as Mexican or key limes or Persian limes are better flavor matches for the limes from Yucatán. Interestingly, lemons are not common in the Yucatán. Also see "lima agria" and side bar, page 114.

Lima agria
Lima agria is a bitter lime and is another citrus fruit that distinguishes many a Yucatecan dish. An off-looking and lumpy lime, it is very sour and very fragrant. Its sister in Yucatecan cuisine is *naranja agria*. If you can't find *limas agrias*, then use regular limes. See side bar, page 114.

Lime - See "lima."

Longaniza
Longaniza is a sausage used in a variety of recipes in the Yucatán. It generally is made of ground pork and beef and seasoned with *recados*. The more common Mexican-style chorizo is a good substitute.

Mamey
Sometimes known as *mamey sapote* or simply *sapote*, *mamey* is a tropical fruit native to Mexico, Central America and the Caribbean. The skin of the fruit is brown and rough, a contrast to its flesh, which is a lush pumpkin or burnt-orange color and resembles a baked sweet potato in texture. You can scoop out the flesh with a spoon to eat or use it in smoothies, shakes, ice creams and other desserts. The seed of the *mamey* is particularly beautiful—big, glossy and smooth. If you find fresh *mameyes*, look for firm fruit that gives slightly when pressed. Or buy frozen pulp.

Maracuyá
Maracuyá, or passion fruit, comes from a vine native to Latin America. The most common ones found in the United States are about the size of a lime and are purple on the outside. When ripe, the papery skin gets wrinkled. Cutting one open reveals small, black seeds swimming in a gooey pulp. That's where all the flavor is. They are expensive, making the frozen pulp an economical option.

Marrow bones
Marrow bones hold bone marrow, the tissue inside bones. They should be easy to find in most supermarkets. If not, ask your butcher, who can also cut them for you. The marrow slides easily from the bones, is very tasty and melts in your mouth.

Masa de maíz
Masa de maíz, or corn dough that has been "nixtamalized" (dried corn treated with quicklime or ash), is the main ingredient for tortillas and tamales. Look for a *tortillería* to purchase *masa de maíz*. It comes in various forms, such as *para tortillas* (for tortillas), *para tamales* (for tamales) or *masa preparada para tamales* (ready-made for tamales with lard and seasonings already added). You can also purchase *masa harina* (corn flour) that requires water to make a dough (see "masa harina"). Do not confuse with corn meal. It is often used as a thickening agent. (See side bar, page 128.)

Masa harina
Masa harina (or *harina de maíz*) is a finely ground corn flour. It is commonly used to make tortillas and tamales. All you have to do is add water and salt to make a dough or *masa de maíz*. If you can't find prepared *masa de maíz*, just follow the directions on the back of the bag to make the dough, and follow the directions for making recipes calling for *masa de maíz*. Two cups *masa harina* (for making about 16 tortillas) will give you about a pound of *masa*. It can be used as a thickening agent. (See side bar, page 128.) Do not confuse with corn meal.

Masa para vaporcito
Masa para vaporcito is the corn dough used to make the tamales called *vaporcito de pollo*, *vaporcito de espelón* and *vaporcito de chaya*. But it is also the *masa* preparation used to make *tamal horneado*. So be prepared to refer to that recipe often.

Media crema
Media crema is a medium-thick cream sauce that comes in 7.6-ounce cans. It is not sweet but adds creaminess to dishes. You can also substitute cream or half and half.

Mexican squash
This squash resembles a stubby zucchini with a thin, pale-green skin. It is almost seedless and its meat is whiter and sweeter. Zucchini is an adequate substitute, but adjust quantity slightly.

Naranja agria
Naranja agria, which refers to a citrus tree and its fruit, is native to southeastern Asia. It is also known as Seville orange, bitter orange, sour orange, bigarade orange and marmalade orange. The roundish fruit has a rough, lumpy surface with a very aromatic, bitter peel. Call it the green, ugly duckling of oranges. In the Yucatán, the acidic juice from the fruit is used to moisten *recados* and plays the role of vinegar to "pickle" onions. Still hard to find in most supermarkets stateside, you can find bottled *naranja agria,* or simply substitute lime juice.

Neck bones (pork and beef)
Pork or beef neck bones add great flavor to stocks, soups and stews. Often they are not served with other meats that might be featured in a dish. But, neck bones have a lot of meat on them and after all the stewing they get, they are quite good. So don't discard them. Either save them for yourself or serve to guests who like finger-lickin' goodness. Just watch out for the small bones.

Octopus ink
For an octopus, its blackish ink might be a defensive tool used to escape a predator. But for humans, it is an ingredient that adds smoky dimensions to seafood dishes. Find it in specialty markets or in seafood section in markets. Squid ink is a good substitute.

Onions - See "red onions."

Pan de sandwich
Pan de sandwich is a Yucatecan white bread whose crust is even white. It is popular as an option to *barras de francés* (French rolls) or *bolillos* (Mexican rolls) for making sandwiches. Folks crave *pan de sandwich* to make sandwiches of *pavo asado* (see recipe). Stateside, your favorite white bread will work.

Papaya
This familiar fruit is native to the Americas and was first cultivated in Mexico. This football-sized fruit, which does come in bigger and smaller sizes, was called the "fruit of the angels" by Christopher Columbus. Look for fruit with skin that is changing from green to yellow or orange and that gives slightly when pressed. It is generally easy to find year-round.

Passion fruit - See "*maracuyá.*"

Pipián
Pipián is a term used for dishes with a pumpkin seed sauce. See "pumpkin seed" and "pumpkin seed oil."

Pitaya
Pitaya is a cactus fruit native to Latin America. Striking in appearance, it is obvious why the fruit is also known as dragon fruit—red or pink *pitayas* sport sparse green "scales." When cut open, their beauty is further revealed; white or red flesh dotted with small, black, edible seeds. More easily found now in specialty markets, look for fruit that gives slightly when pressed. Avoid those with blotches or brown and brittle stems or "scales" or "leaves." The skin is not eaten.

Plantains
Plantains, or "*plátanos,*" are a member of the banana family, but are larger than your common sweet banana. Because they are starchy and low in sugar, they are not eaten raw. They are fried, baked, grilled, boiled or steamed before being consumed. They are widely available in grocery stores where you will find them from green to almost black, depending on their state of ripeness. They are native to Southeast Asia. Regular bananas in Spanish are also called "*plátanos*" so don't confuse the two. For tips on peeling a plantain, see Techniques.

Plátanos - See "plantains."

Plum tomato
In the Yucatán, the oval or egg-shaped plum tomato or Roma (a variety of the plum tomato) is the tomato of choice. It is more acidic than salad or beefsteak tomatoes. It also is very fleshy with a high solid content and fewer seed compartments. As a result, it is ideal for salsas, sauces and stews. And it is widely available year-round. Look for tomatoes that are firm without blemishes.

Pork
Various cuts and parts of the pig from tenderloin to cushion, pork shoulder, baby back ribs, pigs' feet, pork shanks and ground pork are used in the recipes presented here. When given choices in the same recipe, any cut will make you proud of your efforts. Cuts with a higher fat content can be more tender and succulent, but the leaner cuts won't disappoint either. Fatter cuts include pork shoulder and pork butt; leaner cuts include pork loin and tenderloin. Cushion is in between.

Pumpkin seed oil
Pumpkin seed oil for cooking is made from dried seeds that are pressed to produce a green oil with a nutty flavor. It can be derived from boiling pumpkin seeds and skimming the oil that rises to the top. But it's easier to buy in specialty food shops or bought on-line. Here it used to drizzle over *papadzules* (see recipe) or dishes "*en pipián*" to give them that extra something special. Also see "pumpkin seeds."

Pumpkin seeds
Pumpkins are native to the Americas, and since pre-Columbian times their seeds were used as a source of protein and oil. Still today, they are often ground either hulled or unhulled, roasted or unroasted. Dishes with the word "*pipián*" in their name generally refer to dishes with a pumpkin seed sauce. In stores you can find the seeds sold hulled or unhulled as well as ground. As a snack, you can find them roasted, salted and sometimes flavored. Do not confuse with sunflower seeds.

Quicklime
Quicklime—lime or calcium oxide (CaO)—is a chemical compound that has been used by mankind for thousands of years. In Mesoamerica, it was used to treat corn in a process known as nixtamalization. This is a process of soaking dry maize kernels in caustic quicklime to dissolve the outer shell and result in hominy that is needed to make *masa* for tortillas and tamales, etc. In other foods, it acts as a firming, anti-caking or dehydrating agent. Note its use in *papaya en almíbar* (see recipe).

Recado rojo
Recado rojo is ubiquitous in Yucatecan cuisine. It gives food an earthy flavor and great coloring. It is made of ground achiote or annatto seeds (see "achiote") and is also referred to as *recado colorado, pasta de achiote* or achiote paste. In this book, it refers to a paste that contains ground achiote seeds, spices and vinegar or lime juice. Homemade *recados* are always better than store-bought ones.

Recado/s
Recados are to the Yucatán what *moles* are to Oaxaca. They are a regional treasure and figure as important ingredients in Yucatecan cooking. *Recados* are distinctive spice and herb blends that are used in rubs and marinades in a wide range of dishes. Some are used more widely than others (see "recado rojo") Store *recados* in a jar or other tightly sealed container. Refrigerated, they keep pretty much indefinitely. See *recado* recipes in Chapter 1.

Red onions
The most common onion used in the Yucatán is the red onion followed by the white onion. Both are milder and sweeter than yellow or Spanish onions. Debate still surrounds the point of origin of the onion. Some believe it originated in central Asia, others say in the Middle East. However, wild onions were probably found on all continents. Cultivated onions were introduced by the Spanish to the West Indies and eventually spread throughout the Americas. The name comes from the Roman word "*unio*," which means "large pearl."

Rome or Roma tomato - See "plum tomato."

Salpicón
In French cuisine, "salpicon" refers to one or more ingredients that are diced or minced, mixed with a sauce, and used as a stuffing. In the Yucatán, this description applies only so far as the mincing and mixing is concerned. *Salpicón* can refer to minced radishes, cilantro and lime juice (or *naranja agria* juice or vinegar). It is used to top soups and stews, adding a crunchy and bright tanginess, or as key to a good *salpicón de res* or *salpicón de venado* (see recipes).

Scoville scale
Wilbur L. Scoville was a pharmacist who developed a method to measure the heat or bite of a pepper or chile in 1912 called the Scoville Organoleptic Test. Some scientists criticized his method of testing because it relied on the human tongue and was considered too subjective. Many in the chile industry endorse a more objective rating produced by the HPLC machine (High Performance Liquid Chromatography). Regardless, the Scoville scale remains the best-known scale to judge a chile's punch. Also see "chiles."

Sofrito
Sofrito is a combination of aromatic ingredients that are added to many recipes as a flavor base. In the

Yucatán, *sofrito* generally includes tomatoes, onions, garlic and bell peppers—or various combinations of these ingredients—that are sliced, diced or chopped and then sautéed in oil to allow flavors to meld together. Many recipes call for the preparation of a *sofrito*. Do not confuse with "*sofrito de tomate*" (see recipe). (If not stated in a recipe, *sofritos* generally need to be sautéed for 6–8 minutes to cook through.)

SPICES - See "herbs and spices."

TAMAL (tamales)
If you know Mexican cooking, you know tamales. Bundles of stuffed corn dough goodness wrapped and steamed in corn husks, banana leaves or other kinds of wrappers. All kinds of stuffings are used from meat to vegetarian and sweet ones. In the Yucatán, banana leaves are used for its most traditional tamales. See Glossary and Techniques for more on banana leaves and preparing fresh banana leaves. Also see page 128.

TORTILLA/S (corn)
Tortillas are flat, unleavened "bread" made from ground corn (or maize). In the Yucatán corn tortillas are preferred; flour are rarely eaten. So when you see tortillas mentioned in the book, they are always corn.
While little compares to handmade tortillas hot off the *comal* (or griddle or skillet), pre-made and packaged corn tortillas are easy to find almost anywhere and are the convenient way to go. If you really want to make your own corn tortillas, you can start from scratch—a process that requires soaking kernels in lime water, grinding and kneading (see "quicklime"). Or you can take an easier route by using *masa harina* (a corn flour for tortillas or tamales) to which you only have to add water and salt. Also see "*masa de maíz*" and "*masa harina*."

TORTILLA STRIPS - See Techniques.

TOSTADAS - See Techniques.

TROPICAL FRUITS
See separate listings for: *guanábana, lima agria, mamey, maracuyá, naranja agria,* papaya, *pitaya* and plantain.

TURKEY
Turkeys are indigenous to the Americas. The Maya and Aztecs kept both the wild turkey (*Meleagris gallopavo*) and ocellated turkey (*Meleagris ocellata*), particular to the Yucatán, in pens. But it was the wild turkey that was one of the first animals to be domesticated in the Americas, and it was highly revered. The Maya used parts of the bird in sacred ceremonies, the feathers as decorative objects, and the meat and eggs for food. By the time the Spanish arrived in the New World, they found turkey populations spread well beyond Mexico. In the Yucatán, turkeys are called "*pavos*."

VANILLA/VANILLA BEANS
It makes sense that something as lovely and fragrant as vanilla comes from an orchid. And that orchid is native to Mexico. Vanilla was cultivated by Mesoamerican peoples and was one of the great things, along with chocolate, that Hernán Cortés took back to Europe. Attempts to cultivate vanilla outside Mexico were at first unsuccessful because of the symbiotic relationship between the vine that produces the vanilla orchid and the Melipon bee, a local species. Once hand pollination proved successful, it was possible to cultivate vanilla in other parts of the world. Also see "honey."

VENADO (venison) - See "game meats."

VENISON (*venado*) - See "game meats."

YUCATECO/S
Yucateco (or *yucateca*) refers to the someone from the Yucatán Peninsula, the state of Yucatán, or as an adjective in Spanish to refer to something from the Yucatán or of Yucatecan origin. Keep in mind, however, that the different states that make up Mexico's Yucatán Peninsula also have their own identities. The people from Campeche are called "*campechanos*" and the people from Quintana Roo are called "*quintanarroenses.*" Do not confuse "the Yucatán" with "Mundo Maya," which encompasses the areas where the Maya settled. "Mundo Maya" includes not only the Mexican states of Yucatán, Campeche and Quintana Roo, but it also includes the the Mexican states of Chiapas and Tabasco, and several Central American countries.

Chichén Itzá
RESTAURANT

3655 S. Grand Avenue • Los Angeles, CA 90007
213-741-1075 • info@chichenitzarestaurant.com
www.chichenitzarestaurant.com

INDEX

(page numbers in italics refer to photographs)

A

About the authors, 7, 9, 190
About the recipes, 8
Achiote, 84, 176, *176*
Achiote-rubbed Chicken Baked in Banana Leaves, 72, *73*
Achiote-marinated Pork Shanks in Banana Leaves, 84, *85*
Achiote-rubbed Pork Baked in Banana Leaves, 82, *83*
Achiote Sauce for Tamales, 16
Achiote Sauce for Tikin Xic, 16, *112*
Agua de jamaica, *152*, 157
Akat de codillos, 84, *85*
Al-sikbaj, 176, and see "escabeche"
Albóndigas con fideos, *102*, 103
Alcaparrado, 176
Allspice, 17, 176
Andalusian-style Tripe Stew, 60, *60*
Antojitos, see Chapter 2
Appetizers, see Chapter 2
Arrolladitos de repollo, 32, *33*
Arroz, see "rice dishes"
Arroz blanco, *82*, 146
Arroz con azafrán, 147
Arroz con cebolla y tomate, 146, *147*
Arroz con cilantro, *147*, 148
Arroz con leche, *158*, 164
Arroz con plátanos fritos, *18*, 29
Avocado, 176

B

Baby Back Ribs in Pumpkin Seed Sauce, *80*, 87
Baby Edam cheese, *95*, 176, and see "queso relleno"
Baked tamal, *132*, 133

Banana leaves, *127*, 176, and
 - cochinita pibil, 82, *83*
 - pollo pibil, 72, *73*
 - akat de codillos, 84, *85*
 - Get to Know Your Banana Leaf, 128
 - see tamales, Chapter 9
 - Preparing Fresh Banana Leaves, 174
Banana Shake, 156
Barra de francés, 176
Beans, see Chapter 10, and
 - crema de garbanzo, *18*, 31
 - frijol con puerco, 86, *86*
 - vaporcito de espelón, *130*, 131
 - frijoles de la olla, *82*, 143
 - frijoles negros guisados, 143
 - frijoles colados, 144
Beef, see Chapter 7, and
 - kabic de res, 44, 61
 - mondongo kabic, 58, *59*
 - mondongo a la andaluza, 60, *60*
Beef in a Pot, *96* 98
Beef Soup, *44*, 61
Beer/s, 153
Bell peppers, 69, 176
Beverages, see Chapter 11
Bistec de cazuela, *96*, 98
Bistec de venado, 107
Bistec de vuelta y vuelta, 98, *99*
Bitter lime, see "lima agria"
Bitter orange, see naranja agria
Black beans, 149, 176
Black Beans and Pork, 86, *86*
Black Beans in a Pot, *82*, 143
Black Rice and Beans, *147*, 149
Black-eyed Peas, see "espelón"
Black-eyed Peas Tamales Wrapped in Banan Leaves, *130*, 131
Black turtle beans, see "black beans"
Bolillo, 35, 176
Brazo de reina, 136, *137*
Breaded Fish, 124, *124*

Breaded Pig's Feet, *80*, 92
Breaded Shrimp, 121, *121*
Bulgar wheat, 30, 176
Buñuelos de yuca, 167, *167*
Buth negro de carne molida, 105, *105*

C

Caballeros pobres, 166, *166*
Cabbage
 - arrolladitos de repollo, 32, *33*
 - curtido de repollo, 151
Cabbage relish, 151
Calabacitas fritas, *140*, 151
Calamares en escabeche, 119, *119*
Caldillo de huevo, *40*, 41
Caldo de pavo, 46
Caldo de pollo, 48
Camarones, see "shrimp"
Camarones empanizados, 121, *121*
Caramel Custard, 160
Carne molida, 104, *104*
Cassava fritters, 167, *167*
Cattle, 97
Cazón, 122, 177, and
 - empanadas de cazón, 23, *23*
 - chile x'catic relleno de cazón, *18*, 25
 - pan de cazón, *123*, 122
Cebolla para cochinita pibil, *82*, 142
Cebolla para panuchos, *22*, 142
Cebolla para poc chuc, *88*, 142
Cebolla picante de los Cetina, 54
Ceviche de pescado, 114, *115*
Champola, *172*, 173
Charcoaled Pork, 88, *89*
Chaya, 136, 177, *177*, and
 - huevos con chaya, 38, *39*
 - crema de chaya, 49, *49*
 - vaporcito de chaya, *130*, 131
 - brazo de reina, 136, *137*
Chaya Tamales Wrapped in Banana Leaves, *130*, 131
Chayote, 177, *177*

184 SABORES YUCATECOS: A CULINARY TOUR OF THE YUCATÁN

Chichén Itzá Restaurant, 9, 183
Chicken, see Chapter 5, and
- pollo con fideos, *50*, 51
- puchero de tres carnes, *56, 56*
- tamal horneado, *132*, 133
- tamal colado de pollo, 134, *135*
- mucil pollo, *138*, 139
Chicken and Capers, *50*, 65
Chicken and Potatoes, *66*, 69
Chicken in Pumpkin Seed Sauce, 68, *68*
Chicken Soup with Pasta, *50* , 51
Chicken Stock, 48
Chicken Tamal Pie, *138*, 139
Chicxulub Crater, 113
Chile de árbol, 177
Chile dulce, *81*, see "bell pepper"
Chile guajillo, 177
Chile güerito, see "chile x'catic"
Chile habanero, *11, 97, 177, 177*
Chile kut, 14, *14*
Chile serrano, 178
Chile x-catic relleno de cazón, *18*, 25
Chile x'catic, 178, *178*
Chiles, 177
Chilmole de puerco, 90, *91*
Chiltomate, 16, *88*
Chocolomo, 100, *101*
Chopped Pickled Red Onion, *82*, 142
Chorizo, see "longaniza"
Christmas Eve Menu, 74
Cilantro, 178
Cilantro Rice, *147*, 148
Cochinita pibil, *82*, 83
Coconut cream, 178
Coconut Custard, 162, *162*
Coconut Ice Cream, *170*, 173
Coconut milk, see "coconut cream"
Cóctel de camarón, *117*, 120
Codzitos, 24, *24*
Comal, 175
Consomé de pavo, 46

Corn dough, see "masa de maíz" and "masa harina"
Corn dough for tortillas, see "masa harina" and "masa de maíz"
Costillas en pipián, *80*, 87
Cream of Chaya Soup, 49, *49*
Crema de chaya, 49, *49*
Crema de coco, 162, *162*
Crema de garbanzo, *18*, 31
Crema española, *158*, 164
Curtido de repollo, 151

D

Day of the Dead, 127, 139
Day of the Dead Tamal Pie, *138*, 139
Desserts, see Chapter 12
Diced Roasted Pickled Red Onion, *88*, 142
Dog's Nose Salsa, 13
Dogfish, see "cazón"
Donde se compone el mundo, 42
Dragon fruit, see "pitaya"
Dragon Fruit Drink, 156
Drinks, see Chapter 11

E

Egg dishes, see Chapter 3
Egg, Ham and Cheese Sandwich, 42, 43
Eggs Motul Style, 38, *39*
Eggs with Chaya, 38, *39*
Eggs with Chorizo, 37, *37*
Empanadas de cazón, 23, *23*
Ensalada de papa, *18*, 29
Ensalada de pasta, 28, *28*
Ensalada de verduras, 145, *145*
Ensalada mixta de mariscos, 116, *117*
Epazote, 178
Escabeche, 66, 178
Espelón, *127*, 131, and see "vaporcito de espelón"

F

Fideos, 178
Fish Ceviche, 114, *115*
Fish Tortilla Stack, 122, *123*
Fish Turnovers, 23, *23*
Fish-stuffed Blond Chiles, *18*, 25
Flan, 160
Fresh salsa, 13, *112*
Fried plantains, 144
Fried squash, *140*, 141
Frijol con puerco, 86, *86*
Frijoles colados, 144
Frijoles de la olla, *82*, 143
Frijoles negros guisados, 143
From the chef, 7
From the writer, 9
Fruit, see "tropical fruits"

G

Galletas Globitos, *49*, 178, *178*
Galletas María, 178, *178*
Game meats, 179, and
- bistec de venado, 107
- pipián de venado, 108
- sah kol de venado, 109
- salpicón de venado, 110, *110*
- Side bar, On the Wild Side, 110
Garbanzo beans, 31, 179
Garbanzo Dip, *18*, 31
Garnished Corn Tortillas Stuffed with Black Bean Paste, 20, *21*
Garnished Puffed Corn Tortillas, 22, *22*
Get to Know Your Banana Leaf, 128
Glossary, 176
Green leaf lettuce, 179
Grilled Chicken, *70*, 71, *71*
Grilled Fish with Achiote Rub, *112*, 125
Grinding or crushing herbs, spices and chiles, 174

Ground Beef in Recado Negro, 105, *105*
Ground Beef with Sofrito, 104, *104*
Ground Hulled Toasted Pumpkin Seeds, 17
Ground Pumpkin Seeds, 17
Ground Unhulled Toasted Pumpkin Seeds, 17
Guanábana, 179
Guanábana Drink, 155
Guanábana Sorbet, *170*, 171
Guano palm, 83, 179

H

Habanero Chile, see "chile habanero"
Habanero Chile Sauce, 14, *14*
Handling chiles habaneros, 174
Helado/s, see Chapter 12
Helado de coco, 6, *170*, 173
Helado de mamey, *170*, 173
Herbs and Spices, 179
Hibiscus flower, see "jamaica"
Hibiscus-flower Drink, *152*, 157,
Hígado encebollado, 106, *106*
Honey, 179
Honeycomb tripe, 179
Horchata, *152*, 154
Huevos con chaya, 38, *39*
Huevos con longaniza, 37, *37*
Huevos motuleños, 38, *39*

I

Ibes, *141*
Ice cream, see Chapter 12

J

Jamaica, 179, *179*
Jícama, *19*, 180
Jícama Citrus Salad, 27, *27*

K

Kabic de res, *44*, 61

Kibis, 30, *30*, 180
Kol, see "quicklime"

L

Lentil Stew, *55*, 54
Lima, 180
Lima agria, *113*, 180, *180*
Lime/s, see "lima," and 114
Lime Soup, 47, *47*
Limeade, 155
Limonada, 155
Liver Smothered in Onions, 106, *106*
Longaniza, 180, and
 - huevos con longaniza, 37, *37*
 - potaje de lentejas, 54, *55*

M

Mamey, *159*, 180
Mamey con leche, 156
Mamey Ice Cream, *170*, 173
Mamey Shake, 157
Manjar blanco, 163, *163*
Maracuyá, 180
Marrow bones, 180
Masa de maíz, 128, 180
Masa harina, 128, 180
Masa para tortillas, 128
Masa para vaporcito, 129, 180
Mazapán, *159*, *159*
Meat and Bulgur Wheat Patties with Mint, 30, *30*
Meatballs and Pasta, *102*, 103
Media crema, 181
Mexican squash, 181, *181*
Milk Custard, 163, *163*
Mint Omelet, *40*, 41
Mixed Seafood Salad, 116, *117*
Mixed-meats Beef Soup, 100, *101*
Molcajete, 175
Moncho, 35, *42*, 43
Mondongo a la andaluza, 60, *60*

Mondongo kabic, 58, *59*
Moros y cristianos, *147*, 149
Mucbi pollo, *138*, 139
Mundo Maya, 183

N

Neapolitan Custard, 161, *161*
Naranja agria, *113*, 181, *181*
Naranjada, *152*, 154
Neck bones (pork and beef), 181
Nonreactive bowls and containers, 175

O

Octopus
 - ensalada mixta de mariscos, *117*, 166
 - pulpo en su tinta, 118, *118*
Octopus in its Own Ink, 118, *118*
Octopus ink, 181
Omelet with Achiote Sauce, *40*, 41
Onions, see "red onions"
Orange Drink, *152*, 154

P

Pan de cazón, 122, *123*
Pan de sandwich, 74, 181
Pan francés, see "barra de francés"
Panuchos, 19, 20, *21*
Papadzules, 34, 36
Papaya, *153*, 181
Papaya con leche, 157
Papaya en almíbar, *158*, 165
Papaya in Syrup, *158*, 165
Papaya Shake, 157
Passion fruit, see "maracuyá"
Passion Fruit Sorbet, 171
Pasta de achiote, see "recado rojo"
Pasta Salad, 28, *28*
Pasta Soup, 52, *53*
Pastelitos de atropellado, 6, *168*, *169*

Pavo, see "turkey"
Pavo asado, 62, 74
Pavo en relleno blanco, 78, 79
Pavo en relleno negro, 76, 77
Peeling a plantain, 174
Peeling chiles, 174
Pepitas de calabaza tostadas con cáscara, 10, 17
Pepitas de calabaza tostadas sin cáscara, 10, 17
Pescado empanizado, 124, 124
Pezuñas rebosadas, 80, 92
Pib - Pibil, 83, 174
Pickled Squid, 119, 119
Pico de gallo, 13, 112
Pime, 36, 80
Pipián, 181
Pipián de venado, 108
Pitaya, 153, 181, 181
Plantains, 181, 181, and
 - arroz con plátanos, 29, 18
 - huevos motuleños, 38, 39
 - plátanos fritos, 18, 144, 159
 - plátanos fritos con crema, 144, 159
 - pollo ticuleño, 64, 64
Plastic gloves, 175
Plátano con leche, 156
Plátanos, see "plantains"
Plátanos fritos, 18, 144, 159
Plátanos fritos con crema, 144, 159
Plum tomato, 45, 181
Poc chuc, 88, 89
Pollo alcaparrado, 50, 65
Pollo asado, 70, 71, 71
Pollo con fideos, 50, 51
Pollo con papas, 66, 69
Pollo en escabeche oriental, 66, 67
Pollo en pipián, 68, 68
Pollo pibil, 72, 73
Pollo ticuleño, 64, 64
Pork, see Chapter 6, and 182
Poor Boys, 166, 166

Pork dishes, see Chapter 6, and
 - potaje de lentejas, 54, 55
 - pavo en relleno negro, 77, 76
 - pavo en relleno blanco, 78, 79
Pork in Recado Negro Sauce, 90, 91
Pork Milanesa Yucatán Style, 80, 90
Pork Smothered in Tomatoes, 80, 92
Potaje de lentejas, 54, 55
Potato Salad, 18, 29
Preparing fresh banana leaves, 174
Puchero de tres carnes, 56, 56
Puerco empanizado, 80, 90
Puerco entomatado, 80, 92
Pulpo en su tinta, 118, 118
Pumpkin seed oil, 182
Pumpkin seeds, 182, and
 - sikil pac, 27, 27
 - papadzules, 36, 34
 - pollo en pipián, 68, 68
 - costillas en pipián, 87, 80
 - pipián de venado, 108
 - brazo de reina, 136, 137
 - pumpkin seed oil, 182
 - pumpkin seeds, 182
Puréed Black Beans, 144

Q

Queen's Arm Tamal, 136, 137
Queso napolitano, 161, 161
Queso relleno, 93, 93
Quicklime, 182

R

Radish and Cilantro Garnish, 15, 101
Recado blanco, see "recado para bistec"
Recado colorado, see "recado rojo"
Recado de achiote, see "recado rojo"
Recado negro 10, 12
Recado para bistec, 10, 12
Recado para escabeche, 13
Recado para puchero, 13
Recado rojo, 10, 12, 182

Recado/s, see Chapter 1, and 10, 81, 182, 182
Red onions, 182, and
 - cebolla para cochinita pibil, 82, 142
 - cebolla para panuchos, 22, 142
 - cebolla para poc chuc, 88, 142
 - Onions: Red That Is, 143
Refresco de agua de naranja agria, 155
Refresco de guanábana, 155
Refresco de pitaya, 156
Refresco de sandía, 156
Rice dishes,
 - arroz con plátanos, 29, 18
 - arroz blanco, 82, 146
 - arroz con cebolla y tomate, 146, 147
 - arroz con cilantro, 147, 148
 - arroz con azafrán, 147, 148
 - moros y cristianos, 147, 149
 - suflé de arroz, 150, 150
 - horchata, 152, 154
 - manjar blanco, 163, 163
 - arroz con leche, 158, 164,
Rice Drink, 152, 154
Rice Pudding, 158, 164
Rice Soufflé, 150, 150
Rice with Cilantro, 147, 148
Rice with Fried Plantains, 18, 29
Rice with Onions and Tomatoes, 146, 147
Roasted Habanero Chile Salsa, 14
Roasted Tomatoes and Ground Pumpkin Seed Dip, 27, 29
Roasted Tomato Sauce, 16, 89
Roasted Turkey, 62, 74
Roasted Turkey with Pork Meatballs in Recado Blanco, 78, 79
Roasted Turkey with Pork Meatballs in Recado Negro, 76, 77
Roasted Turkey with White Sauce, 75, 75

Roasting chiles, garlic, tomatoes, etc., 174
Recipe tips, 8
Rolled and Fried Tortillas, 24, *24*
Rome or Roma tomato, see "plum tomato"

S

Sacred Toppings, 21
Saffron Rice, *147*, 148
Sah kol, 17
Sah kol de pavo, 75, *75*
Sah kol de venado, 109
Salads
  - xec, 27, *27*
  - ensalada de pasta, 28, *28*
  - ensalada de papa, *18*, 29
  - suflé de arroz, 150, *150*
Salbutes, 22, *22*
Salpicón, 15, *101*, 182
Salpicón de res, 100
Salpicón de venado, 110, *111*
Salsa blanca, see "sah kol"
Salsa de achiote para tamales, 16
Salsa de achiote para tikin xic, 16, *112*
Salsa de chile habanero, 14, *14*
Salsa de tomate, 15, *24*
Salsa tártara, 17, *124*
Salsas, see Chapter 1
Scoville scale, 11, 182
Seafood, see Chapter 8, and
  - empanadas de cazón, 23, *23*
  - chile x'catic relleno de cazón, 25, *18*
  - pan de cazón, 122, *123*
Seasoned Tomato Sauce, 15
Seville orange, see "naranja agria"
Seville Orange Drink, 155
Shredded Beef Salad, 100
Shredded Venison Salad, 110, *111*
Shrimp, see Chapter 8, and
  - ensalada mixta de mariscos, 116, *117*

- cóctel de camaornes, *117*, 120
- camarones empanizados, 121, *121*
Shrimp Cocktail, *117*, 120
Side bars
- Achiote: The Color of the Yucatán, 84
- Allspice: An All-in-one Spice, 17
- America's Bird, 74
- Black Beans: Protein Powerhouse, 149
- Cazón: To Catch or Not to Catch, 122
- Chaya: Leafy Green, 136
- Crustaceans of the Sea: Shrimp, 120
- Donde se compone el mundo, 42, *42*
- Escabeche: Nice and Tangy, 66
- Lime, By Any Other Name, 114
- Masa de maíz, 128
- Menú para Nochebuena, 74
- On the Wild Side, 110
- Onions: Red That Is, 143
- Pibil: A Way of Cooking, 83
- Recados: Spicey Surprises, 12
- Recado Tips, 77
- Sacred Toppings, 21
- Snacks, 125
- The "Bell Pepper" Story, 69
- Tortillas: Corn Only, 36
Side dishes, see Chapter 10
Sikil pac, 27, *27*
Sliced Pickled Red Onion, *22*, 142
Snacks, 19, 125
Sofrito, 182
Sofrito de tomate, 15
Sopa de lima, 47, *47*
Sopa de pasta, 52, *53*
Sopa de tortilla estilo Quintana Roo, 48
Sopa de verduras, 52, *53*
Sopas y guisos, see Chapter 4, and

- pollo alcaparrado, *50*, 65
- pollo en escabeche oriental, 66, *67*
- pollo con papas, *67*, 69
- albóndigas con fideos, *102*, 103
Sorbete de guanábana, *170*, 171
Sorbete de maracuyá, 171
Sorbets, see Chapter 12
Soups and stews, see Chapter 4, and
  - pollo alcaparrado, *50*, 65
  - pollo en escabeche oriental, 66, *67*
  - pollo con papas, *67*, 69
  - albóndigas con fideos, *102*, 103
Sour orange, see "naranja agria"
Soursop, see "guanábana"
Spanish Custard, 158, 164
Spices, see "herbs and spices"
Squid
  - ensalada mixta de mariscos, *117*, 116
  - calamares en escabeche, 119, *119*
Starters, see Chapter 2
Strained Chicken Tamal, 134, *135*
Stews, see "soups," and Chapter 4
Stuffed Cabbage Leaves, 32, *33*
Suflé de arroz, 150, *150*
Sweet Potato and Coconut Turnovers, 6, 168, *168*

T

Tamal/tamales, see Chapter 9, and 183
Tamal colado de pollo, 134, *135*
Tamal Folding 101, 128
Tamal horneado, *132*, 133
Tamalera, 175
Tartar Sauce de Chichén Itzá Restaurant, 17, *124*
Techniques, 174
Tenderloin of Venison, 107
Three-meat Stew, 56, *56*
Ticul-style Chicken, 64, *64*
Tikin xic, *112*, 125

Tools, 175
Torta de huevo con hierbabuena, 40, 41
Tortilla/s (corn), 36, 183
Tortilla making, 174
Tortilla press, 175, *175*
Tortilla Soup Quintana Roo Style, 48
Tortilla strips, 175
Tortilla test, 175
Tortillas Stuffed with Hard-cooked Eggs in Pumpkin Seed Sauce, *34*, 36
Tostadas, 38, 64, 175
Tree spinach, see "chaya"
Tripe Soup, 58, *59*
Tropical fruits, see
 - guanábana, 179
 - lima agria, 180
 - mamey, 180
 - maracuyá, 180
 - naranja agria, 181
 - pitaya, 181
 - plantains, 191
Tropical Ice Cream Float, *172*, 173
Turkey, 183, and
 - consomé de pavo, 46
 - caldo de pavo, 46
 - pavo asado, *62*, 74
 - sah kol de pavo, 75, *75*
 - pavo en relleno negro, 75, *76*
 - pavo en relenno blanco, 78, *79*
Turkey Soup, 46
Turkey Stock, 46
Turkey, recipes, see Chapter 6

V

Valladolid-style Marinated Chicken, 66, *67*
Vanilla/vanilla beans, 183
Vaporcito de chaya, *130*, 131
Vaporcito de espelón, *130*, 131
Vaporcito de pollo, *126*, 129

Vegetable pear, see "chayote"
Vegetable Salad, 145
Vegetable Soup, *52*, 53
Vegetables
 - sopa de verduras, 52, *52*
 - ensalada de verduras, 143, *143*
 - calabacitas fritas, *140*, 151
 - curtido de repollo, 151
Vegetarian dishes
 - papadzules, *34*, 36
 - codzitos, 24, *24*
 - xec, 27, *27*
 - sikil pac, 27, *27*
 - ensalada de papa, *18*, 29
 - arroz con plátano, *18*, 29
 - crema de garbanzo, *18*, 31
 - vaporcitos de espelón, 131, *130*
 - vaporcito de chaya, *130*, 131
 - see various recipes, Chpater 10: Sides
Venado (venison), see Chapter 7, and "game meats"

Venison (venado), see Chapter 7, and "game meats"
Venison in Pumpkin Seed Sauce, 108
Venison with White Sauce, 109

W

Watermelon Drink, 156
White Rice, *82*, 146
White Sauce, 17

X

X'nipek, *13*, 14
Xec, 27, 27
Xtabentún, 153

Y

Yucatán-style Steak, 98, *99*
Yucatecan Tartar Sauce, 17
Yucatecan tomato sauce, 15, *24*
Yucateco/s, 183

Rule-of-thumb Guide

A little bit of this . . . a little bit of that

As we noted in our introduction, we have tried to be as accurate as possible with the measurements given in our recipes. Regardless, here's a quick, rule-of-thumb guide for some ingredients, as well as some additional tips.

Naranja agria:*

3–4 fruit = about 1/3 cup juice

5–6 fruit = about 1/2 cup juice

*If you can't find fresh *naranjas agrias*, just substitute limes. You can also use bottled *naranja agria* juice except for making *refresco de naranja agria* (see recipe). You will sometimes see recipes that mix a variety of citrus juices to make an equivalent of *naranja agria* juice. But I find that using limes is just fine to achieve the desired results.

Limes:

4–5 fruit = 1/4 cup juice,

5–6 fruit = about 1/3 cup juice

6–8 fruit = 1/2 cup juice

Recados:

1 ounce of any *recado** = about 1 1/2 tablespoons

*Using the *recados* following my recipes (see Chapter 1)

Masa harina

There's nothing like fresh *masa de maíz* (corn dough) for making *panuchos, salbutes,* empanadas and tamales (see recipes). If you only have access to *masa harina* (corn flour), just follow the directions on the back of the bag. (See Glossary for more information on *masa de maíz* and *masa harina*.)

1 1/2 cups *masa* harina (wth water and salt) = just under 1 pound of *masa*

2 cups masa harina (wth water and salt) = a little over 1 pound of *masa*

Fresh herbs

Bunches of herbs vary in size, so it's hard to give an accurate measurement. Use your judgement. However, if the herbs are just flavoring a stock, go ahead and toss in whole stems. For other uses, cut off and disgard the thicker ends of the stems.

Heat Control

To reduce a bit of the heat of chiles, remove the seeds and veins. Just remember that a *chile habanero* is hot, with or without seeds or veins.

Plum Tomatoes

6–8 plum tomatoes = about 1 1/2 pounds

This is only a guide as plum tomatoes can be petite in size or large.

Naranja agria

Recados

Plum tomatoes

Chiles habaneros

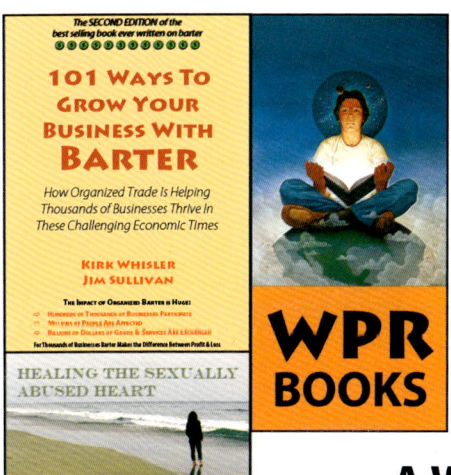

WPR BOOKS

is dedicated to improving protrayals and expanding opportunities for Latinos in the USA

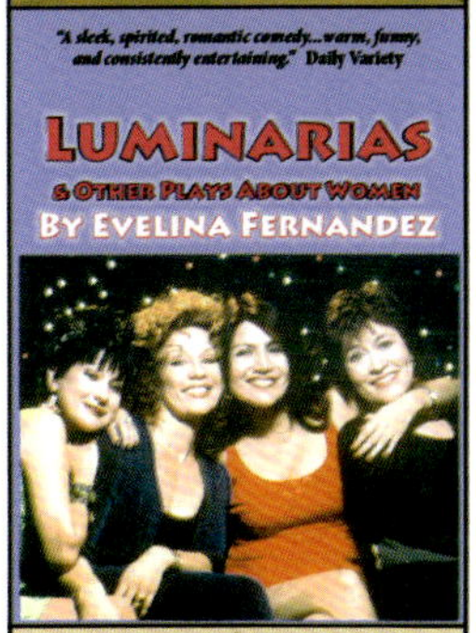

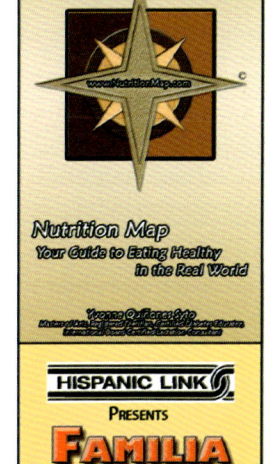

A Wide Variety of Opportunities

WPR BOOKS, formerly known as WPR Publishing, has been publishing books and directories since 1983. WPR Books has seven imprints: *Comida, Helping Hands, Heroes, Latino Insights, Latin American Insights, Para los Niños,* and *Total Success.*

Latino Print Network, **WPR BOOKS** sister organization, works with over 625 Hispanic newspapers and magazines. These publications have a combined circulation of 19 million in 177 markets nationwide.

Latino Literacy Now is a 501(c)3 organization that has produced 48 **Latino Book & Family Festivals** around the USA since it's founding in 1997. Over 800,000 people have attended these events. It also has carried out the **International Latino Book Awards** since 1997 and the **Latino Book into Movies Awards** since 2010.

Hispanic Marketing 101 is a twice-weekly enewsletter that provides a variety of helpful information. A subscription is free at **www.HM101.com**

We have these and other programs that may be of interest to you. For more information please go to **www.WPRbooks.com** or call us at 760-434-1223.

We're adding more books every month

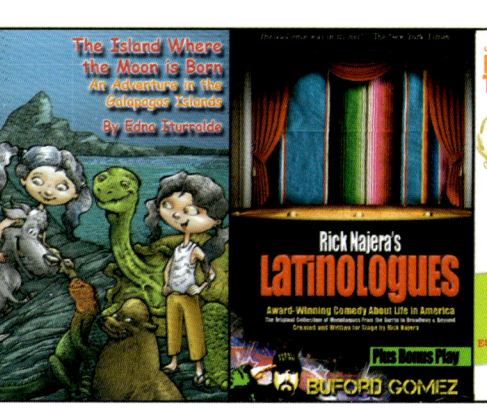

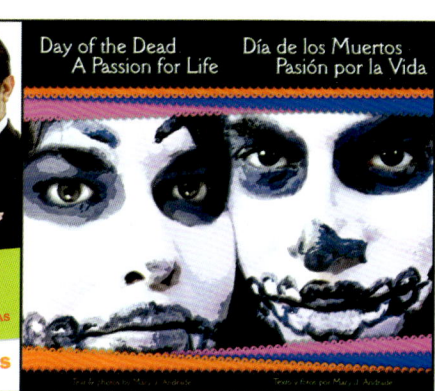

About the Authors

Chef Gilberto Cetina

Gilberto Cetina learned the secrets of cooking from his mother in a timber town in the Tizimín province of the state of Yucatán. A trained engineer, he moved with his family to the United States in 1986 where he was finally able to dedicate himself to the culinary arts. He worked in various restaurants and learned the ins and outs of the business.

He opened Chichén Itzá Restaurant in 2001, and his Yucatecan dishes soon became the talk of the town among customers, foodies, food critics and other restaurateurs.

Chef Cetina and the food of Chichén Itzá Restaurant have been lauded in such publications as *GQ Magazine, Los Angeles Times, Travel and Leisure Magazine, People en español, Hispanic Magazine, L.A. Weekly, La Opinión, City Beat* and *Adelante;* as well as on television and radio.

Jonathan Gold, the Pulitzer Prize-winning food writer from *L.A. Weekly,* wrote of the restaurant, "Chichén Itzá, named for the vast [Mayan] temple complex near Mérida, is indisputably the real thing."

Chef Cetina has been a spokesperson for Splenda, was featured in a national Hyundai ad campaign, teaches classes in Yucatán cuisine, and is in demand for events showcasing the best of Mexican culture and cuisine. His restaurant is invariably named as one the top Mexican restaurants in the greater Los Angeles area.

This is his first cookbook. He is already developing additional cookbooks and is planning a series of cooking classes as Webinars. He can be reached at: chefcetina@chichenitzarestaurant.com.

Katharine A. Díaz (A *much* younger Díaz at the Mayan ruins of Xpujil in Campeche.)

Katharine A. Díaz is a self-described foodie. She is also a food and travel writer specializing in Latin America, where she has traveled widely.

She has worked as editor of several publications, including such national magazines as *Hispanic, Caminos* and *Mexico Events and Destinations.* Her work has also appeared in other publications, including *Segunda Juventud* (an AARP publication now titled *AARP Viva), Latino Magazine, VISTA, Aboard Magazine, Hispanic Magazine, Corporate and Incentive Travel Magazine, Insurance Meetings Management Magazine, Recommend Magazine, Hispanic Trends,* and *San Fernando Sun.* Díaz also authored several entries, including ones about Latino cuisine and restaurant culture, in the *Encyclopedia Latina* (Scholastic Library Publishing).

She also is the long-time host of "Canto Tropical," an Afro-Cuban/salsa music show on KPFK-90.7 FM in Los Angeles.

This is her first cookbook. She is currently editing and writing other cookbooks as well as young-adult, historic fiction. She can be reached at: kanndiaz@yahoo.com.

Gilberto Cetina, Jr.

Gilberto Cetina, Jr., was on a different career path before the family business got under his skin. In Mérida he was studying computer science before his studies were interrupted, and he returned to the United States to rejoin his family in 2000.

Back in the States he worked at various restaurants, including on the catering side of some. He didn't begin working at Chichén Itzá Restaurant until a week after it opened in 2001. In the beginning he worked the front of the house.

Eventually, he began to focus on the kitchen and learn the secrets of his father's (and grandmother's) cooking. It wasn't too long before he mastered them and brought innovations to the kitchen.

When time permits, Gilberto enjoys experimenting and putting new twists on traditional dishes. It might not be too long before he publishes his own cookbook on *la nueva cocina yucateca*—the new Yucatecan cuisine. In the meantime, he is his father's right-hand man. He can be reached at: gcetina@chichenitzarestaurant.com.